Henry Purcell

HENRY PURCELL

Glory of His Age

MARGARET CAMPBELL

Hutchinson
London

This edition first published in 1993 by
Hutchinson

Random House UK Limited
20 Vauxhall Bridge Road, London SW1V 2SA

Random House Australia (Pty) Ltd
20 Alfred Street, Milsons Point, Sydney, NSW 2061, Australia

Random House New Zealand Ltd
18 Poland Road, Glenfield, Auckland, New Zealand

Random House South Africa (Pty) Ltd
PO Box 337, Bergvlei, 2012, South Africa

A CIP catalogue record for this book is available from the British Library

ISBN 0 09 174272 2

Photoset in 11/13pt Linotron Sabon
by Deltatype Ltd, Ellesmere Port, Cheshire
Printed and bound in Great Britain by
Mackays of Chatham PLC, Chatham, Kent

To my husband, my children and their children

CONTENTS

ILLUSTRATIONS

Henry Purcell Family Tree

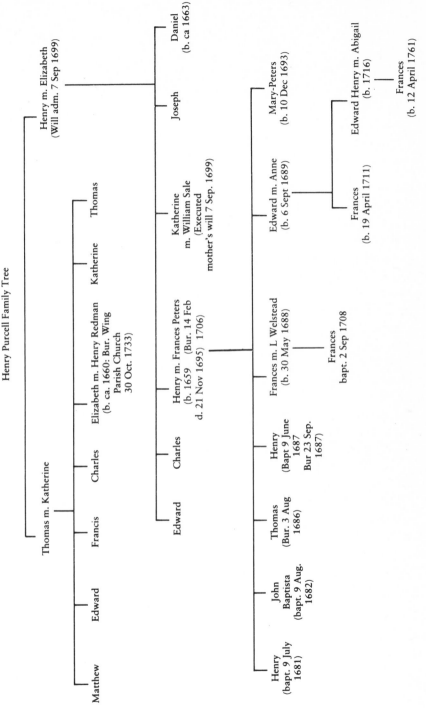

ACKNOWLEDGEMENTS

I would like to thank all the people who have assisted me in my researches for this book, even though it is not possible to name them all individually. None the less, there are a few who must be singled out for special mention. Layton Ring has loaned me books from his personal library and made available his own researches on Purcell; also, after an early reading of the manuscript, he made some useful suggestions, many of which have been incorporated. Robert Spencer, who saw it at a later stage, advised me in a similar capacity, gave me access to his personal library and provided me with countless examples for illustrations. David Baldwin, Sergeant of the Vestry at HM Chapel Royal, St James's Palace has supplied copious information on the Chapel Royal, and Dr Richard Luckett, Pepys Librarian at Magdalene College, Cambridge, gave me the benefit of his immense knowledge of the period and directed me to sources quite new to me. Dr Andrew Ashbee, whose *Records of English Court Music* has been consulted with some frequency, has also provided me with his personal notes on related queries.

Andrew Pinnock and Bruce Wood have generously given me unrestricted access to their fascinating researches on the dating of *Dido and Aeneas*, and Julie Muller, in a similar capacity to her thesis on *Dioclesian*; her husband, Franz, whose studies on the Dorset Garden Theatre proved invaluable, also read and advised me on the relevant chapters.

Dr Curtis Price, King Edward Professor of Music at King's College, London and Secretary of the Purcell Society Edition, has given me much of his time, and access to the archives of the Purcell Society. Dr Carl Dolmetsch has given me access to the Dolmetsch Library and assisted me with some French translation. I am grateful also to the following who will recognize their individual contributions: Lady

Evelyn Barbirolli, Philip Bate, John Belcher, Andrew Best, Dr Patricia Howard, Benigna Lehmann, Marie Leonhardt, Gwen Montagu, Fumihiko Mori, Andrew Pearmain, Trevor Pinnock, Anthony Rooley, Dr Stanley Sadie, Lionel Salter and Dr John M. Thomson.

My thanks also to Philip Robinson and the staff of the Music Library at Welwyn, Hertfordshire and my local library in Berkhamsted. I am grateful for the courtesy and help I have received from Cathy Haill and the staff at the Theatre Museum, the Reading Room of the British Library and Westminster Abbey. I am particularly indebted to Anthony Perch who unearthed for me the Cummings notebook in the library at the Guildhall School of Music and Drama.

Much gratitude is due to my son, Steve, whose ability to tame the antics of an errant word-processor passeth all understanding; and finally, to my husband who, despite having acted as an unpaid assistant to an often over-demanding researcher, has supported the project throughout.

I am grateful for permission to publish extensive extracts from the Muniment Room and Library of Westminster Abbey which appear by Courtesy of the Dean and Chapter of Westminster. The letter from Thomas Purcell to John Gostling is published by kind permission of the Nanki Library at Tokyo Music University. I would also like to thank Cambridge University Press for allowing me to publish numerous extracts from *Henry Purcell & The London Stage* by Curtis Price, *Foundations of English Opera* by E. J. Dent and *Music in Eighteenth Century England* edited by Hogwood & Luckett, and to Oxford University Press for permission to publish numerous extracts from *Henry Purcell* by Dennis Arundell, *Purcell* by Imogen Holst, *Charles II, King of England, Scotland & Ireland* by R. Hutton, *The Puritans & Music* by Percy Scholes and *Up to Now* by Martin Shaw.

I am also indebted to all the other publishers who have given me permission to print short extracts from their books, each of whom is listed in the Bibliography and in references at the end of each chapter. I have made every effort to trace owners of the copyright in all material quoted but in some cases this has proved impossible. I hope that any publishers who fall into this category will understand my difficulties and at the same time appreciate that I have clearly named every source in detail.

Margaret Campbell

PREFACE

The Author's extraordinary Talent in all sorts of Musick is sufficiently known, but he was especially admir'd for the Vocal, having a peculiar Genius to express the Energy of English Words, whereby he mov'd the Passions of all his Auditors.

Thus wrote Henry Playford the bookseller in 1698 in his note *To the Reader*, at the beginning of *Orpheus Britannicus*, the first collection of Purcell's songs. No one since then has better expressed Purcell's contribution to music.

In the eighteenth century, Purcell's music was still played in church and at the theatre and the demand for his published songs continued throughout. Even in the early nineteenth century, when public taste had changed considerably, the celebrated organist and composer, William Crotch, described him as 'not only the greatest master of his time, but the most extraordinary genius that this nation has ever produced' (Crotch, William, *Substance of Several Courses of Lectures on Music*, Longman, Rees, Orme, Brown and Greene, 1831, p 109).

Today his genius is being more widely recognized. As a melodist, he was supreme – witness the perennial beauty of such songs as 'Fairest Isle' from *King Arthur* or 'I attempt from love's sickness to fly' from *The Indian Queen*, just two from hundreds of possible examples.

His harmonic mastery is again evident in both his 'early' styles and his latest 'Italianate' ventures. One has only to hear the simple yet profound chords of the Funeral Sentence, 'Thou Knowest, Lord' to realize this.

Layton Ring confirms that Playford's comment three centuries ago is still true today:

If there were one quality which all ears, whether 'innocent' or sophisticated, can appreciate, it is his word-setting of the English language. This is a knack given to few composers – among them Sir Arthur Sullivan and, perhaps, Benjamin Britten – i.e. the ability to frame words at once elegantly *and* naturally. Purcell has this gift *in excelsis* – he literally – still less figuratively – never goes wrong. Two examples from *The Faerie Queene* will suffice to prove the point: one, the well-known 'Drunken Poet's' words from Act I, 'tu-tu-turn, tu-tu-turn me round, and stand away, sta-stand away, sta-stand away' to a syncopated rhythm in triple time; and again, the less-familiar entry of Phoebus from Act IV, 'When a long cruel winter has frozen the earth and Nature imprison'd seeks in vain to be free'. Until one has heard Purcell's actual setting of this 'prosy' statement, all on one level, as it were, one cannot imagine how such seemingly unpromising material could be given such an intensity of utterance as the singer is asked to realize. Indeed, the art of the vocal 'melisma' has never had a greater exponent. He sings from, and speaks to, the heart at all times. Others may abide the question. Like Shakespeare, Purcell is free.

Unfortunately there is a dearth of information about his private life. Even his actual date of birth is uncertain. It is generally accepted as being sometime in the latter half of 1659, deduced from the inscription on the memorial tablet in Westminster Abbey which states that he died on 21 November 1695 in his 37th year.

We know that he lived in Westminster and his father and uncle were 'Gentlemen' of the Chapel Royal. We know also that his father died when he was six years old and from this time on his uncle Thomas was in charge of his upbringing. Shortly afterwards young Purcell became a 'Child' of the Chapel Royal and, serving under four monarchs, remained in the employment of the royal court until his death. It also happened to be one of the most exciting periods in the history of his country.

Of his domestic life we know next to nothing. He married at the age of 20 or thereabouts and his wife, Frances, bore him seven children, only two of which survived infancy.

I have been fortunate in having access to some recent reappraisal concerning the re-dating of the opera, *Dido and Aeneas*, and other researches which have not as yet been published. I have also discovered in the Guildhall School of Music and Drama Library a notebook belonging to the nineteenth-century scholar and authority on Purcell, W.H. Cummings; these notes were intended to be used in a second revised edition of his biography of Purcell, where he corrects errors for which several generations of scholars have castigated him.

This was a particularly exciting discovery as Cummings was a fine scholar and it is always satisfying to be able to put the record straight.

As for the 'life' itself, I have tried to reconstruct the period in which Purcell lived, not only through the social, religious and political history, but also through his friends and colleagues at court, in the church, and the theatre. It is through a study of these personalities that we catch brief but often compelling glimpses of Henry Purcell as a man.

One has only to look at the infinite variety of his compositions to imagine the breadth of his personality. He was equally at home in writing for the church, the theatre, or the grand court occasion. He also had a sharp wit and took an obvious delight in setting bawdy catches – it is believed that on many occasions he also wrote the words.

In all we see a man of incredible industry right up to the day he died, but despite his tremendous output, he was a perfectionist who never presented work that fell below his own high standards. He did not suffer fools gladly and could give a sharp retort when needed, although, despite his busy schedule, he was always willing to help others. Above all, he was greatly loved and respected by his colleagues who clearly recognized and applauded his genius. His musical output was tremendous, but, like Mozart a century later, he died early in the full flower of his creative genius.

For those who wish to pursue further the subject of Purcell's music, I recommend the works of the scholars who have written extensively in analytical terms from the earliest promise to the full flowering of his genius. The main aim of this book is to discover something about the man and the times in which he lived, and, where possible, the effect his music had on his contemporaries who, as we know, proclaimed him the greatest of English musicians – their *Orpheus Britannicus*.

Margaret Campbell
Berkhamsted, 1992

ABBREVIATIONS

The following abbreviations are used in the references:

AA   Andrew Ashbee, *Records of English Court Music*
BM   British Museum
Cal Treas Books Calendar of Treasury Books
ED   Evelyn's *Diary*
Grove's   *Grove's Dictionary of Music and Musicians*, 5th edition
LS   *The London Stage*
Lutt   Narcissus Luttrell *A Brief Historical Relation of State Affairs*
NG   *The New Grove Dictionary of Music and Musicians*
PD   *The Diary of Samuel Pepys*
WAM   Westminster Abbey Muniments

1

BEGINNINGS

In tracing the Purcell family back to its origins, we must rely more on legend than fact. The most likely ancestor would seem to be one Sir Hugh Porcel, who first set foot on British soil in the Norman invasion, although his name does not appear in the Battle Abbey Roll. Several branches of this family were known in Britain in the Middle Ages and an Irish branch emerged in Kilkenny in the twelfth century. There were also Newton-Purcells living in Oxfordshire about the same time, and Roger Purcell from this family founded the Shropshire branch, both of which flourished well into the seventeenth century. During this period there were also a large number of Purcells in London but again there is no proof that they were related to the family of the composer.

It is probable that Henry Purcell was descended from the Shropshire branch. One of the reasons for this assumption is that on the title-page of Purcell's *Sonnatas of III Parts* he published his coat of arms depicting the three boars' heads which are common to both the Kilkenny and Shropshire Purcells. A detail which could have some bearing on the subject is that a German eighteenth-century lexicographer uses the French spelling, 'pourcelle' (now obsolete), meaning 'boar'. So since the three boars' heads insignia was of Gallic origin, we may presume that Henry Purcell had French connections.[1]

On a much more positive trail, recent research now suggests that Henry Purcell's family came from Thornborough in Buckinghamshire. There were several Purcells – mainly carpenters and artisans – in that village who favoured the names Henry and Thomas for their children. An inscription on a stone in St Katherine's Chapel in the parish church at Wing, Buckinghamshire, states:

Here lies [the body of] Elizabeth, the wife of Henry Redman late of Ascot [and daughter of] Catherine and Thomas Purcell, yeoman of the robes and one of the Gentlemen of the Chapel Royal to Charles 2nd [she died] Oct. 29 1733, Aged 73.

The parish records show that Elizabeth Redman died on the date indicated by the memorial stone, and in fact Redmans and Purcells had lived side by side for over a hundred years in Oving, a small village near Wing lying between Aylesbury and Leighton Buzzard in Bedfordshire.

A local Buckinghamshire legend claims that both Henry the elder and Thomas were kidnapped to serve as choristers in the Chapel Royal, and settled in Westminster in the mid-seventeenth century. Quite recently, records have revealed that a John Purcell, employed by the Verney family as a carpenter, had two sons, Henry and Thomas, both born at about the right time to have been the two musical Purcells of Westminster. From the time of Richard III, it was common practice to press-gang boys from poor families into service in the Chapel Royal. It would therefore seem likely that these could be the ancestors of Henry the younger. Moreover, there have since been discovered a number of links between the Westminster Purcells and some prominent Buckinghamshire families which cannot be explained away as coincidental: an example is the following excerpt from a letter written on 22 February 1939 by a Mr F.G. Gurney of Wing, Bucks, to a Mr A. Vere Woodman:

There is hardly the slightest doubt that the great musician was a Bucks. man. His father, Henry, used for his sons the names used by the Oving Purcells throughout. Henry Purcell, the father, was married by 1652 and was probably born between c. 1622 and 1631 (a statement according well with the fact that Henry Purcell of Thornborough was baptized in 1627, and Thomas Purcell in 1629–1630)[2]

A controversy that has persisted for centuries is which of the two brothers was the father of the great Henry Purcell. Jack Westrup favours Thomas, basing his assumption on a letter written in 1678 by Thomas to John Gostling, celebrated bass singer in the Chapel Royal, in which he calls Henry his son. However, recent research presents a more convincing argument for Henry the elder as the true father. The will of the organist John Hingston – Henry's godfather – clearly states that Purcell was the son of Henry's wife Elizabeth; Thomas's wife was called Katherine. We know that after the death of his brother in 1664, Thomas took over the child's upbringing from the age of five. It would therefore seem reasonable for him to regard Henry as more of a son than a nephew. Until further evidence is unearthed, we must accept this as being so.

Henry the elder was a practising musician and singing actor. The Commonwealth years were difficult times for a musician and he would have earned his living by giving lessons, and probably also composed music for private performance by those who could afford to pay. He certainly had very little money, for when he lived in Great Almonry, Westminster, his payment of 1s 6d for the poor rate was considerably less than that paid by his better-off neighbours. Great Almonry was in the residential area south of Tothill Street, just a short distance from the Abbey. His next-door neighbour was the famous composer Henry Lawes, and another, Christopher Gibbons, who moved there some time after. Amongst other well-known musicians who lived within a stone's throw of Great Almonry were John Banister in King Street West, Captain Henry Cooke in Little Sanctuary, Thomas Farmer in New Palace, and Dr John Wilson in Dean's Yard.

Henry and Elizabeth's first child, Edward, was born in 1653, their second, Charles, about 1657 and Henry in 1659, somewhere between summer and autumn a year after the death of Cromwell. Parish registers for the Commonwealth period are unreliable, so no details of the registration of his birth have ever been found. The year has been deduced from the memorial tablet in Westminster Abbey which records that he died on 21 November 1695 in his thirty-seventh year. The Purcells produced three more children, a daughter, Katherine, and two sons, Joseph and Daniel. The latter followed the family tradition by becoming a professional musician; he was also a composer and assisted his elder brother in his final years, but never approached his genius.

The Westminster in which the young Henry Purcell was born was quite a small place in the parish of St Margaret's, concentrated closely round the Abbey Church of St Peter. These districts were known as the 'Liberties' of London. A short stroll down any of the streets led to open countryside, and north of Piccadilly lay nothing but pasture and heathland. Parliament House and Westminster Hall were the only two large buildings in the parish. Parliament itself saw little activity after the restoration of Charles II, since he called the House infrequently and even then the sessions were short. By contrast, Westminster Hall was a hive of industry. It was a kind of covered market with stalls where law stationers, dealers in toys, booksellers and seamstresses sold their wares to the public. Samuel Pepys was a frequent visitor and always bought his haberdashery there. He also quenched his thirst at one or both of the two taverns, 'Heaven' and 'Hell', which flanked the hall on either side. Both buildings had once been part of the Exchequer: 'Heaven' was so called because it was on the upper storey, and 'Hell' as it was partly underground and possibly had been used as a prison.

The taverns, inns and eating-houses, of which there were hundreds within the square mile of the city of London, were an integral part of everyday life. No man was ever more than a few yards from a house where refreshment could be obtained, the only restriction on the sale of alcoholic drinks being during service times on Sundays.

In 1652 the first coffee-house was established in Holborn and its immediate success led to the opening of a number of others where friends could meet and partake of coffee, tea or chocolate whilst the latest news or gossip was exchanged. It was also convenient for businessmen undertaking transactions. Fellows from the Royal Society would meet at the 'Grecian' in Threadneedle Street after their official meetings, and 'Will's' became famous as a rendezvous for the wits and writers, mainly because Dryden – known as the 'Monarch of Will's' – was a regular visitor and even enjoyed the privilege of his own special chair. Lloyd's, which became the insurance exchange, was formerly a coffee-house and two others survive today as the well-known clubs, Boodle's and White's.

The River Thames was the main artery of London life and the only highway. To go by water was the quickest form of transport, especially for those bound for the City, and boats could be hired at the quay near Palace Yard. For some six miles along the north bank were the imposing houses and palaces of the wealthy, whilst on the south, the empty wastes of the Lambeth Marshes stretched as far as the eye could see.

These waterways were ruled by the Wapping watermen, who brooked no competition. Their ribaldry was proverbial and even the nobility knew better than to challenge them on an issue. In fact it was for fear of the Wapping watermen that London Bridge remained for so long the only crossing to the Southwark side: King Charles II, who called them his 'nursery of seamen' supported them in their objection to another being built.

Their rivals on the streets were the hackney coachmen who waited underneath the Maypole in the Strand for those who could afford their exorbitant charges. If questioned, they were always ready with a whip or fist to vindicate themselves, but few were brave enough to argue with them. Whenever political feelings ran high, these two trades would automatically take opposite sides and much blood was shed in the process.

Travelling in the streets of London was not easy, and 'at any hour of the day, coaches, drays and cattle were mingled in profane confusion'.[3] On two successive days, Pepys in his fine new coach protests that he was held up for half an hour by a traffic block in Exchange Street.

In 1660, when Henry Purcell was only a year old, the City of London was an agricultural town surrounded by green fields. In the tree-lined squares many of the houses had fine gardens, and nightingales were frequently heard in Lincoln's Inn Fields. On May Day, the milkmaids, their pails decorated with garlands, danced down the Strand with a fiddler playing at the head of the procession. In contrast to this pastoral merry-making was the stench of the effluent running in the gutters and the perpetual noise of carriages and farm carts trundling over the cobbled streets, accompanied by the ear-splitting cries of apprentices and hawkers bawling their wares.

The English people had suffered for more than 20 years, at first under Charles I whose long period of non-parliamentary government had solved none of the current problems, followed by the iron rule of Cromwell. With the Restoration in 1660, their pent-up feelings were suddenly released so it is not surprising that the favourite pastime was fighting. In the City of London, on holidays, the rival trades would challenge each other without provocation whilst the people looked on and cheered. In Moorfields the butchers and weavers who had a hereditary hatred of each other, needed no encouragement to open battle. If the weavers won they would shout 'A hundred pounds for a butcher!'[4] As there was no police force their savagery went unchecked. This behaviour was not confined to the lower echelons of society. When the Lord Mayor decided to ride to the Temple with his sword borne before him, students pulled it down and besieged him all day in a councillor's room. Even at Oxford a respected academic who had a grudge against one of his fellow dons was known to attack him whenever they chanced to meet, resulting in bloody noses and black eyes.

Duels were a constant hazard for the pedestrian who walked abroad after nightfall. Quite frequently two strangers bumping into each other would think nothing of whipping out their swords and engaging in a fight. In the case of a death, unless a witness came forward, it was unlikely to be reported. Everyone, from the nobility to the boatmen, was interested in matters of State, and the ordinary Englishman would react strongly to anyone who disagreed with his views. When the French ambassador forgot to light a bonfire to celebrate the English victory over the Dutch, the mob smashed his windows and 'all but grilled him on his own furniture'.[5]

The main target for political aversion was popery. Anyone showing the slightest sympathy for Catholics would arouse the most warlike tendencies in the mildest of Englishmen. Once a year on 17 November, the anniversary of Queen Elizabeth's accession to the throne, a mob marched through the City with effigies of the Pope, cardinals and devils which they stuffed with live cats to make their squalling realistic. Finally when they were burned at Smithfield, the crowds looked on screaming with delight.

However, a gentler side to the English temperament was apparent in their love of music. The common people danced and sang to the fiddlers who played in the taverns; the theatre, which put on plays with musical excerpts, catered for all classes of society. Most of the more substantial families both in the town and country made their own music on viol, harpsichord, virginals, lute or guitar. Pepys tells us that once going down the river he shared a boat with a stranger who sang with him all the way, 'with great pleasure'.[6] And again, on a fine moonlight night, how Pepys, his wife and her companion went into their garden and sang until midnight 'with mighty pleasure to ourselfs and neighbours' who showed their appreciation 'by their Casements opening'.[7]

This then was the London in which young Henry was reared. When the Restoration took place he was only one year old, but in time he would have learned of the colourful details of the Coronation and other court occasions through his father and uncle who were Gentlemen of the Chapel Royal. Of one thing we are certain: from birth his environment was steeped in music and, since his talent manifested itself at an early age, it would have been encouraged and given room to grow.

References

1. Zimmerman, Franklin B., *Henry Purcell, 1659–1695, His Life and Times*, 2nd edition, University of Pennsylvania Press, Philadelphia, 1983, p 332.
2. Ibid, p 335.
3. Bryant, Arthur, *King Charles II*, Longmans, 1949, p 92.
4. Ibid, p 87.

5. Ibid, p 88.
6. *The Diary of Samuel Pepys*, ed R.C. Latham and W. Matthews, Bell, 1970–83, Vol 6, p 156 (1665).
7. Ibid, Vol 7, p 117.

MUSIC UNDER THE PURITANS

We know that from the Restoration onwards music played an important part both in the church and at court. But how did it fare under the Puritans? When Henry Purcell was born, Oliver Cromwell, His Highness Lord Protector of the Commonwealth of England, Ireland and Scotland had been dead for a year, but the country was still under the influence of Puritanism. It is a common belief that a dark curtain was lowered over the performing arts during the eleven years of the Commonwealth and that all music and entertainment was frowned upon. This is one of those biased assumptions that gain momentum throughout the centuries, with successive writers perpetuating half-truths that grow into historical fact.

From the religious aspect there had been stirrings of protest since the Middle Ages when the expanding wealth and influence of the Catholic Church bred corruption in high places. John Wyclif in England, John Hus in Bohemia and Girolamo Savonarola in Italy were the leading protesters and their writings, pleading for simpler and more direct forms of worship were widely circulated. The most effective and enduring protest came from Germany with Martin Luther, but it was the French John (Jean) Calvin who became the most enthusiastic advocate of Protestantism and can be regarded as the virtual father of Puritanism.

In England, Henry VIII had broken away from Rome following his divorce from Catherine of Aragon. When Queen Elizabeth succeeded to the throne in 1558, England was still bitterly divided, but fearing the influence of Catholic Spain, it gradually came to accept a moderate form of Protestantism together with the Anglican Book of Common Prayer. In Scotland, where feelings ran much higher, the zealots had driven Mary Stuart from the throne. Her son, James VI, who took her place in 1567, was prepared to pay lip-service to them, but on his succession to the English throne as James I in 1603, he threw away all pretence and in 1617 published the *Book of Sports*. This decreed that on Sundays, after divine service, 'no lawful recreation should be barred'. Dancing, including morris-dancing, archery, leaping, vaulting, May-games, Whitsun-ales, and anything that provided a diversion for pleasure were specified. The one proviso was that these pursuits could only be enjoyed if the participants had attended church.

Could it be that the legend of the Puritan hatred of amusements stems from these decrees? The Puritans always favoured a religious observance of Sunday and, despite fierce opposition, never ceased to petition against the decree set down in the *Book of Sports*.

How then did the Puritans regard the pleasures of music and dancing? Dancing and the Devil have been closely associated since time immemorial, and zealots from all religions including the Puritans have condemned it as ungodly. The Spanish Jesuit, Father Mariana, says that 'the sarabande worked more mischief than the plague', and the English bishop Babington claimed that dancing was 'an incitement to whoredome'.[1] The Puritan view is clearly expressed in *The Heart of the Puritan*: 'Only lascivious dancing to wanton ditties and in amorous gestures and wanton dalliances, especially after great feasts, I would bear witness against, as great *flabella libidinis*'.[2]

We are told constantly that dancing practically disappeared with the Puritans, but when one of Oliver Cromwell's daughters married the Earl of Warwick's grandson in 1657, the wedding feast was held at Whitehall where they had '48 violins, 50 trumpets and much mirth with frolics, besides mixt dancing [formerly considered profane] till five of the clock yesterday morning'. And there would seem to be little sign of restraint when John Milton, that pillar of Puritanism, describes the summer pastimes of village life in his *L'Allegro*:

> Come and trip it as you go
> On the light fantastic toe . . .
> When the merry bells ring round,
> And jocund rebecks sound,
> To many a youth and many a maid
> Dancing in the chequered shade.

There are many other examples of staunch Puritan families educating their children in dancing, fencing and music as well as in languages and sciences. Even John Bunyan in that great Puritan allegory, *Pilgrim's Progress*, cannot disguise his enthusiasm for spectacle and music:

But glorious it was to see how the upper region was filled with horses and chariots, with trumpeters and pipers, with singers and players on stringed instruments, to welcome the pilgrims as they went up, and followed one another in at the Beautiful Gate of the City.[3]

However, there is no denying that under the Puritans, Parliament decreed the destruction of all church organs: but this was not a precedent. Ever since Henry VIII broke with the Pope and reformed the Church, there were those who felt that where ritual was concerned, reform had not been carried far enough. 'Curious singing' (polyphonic) and instrumental music were anathema to them and they wanted to dispense with it. In fact, in 1536, a century before the Puritans came into power, the lower House of Convocation included organ-playing amongst the '84 Faults and Abuses of Religion'.[4] In 1552, the organ of St Paul's Cathedral was silenced for a time and reopened only when Mary came to the throne the following year. In 1563, during the reign of Queen Elizabeth, a resolution for the removal of all organs was defeated by only one vote. Some organs were removed at this time and the pipes sold to make pewter dishes.

None the less, the Roundhead soldiers cannot be excused for their wanton desecration of the churches and organs; a typical example concerns Westminster Abbey in 1643:

The soldiers . . . were quartered in the Abbey Church, where they brake down the rayl about the Altar, and burnt it in the place where it stood; they brake downe the Organs, and pawned the pipes at severall ale-houses for pots of ale. They put on some of the Singing-men's surplices, and, in contempt of that canonicall habite, ran up and down the Church; he that wore the surplice was the hare, the rest were the hounds.[5]

Percy Scholes, in his informative study on the subject, maintains that it was not the *presence* of the organ in church that offended the Puritan, but the implication that it was to be used in worship. And although they regarded the organ as a secular instrument, the meeting-house itself was not considered sacred. In fact, it was used for worship only on Sundays, secular recreations, musical or otherwise being allowed on weekdays. Recitals and concerts of secular music have been given in nonconformist churches and meeting-houses for many generations. It is only in recent years that Anglicans and Catholics have permitted their churches to be used for this purpose.

Cromwell himself was known to be a lover of music and it was he who saved the organ at Magdalen College, Oxford, by ordering its removal to Hampton Court, where it was placed in the Great Gallery. In 1660, the organ was restored to Magdalen, and sold to Tewkesbury Abbey in 1736 where it remains today.*

As to the kind of music allowed in church services, the Puritans were very precise. The English Puritans, being Calvinistic rather than Lutheran held the view that the only proper worship in singing should be the Psalms of David and Biblical canticles. This was Calvin's conviction and a metrical psalm before and after the sermon was common practice at Geneva. Singing should be in unison and syllabic. The polyphonic weaving in and out of voice-parts and the setting of several notes to one syllable was the 'curious singing' already mentioned, to which the Puritans were so opposed.

The meaning of the psalms was very personal to the Puritans and they would choose according to the immediate need. Scholes quotes an amusing story concerning Charles I in 1646 in the hands of the Scots:

a Scotch minister preached boldly before the King at Newcastle, and after this sermon called for the fifty-second psalm, which begins: 'Why dost thou tyrant boast thyself, thy wicked works to praise?'. His majesty thereupon stood up, and called for the fifty-sixth psalm, which begins: 'Have mercy, Lord, on me I pray, for men would me devour'. The people waived the minister's psalm and sung that which the king called for.[6]

Instrumental music was entirely banned in churches, and it is in this field that musicians were hardest hit. Many had to seek employment outside their profession, and some earned their living by teaching, and, if we are to believe the various accounts by contemporaries, there was a constant demand for good teachers throughout the Commonwealth years. John Playford's *Musicall Banquet*, issued in 1651 during the Commonwealth, assures the reader that 'many excellent and able Masters' were then available as teachers, and gives two lists of some 30 names, one for 'the Voyce or Viole' and the other for 'the Organ or Virginall'.

It is this distinction between church music and music in the home, which has caused the main misconception that Puritans were opposed to all music. It was only elaborate church music that they disliked. Scholes cites the case of Bach, some sixty years after the Commonwealth

* The organ was built by Robert Dallam for Magdalen in 1631 and remodelled by Harris in 1690. It was rebuilt by 'Father' Willis in 1848 and again by Walker in 1948. Much old pipework still exists and is in use, in addition of course to the magnificent Dallam case which is much admired.

ended. Employed by a Puritan court, he lived for six years at Cöthen, which was Calvinist, not Lutheran and therefore used the simplest music in all its services. None the less, the Prince was a keen musician who had studied with the best teachers and travelled to Italy in order to understand better the music of that country. On his return he actively organized the music of his court, with the result that Bach focused his attention on secular music and produced, among other masterpieces, the First Book of the 48 Preludes and Fugues, the Brandenburg Concertos and the French Suites. Had he been required to deliver an endless flow of cantatas and other liturgical music for regular Sunday performance, his output of secular music might have been considerably less.

There were also a number of musicians who still managed to earn a living as professional performers. We have the following account from Anthony Wood in his Diary of March 1658:[7]

In the latter end of this yeare Davis Mell, the most eminent violinist of London, being in Oxon, Peter Pett, William Bull, Kenelm Digby and others of Allsoules ... did give him [Wood] a very handsome entertainment in the taverne cal'd The Salutation in S. Marie's parish Oxon.

He also gives a vivid description of the playing of the virtuoso violinist, Thomas Baltzar from Lübeck. It is interesting that Baltzar came to England in 1655 at the height of the Puritan regime and stayed throughout the period, no doubt earning sufficient money to make it worth while. So great was his fame, he would have been welcome anywhere in Europe. John Evelyn was invited to hear him and declared there was: 'nothing, however cross and perplexed, brought to him by our artists, which he did not play off at sight with ravishing sweetness and improvements [improvisation], to the astonishment of our best masters. In sum, he played on the single instruments a full concert, so as the rest flung down their instruments, acknowledging the victory.'[8] Unfortunately, Baltzar was inclined to 'drink more than was ordinary' which, combined with the effects of 'the French pox and other distempers' sent him to an early grave at the age of 33. Characteristically, the English, who at the time held an abnormal respect for foreign musicians, showed their appreciation of his artistry by burying him in the cloisters at Westminster Abbey.

It is known that Charles II was fond of the violin, which he had grown to love during his exile in France. It is therefore assumed that it was virtually unknown before the Restoration. If we consider the accomplishments of Mell, Baltzar and many others, we must believe Anthony Wood when he says that England had as many good violinists as any in Europe. Also in Playford's *Introduction to the Skill of Musick* there is a section devoted to the 'Treble-Violin, a cheerful and sprightly instrument and much practised of late'.

Another aspect of musical skill which reached its peak in the seventeenth century was performance on the viola da gamba. Van der Straeten tells us: 'Throughout the seventeenth century England was considered the "high school" for viol da gamba playing, and many eminent musicians came to London to perfect themselves in that art'.[9] Significantly, the period in which these musicians visited England, spanned from 1620–85.

John Hingston, Henry Purcell's godfather, was Cromwell's chief of musical staff for which he received a salary of £100 per annum, a princely sum in those days. He also taught both Cromwell's daughters. Hingston trained two choirboys to sing Deering's Latin motets for three voices with himself as bass, because they were particular favourites of the Protector, who frequently dropped in on the musical gatherings at Hingston's own house.

Cromwell's body of court musicians was small. Besides John Hingston and the violinist Davis Mell, there were six other men (John Rogers, Thomas Mallard, William Howe, Thomas Blagrave, William Gregory and Richard Hudson), and two boy singers. Scholes considers the employment of these boys as significant. Since all the choirs had been dispersed, they were probably the only trained boy singers in the country; although it is possible that some might have been retained by a few of the noble houses.

When Cromwell needed larger forces they would have been *ad hoc*. After the death of Charles I the Chapel Royal had been disbanded and was reconstituted only at the Restoration. There are no entries between 1644 and 1660 in the records of court musicians, but it has been suggested that had Cromwell become 'Lord Protector' at the beginning of the Commonwealth, it might never have been dissolved. His love of music and the employment of it in state matters would point to this possibility, though for financial reasons he might have reduced its numbers.

There was also a 'Committee for Advancement of Musicke' set up in 1657 when Puritan rule was at full strength. It came about through a petition signed and presented by John Hingston, Davis Mell and four other 'Gentlemen of his Highness Musique'. Here is part of the text:

That by reason of the late dissolucion of the Quires in the Cathedralls where the study and practice of the Science of Musick was especially cherished, Many of the skilfull Professors of the said Science have during the late Warrs and troubles dyed in want, and there being now noe preferrment or Encouragement in the way of Musick, noe man will breed his child in it, soe that it must needes bee, that the Science itselfe, must dye in this Nacion, with those few Professors of it now living, or at least it will degenerate much from that perfection lately attained unto. Except some present maintenance and Encouragement bee given for educating of some youth in the Study and practice of the said Science.[10]

The petition goes on to plead for a College of Music to be set up in London with reasonable powers to 'read and practise publiquely all sorts of Musick', and to suppress the singing of obscene, scandalous and defamatory songs and ballads. They ask also for reasonable powers to purchase lands and to use the revenue in respect of rents etc., to pay the professors and generally maintain and encourage the 'Science of Musick'.

That such a petition could be drawn up at all proves that study of music in itself was respected, although unfortunately nothing came of it. Cromwell's personal interest in music was well known, so that had it been possible, he would probably have supported the idea.

Another fact not much publicized is that the Puritan government actually paid arrears of wages of musicians incurred during the reign of Charles I. Clement Lanier, one of the instrumentalists (recorder and sackbutt) ordered to play during the principal feasts given by the monarch, had money owing to him when the Civil War caused the dissolution of the royal band. The government promised to pay this debt and records show a sum paid on account the following year.

Furthermore, it seems that a wider plan for relief was envisaged. Parliament, having ordered the sale of land belonging to the bishops, deans and chapters, invested the money, part of the income from which was to go towards the support of the dispossessed bishops, deans, singing men, choristers and the like.[11] It is uncertain whether this plan was effectively carried out, but at least the intention was far more compassionate than that shown by the Church of England for the nonconformists after the Restoration.

Another cultural development in Puritan times is that the printing of music took on a new lease of life with no restrictions upon the content. Many erudite and learned treatises and secular musical instruction books were published under the Commonwealth regime. Here are a few outstanding examples from a long list published by John Playford, the first regular music publisher in Britain.

1651, *The English Dancing Master; or Plaine and easy Rules for the Dancing of Country Dances, with the tune to each dance.*

1652, *Catch as Catch Can, or a Choice Collection of Catches and Rounds.*

1653, *Ayres and Dialogues for one, two and three voyces by Henry Lawes* . . .

1654, *An introduction to the Skill of Musick in two books; first a brief and plaine introduction to musick, both for singing and for playing the violl, by John Playford; second the Art of setting and composing musick in parts . . . formerly published by Dr Tho. Campion, but now republished by Mr Christopher Sympson.*

It should also be remembered that the collection of catches from various composers mostly had words that were either bibulous or bawdy or both. Yet the delightfully illustrated cover of the 1652 publication mentioned above, does not give the impression that the 'Puritan' singers were in the least inhibited in their enjoyment of this very popular pastime.

But when it came to the stage, it was a very different matter. Here the Puritans were intractable. In their view, the play was totally corrupt and the theatres were closed. On 2 September 1642, a provisional ordinance demanded that 'the stages, seats and galleries were to be pulled down, players to be punished as rogues, and spectators fined five shillings for the use of the poor'. Many actors took to the road and performed at fairs which were held all over the country, others braved the ban and took part in performances of sorts at the Red Bull Theatre. Here there were sporadic raids by soldiers who would arrest the actors and carry their clothes on their pikes. 'Pieces, known as "drolls" understandably became shorter and sharper, to cope with the possibility of interruption. Other plays were given in noblemen's houses, principal among them Holland House, safely tucked away in Kensington two or three miles away from the centre of London.'[12] So the theatre continued underground because the need existed.

However, there was a persistent band of actors and managers who tried to reinstate the theatre under a number of pretexts which included works of moral value and described as 'entertainment' instead of a 'play'. A typical example was the semi-private performance of *The Siege of Rhodes* put on in 1656 at the back part of Rutland House in the upper end of Aldersgate Street in London, by

William Davenant, a famous actor-manager. It was so successful that it was revived two years later at the newly reopened Phoenix Theatre. The restrictions were gradually being eroded and the door to the re-establishment of the theatre proper was, at least, ajar. Fortunately for all concerned, there were but two more years to go before the monarchy was to be restored in all its glory, and the theatre would come into the most colourful period in its history.

References

1. Scholes, Percy A., *The Puritans and Music in England and New England*, Clarendon, 1969, p 58.
2. Hanscom, C., *The Heart of the Puritan*, p 177, quoted in Scholes, p 58.
3. Scholes, op cit, pp 144, 61.
4. Davey, C., *History of English Music*, 2nd edition, 1921, p 107, quoted in Scholes, p 230.
5. Ryves, B., *Mercurius Rusticus*, 1642, quoted in Scholes, p 233.
6. Scholes, op cit, p 271.
7. Ibid, pp 277–8.
8. *The Diary of John Evelyn*, ed Ernest Rhys, Dent, 1945, Vol 1, p 315 (4 March 1656).
9. Van Der Straeten, Edmund S.J., *History of the Violoncello, the Viol da Gamba, Their Precursors and Collateral Instruments*, Reeves, 1971, p 52.
10. Public Record Office, *State Papers*, 18, Vol 153, no 123, fo 254, quoted in Scholes, pp 282–3.
11. Neal, C., *History of the Puritans*, 1732–8, quoted in Scholes, p 281.
12. Fraser, Antonia, *Cromwell, Our Chief of Men*, Methuen, 1985, p 465.

3

THE RESTORATION

Charles II was born in 1630 and had become king at 18 after his father's execution. Following many attempts to reinstate his right to the throne, he was defeated by Cromwell at Worcester and on 16 October 1651, landed in France, where, apart from some time in Flanders, he spent most of his exile.

It was General George Monck, a colonel under Charles I in the Scottish wars and later Cromwell's commander-in-chief in Scotland, who saved the situation. On 11 February 1661, he marched into the city of London, where, at the Guildhall, he told the mayor and aldermen that he had organized a dissolution to make way for a free parliament. The people were ecstatic: bonfires were lit and church bells rang throughout the night. Not to be outdone, the butchers in the Strand rang a peal on their knives whilst in every street a rump was roasting.

On 25 May 1660 a tall, dark young man, looking more southern European than English, landed at Dover and was presented with a Bible by the mayor. Charles assured him 'it was the thing that he loved above all things in the world' which delighted the mayor who fortunately did not recognize that 'the wittiest company of comedians that history records had come to tread the stage for a while'.[1] Charles II had returned to his country and England would never be the same again.

When it was time to crown the new King, it seemed appropriate to choose St George's Day, 23 April. The two-year-old Henry Purcell would have heard much music going on in the household at this time, for both his father and his uncle Thomas were members of the Chapel Royal who were an integral part of the music on this grand occasion.

On Monday 22 April, according to ancient custom, the King left Whitehall at dawn by barge for the Tower of London. At 10 am the procession made its way through the City back to Whitehall arriving at three in the afternoon. A colourful description comes from John Evelyn who first lists all the dignitaries in order of procession and the:

KING, in royal robes and equipage . . . This magnificent train on horseback, as rich as embroidery, velvet, cloth of gold and silver, and jewels, could make them and their prancing horses, proceeded through the streets strewed with flowers, houses hung with rich tapestry, windows and balconies full of ladies; the London militia lining the ways, and the several companies, with their banners and loud music, ranked in their orders; the fountains running wine, bells ringing, with speeches made at the several triumphal arches . . . Thence, with joyful acclamations, his Majesty passed to Whitehall. Bonfires at night.[2]

Samuel Pepys had been seven years old at the time of the Civil War and was determined not to miss the Coronation. On 23 April, he rose at 4 am and made his way to the Abbey and found a place on the scaffold at the north end, where he sat patiently until eleven o'clock when the King arrived by barge from Whitehall. He noted the splendid colours of the robes of the various dignitaries and also remarks upon how good the fiddlers looked in their red vests. He complains that because of the great noise he heard little of the music. But he also had another pressing problem: 'I had so great a list to pisse, that I went out a little while before the King had done all his ceremonies.' There were no public conveniences in those days and any street was as good as another for the purpose.

Pepys spent the rest of the day feasting at Whitehall and the evening drinking with friends. He recounts that when they went into Axe Yard, several gallants, men and women 'laid hold of us and would have us drink the King's health upon our knee, kneeling upon a fagott; which we all did, they drinking to us one after another – which we thought a strange Frolique'. Pepys and most of his friends went to bed in various states of intoxication that night, but in his diary he admits he is 'sure never to see the like again in this world'.[3]

After the coronation of Charles II, the next important royal occasion in which the Purcells took part, was the King's marriage to Catherine of Braganza of Portugal the following year: a union that was to establish a congenial association between the two nations lasting to the present time. It is likely that the three-year-old Henry heard his father practising music to be played at the service; what was probably not discussed within hearing of the young child was the gossip regarding the king's numerous mistresses, especially the favourite, Barbara Palmer (later to become first Countess Castlemaine and finally Duchess of Cleveland), and what would happen now that he had taken himself a queen. The excitement mounted when it was rumoured that the king found his bride much plainer than her portraits had led him to anticipate, although afterwards he admitted that she had 'lovely hands and feet'.[4]

None the less, Charles knew very well why he had chosen Catherine. When he first arrived back in England he had been confronted with enormous debts. Those of the Fleet and the Army, even after the disbanding of a million men were extremely high. Then there was a Commonwealth civil debt of about £400,000, £320,000 incurred by Parliament before 1648 and £530,000 by Charles I, not counting the debts amassed during his own exile. The assets of the Exchequer at the moment of the King's return were £11 2s 10d. The gods came to his rescue. The Queen Regent of Portugal offered a dowry for her daughter that exceeded any brought to England by previous foreign brides – over half a million pounds in cash, Tangier, the island of Bombay, and most lucrative of all, free trade with Brazil and the East Indies, 'a key for English merchants to the treasure trove of the world'.[5] What could Charles do but accept?

The impecunious circumstances in which the monarch found himself did little for those in his employ, a situation not improved by the extra costs of running the court itself, and his generosity to his many mistresses. He had doubled the membership of the Chapel and raised their annual salaries from £40 to £70. In November that year, Henry the elder gained himself another appointment shared with the ageing Angelo Notari as musician with a yearly wage of £40. No doubt this was welcomed by the Purcell family since their first daughter, Katherine, was born in March of that year. Unfortunately, however good his intention, promises of money by the King tended to remain unfulfilled. There are countless records of arrears outstanding for anything from a year to a decade, so the actual finances of the Purcell family would not have been impressive.

In December 1663, Notari died and Henry the elder succeeded him as one of the King's Band of Music, but it was to be a short-lived appointment. He died quite suddenly in August 1664 and was buried in the cloisters at Westminster Abbey. He would have been still relatively young so that there remains some doubt as to whether he had a weak constitution: he could have been suffering from tuberculosis, a common incurable disease in those days. Inevitably it leads to the question of the possibility that his son Henry inherited the disease which brought about his own early death.

Henry was only five years old when his father died, so he would have suffered not only the grief of losing a parent, but probably missed hearing the sound of music about the house. After her husband's death, Elizabeth moved to Tothill Street with her six small children – Joseph and Daniel having been born in quick succession after Katherine. She supported them on her widow's pension and what small income she could get from taking in lodgers. It must have been much to her relief that her brother-in-law Thomas took over young Henry's welfare from this time and treated him as a son.

Thomas Purcell held a privileged position at Court. Right at the beginning of the Restoration he had been named as the first of ten musicians 'that do service in the Chapel Royal whose salaries are payable in the Treasury of his Majesty's Chamber' which may have indicated that the payment was more regular than most. In November 1662 he had been appointed to the Private Music for the lutes, viols and voices, in place of Henry Lawes who had died the previous month. For this he received an annual allowance of £36 2s 6d for wages and livery. The latter would seem to be rather splendid made of 'camlet [silk and wool mixture] gown, garded with black velvet and furred'. In addition there was a damask jacket and a velvet doublet. Thomas's knack for gaining extra duties brought him yet further income when he was appointed Groom of the Robes to Charles II. In 1673 he was appointed 'composer in ordinary to his Majesty for the violins', a position he shared with Pelham Humfrey.[6] All in all he would have received about £250 a year, a substantial sum in those days. Thomas Purcell had considerable influence at court and was in a strong position to make it known that his adopted son Henry was showing remarkable talent which should be encouraged.

King Charles II may not have enjoyed a particularly congenial relationship with his imperious mother, Queen Henrietta Maria, but he had inherited her French blood. When he returned to England from his exile at the court of his cousin Louis XIV, he emulated everything French. His 24 violins* were in imitation of the French *Vingt-quatre violons du Roi* to play at court functions whenever he was in residence and particularly 'while he was at meales, as being more airie and brisk than Viols'.[7]

However, there were those who would have been happier had he confined his 'four-and-twenty fiddlers' to meal-times. Evelyn, following a visit to the royal chapel, complains:

---

* These consisted of 24 members of the violin *family*; i.e. trebles, altos, tenors and basses.

One of his Majesties chaplains preached; after which, instead of the ancient, grave, and solemn wind music accompanying the organ, was introduced a concert of twenty-four violins between every pause, after the French fantastical light way, better suiting a tavern, or playhouse than a church.[8]

Charles' taste in general was for light instrumental music from the French School. He had collected around him the few surviving English musicians who had served under his father and, in addition, imported several foreign players whom he had known in his exile. This practice did nothing to endear him to the natives struggling to earn a living after the privations of the Commonwealth.

John Banister, one of Charles's favoured few, had been sent by him to France on 'Special Service', presumably to take a closer look at the musical establishment of Louis XIV. On his return he was appointed director, not only of the 24 violins but also of 12 selected from their number to form a special band 'for better performance of service'. Banister was bitterly opposed to any foreign imports, and is said to have used 'saucy words' to the king when some Italian violinists were called for. Whatever the reason, he was deprived of his post and the Italian Louis Grabu appointed in his place. He was furious and tried to stop the passing of the King's privy seal confirming Grabu's appointment, on the grounds that his own wages were in arrears. Unfortunately, Banister himself was found guilty of misappropriating funds due to his players: none the less he continued to serve for a few years as a member of the band. Eventually, Grabu, too, fell by the wayside, his place being taken in 1674 by the 'bandy-legged' Nicholas Staggins.[9]

The Gallic influence predominated so that a continuous stream of French ideas, fashions and manners flowed across the Channel. There were sedan chairs, little silver brushes for cleaning the teeth and, for the first time, French cuisine, by way of fricassées, ragôuts and salads which could be sampled at Chatelin's famous restaurant in Covent Garden. In 1666 Charles wrote to his sister Minette in France asking her to send some gold sealing-wax as he could find none in London, and a few years later, the English ambassador to Paris reported that four thousand gilt mirrors had been sent to England in one summer.[10] Pepys was struck with the French manner of drinking healths: 'Bow to him that drunk to you, and then apply yourself to him whose lady's health is drunk, and then to the person that you drink to.'[11]

There were those who criticized his extravagance and elastic morals, but perhaps it was because of these facets of his personality that Charles II did achieve 'a change in English taste far greater than any transient turn of fashion. For it affected everything: our architecture, our dress, food and manners, our books, our whole attitude of life . . . The calm, the balance and beauty of the eighteenth century is Charles's legacy to his people.'[12]

References

1. Trevelyan, G.M., *England under the Stuarts*, 19th edition, Methuen, 1947, p 274.
2. ED, Vol 1, pp 354–55 (23 April 1661).
3. PD, Vol 2, pp 84, 88 (23 April 1661).
4. Bryant, *King Charles II*, p 146.
5. Ibid, p 135.
6. Ashbee, Andrew, *Records of English Court Music* (1660–85), Vol 1, Ashbee, 1986, p 128.
7. North, Roger, *Memoires of Musick*, ed Edward Rimbault, Bell, 1846, p 98.
8. ED, Vol 1, p 379 (21 December 1662).
9. Westrup, J.A., *Purcell*, 'The Master Musicians', 3rd edition, Dent, 1947, p 32.
10. Bryant, op cit, p 109.
11. PD, Vol 4, p 189 (19 June 1663).
12. Bryant, op cit, p 110.

4

CHILD OF THE PLAGUE

Five years after the Restoration, when Henry Purcell was six years old, London was decimated by the Great Plague. The entire population of the City, Liberties of Westminster and outlying parishes was just short of 500,000: in a few months the Plague brought death to close on 100,000 in London alone. The disease was thought to have been carried by seamen from the Netherlands, but the declaration of war on the Dutch on 22 February 1665 cut off further direct contact with that source of infection.

There had been sporadic outbreaks of plague throughout the centuries, so when the first few cases were discovered, there was no great concern among the people. The attitude to death was casual and relatives were under no obligation to make known loss of life whatever the cause. Similarly, doctors were not required to report causes of death. In time of plague the Bills of Mortality came into operation, but since there was so much corruption in presenting true records of the cause of death, the figures for the year are unreliable.

Once the Plague had reached epidemic proportions, the authorities tightened the rules and appointed 'searchers of the dead'. These were illiterate, elderly female paupers without any knowledge of disease who worked in pairs. They were sent by the parish to the house of bereavement to exercise their rights of viewing the body and receiving a fee of 4d per corpse. If distressed relatives offered them a shilling or maybe half a crown, they were content to leave without even looking at the body. The searchers were virtual outcasts who lived in specially appointed houses where they had no contact with their own families. When they walked in the streets they kept their distance and warned the public by carrying a white wand.

Most of the buildings in London in 1665 were still those of the Plantagenets and Tudors; timber-built, red-tiled and gabled houses

which overhung gregariously towards their neighbours on the opposite side. Their picturesque beauty can be seen in many prints and
engravings of the period, but inside these rat-infested houses the
reality was somewhat different. The slender timber framework filled
in with lath and plaster harboured dirt and damp and the rooms were
small and dark. The effluent drained, if at all, into a cesspool and in
many cases simply flowed into the streets where the smell must have
been revolting. There had been little improvement since Cardinal
Wolsey passed through London some two centuries before, holding to
his nose an orange stuck with cloves.

Such filth and squalor became a natural breeding ground for plague,
and it was almost impossible to prevent the disease from spreading. In
desperation, the authorities brought back the medieval practice of
shutting up any house where a plague victim had lived. The doors were
padlocked and guards stood on duty day and night. The houses of the
'visited' were marked with a large red cross and no one was allowed to
leave or enter except the dreaded 'searchers'. Pails of water and food
were handed in so that the inhabitants could remain confined. As a
result entire families died of the disease.

Although Westminster and St Margaret's were situated so close to
the out-parishes that were so badly infected, they held a clean bill of
health until May when the first victim was reported in Long Ditch, a
squalid quarter near the Abbey. Westminster had its own permanent
pest-house as did the City of London. Since the old building in Tothill
Fields had fallen into disrepair, a 'New Pest-house' was built, for
which John Goodchild, a carpenter, was paid £93 5s.

Also in Tothill Fields were the terrible plague pits where the dead
were committed nightly without any rites. The sight of the cartloads
being emptied by the flare of torches was unforgettable. Today, the
boys of Westminster School play games on the green playing field in
Vincent Square. When later excavations were made to prepare
foundations for new building on another part of the site, heaps of
bones – evidence of the cramming together of the corpses – were
found. There were also broken remains of clay pipes which the diggers
used to disinfect themselves as they carried out their obnoxious task.

'The poore's Plague' was not at first the concern of the wealthier
inhabitants of London. But as the disease spread to the out-parishes,
many noble families retired to their country homes to await the decline
of the pestilence.

By June, most of the nobility had fled to the country and in July the
King took his court to Sion House at Isleworth, where he stayed two

nights before departing for Hampton Court. Subsequently he stayed at Salisbury and Oxford, returning to London early in the New Year of 1666 when the Plague was safely on the wane.

As far as we know, the Purcells remained in Westminster throughout the epidemic, although as Thomas was one of the King's musicians, he would have been obliged to serve at court wherever it was domiciled. Unfortunately no records exist to give exact information about the movements of Thomas or the rest of the family. But at some time during those dreadful months, the six-year-old Henry would have seen the searchers with their white canes and heard the continual knell of the sexton's bells. The smell of death and the sound of the carts trundling over the cobbles at night with their dreaded call 'Bring out your dead!' are experiences a child could not easily forget.

As if this were not enough, the very next year when Henry was seven, the City of London was demolished by the Great Fire. It broke out during the night of Sunday 1 September in Pudding Lane and was driven by a hot easterly gale into the City. The King ordered the houses in its path to be destroyed, but the terrified inhabitants frantically removing their goods, prevented the Lord Mayor enforcing the order. Consequently, the flames continued to spread and nothing could be done to stem its growth. In the evening Charles came down the river to see for himself. As it grew dark the fire took 'a most horrid, malicious and bloody aspect' stretching for at least a mile across the sky. The following day the flames reached the top of St Paul's and the melting lead of the roof poured into the aisles below. Charles took control of the fire-fighters and was himself in the forefront.

All that day he was King of England, riding up and down the line of his workmen with a bag of guineas at his side, commanding, threatening, rewarding, sometimes dismounting at the fiercest points to pass the buckets with his own hands [the only water supply was from the Thames], or standing, ankle deep in water, amid sparks and falling masonry, to see his orders for blowing up houses carried out.[1]

It raged for two more days and finally subsided on the Thursday morning leaving a mass of blackened stones and charred timber stretching for 450 acres. Altogether 13,200 houses were destroyed either by fire or demolition and the majority of the City of London's inhabitants were homeless.

The destruction caused by the Fire affected the lives of everyone who worked in London. The following petition, one of many, is typical, not only of the results of the Fire itself but of the way in which musicians suffered through the impecuniosity of their monarch:

John Gamble, one of His Majesty's wind-instrument concert, pleaded for payment of £221.10s. 4½d, arrears of his salary over four and three-quarter years. All he possessed he had lost by the dreadful Fire, and he had contracted a debt of £120, for which one of his sureties had been sent prisoner to Newgate. Ruin awaited them and their families without this payment. Twenty-two musicians on the violin made similar plaint, having had houses and goods burnt in the Fire.[2]

On 10 October 1666, Londoners held a feast day to celebrate the end of the Great Fire and a month later a thanksgiving for the end of the Plague. There was also another which took place at the Chapel Royal, for the victory over the Dutch on 25 July when Admiral Opdam was blown up in his own flagship and 10,000 Dutch seamen were either slain or drowned. Matthew Locke composed a special anthem, 'The King Shall Rejoice', for the occasion.

It was a year for celebration. Pepys writes about a ball held in honour of the Queen's birthday in November 1666. Having obtained for himself an excellent place from which he could see everything, he tells us that the house was full and all the candles were lit. He describes in considerable detail the gowns and jewels worn by the ladies and 'the King in his rich vest of some rich silk and silver trimming'. He was not greatly impressed with the dancing which consisted of Bransles, Corants and 'French' dances, with the exception of one called the 'New Dance': this he thought 'very pretty'.[3]

The King's violins, who were playing on this occasion, had, as we know, recently complained strongly about their arrears of salary. It is to be hoped that these differences had been ameliorated before the gala ceremony for the Order of the Garter on 23 April 1667, the anniversary of Charles II's coronation, held first in the Chapel and then at the Banqueting House at Whitehall. Evelyn gives a vivid account beginning with the morning service in which the ceremony and the rich robes are described in evocative detail. There was a full music programme with the choir singing in procession and anthems for each stage of the ceremony, after which they proceeded to the Banqueting House for the great feast:

The King sat on an elevated throne at the upper end at a table alone; the Knights at a table on the right hand, reaching all the length of the room; over against them a cupboard of rich, gilded plate; at the lower end, the music; on the balusters above, wind music, trumpets, and kettle-drums. The King was served by the Lords and pensioners who brought up the dishes. About the middle of the dinner, the Knights drank the King's health, then the King, theirs, when the trumpets and music played and sounded, the guns going off at the Tower. At the Banquet, came in the Queen, and stood by the King's left hand, but did not sit. Then was the banqueting-stuff flung about the room profusely ... I now stayed no longer than this sport began for fear of disorder. The cheer was extraordinary, each Knight having forty dishes to his mess, piled up five or six high.[4]

The various members of the King's Musicians-in-ordinary were accustomed to such situations, but the choristers of the Chapel Royal – either 'gentlemen' or 'children' – were concerned with more serious matters. Their fine singing and colourful uniforms are still today an integral part of the splendour of royal occasions for celebration.

The term, Chapel Royal, refers not to the building in which the monarch attends divine service, but to the body of clergy and musicians, the vestments, the plate and the service books – musical and otherwise – which constitute the religious establishment attached to the household of a sovereign. The origins of the Chapel Royal can be traced back to the earliest Christian rulers of the Anglo-Saxon kingdoms, when 'The king and his court moved on as dictated by the seasonal food supplies and thus ... the Chapel Royal had to become "portable".'

All members of the King's Chapel, furthermore, and all his servants, enjoy the right by apostolic privilege to hear mass and to conduct all other divine service in any suitable place, and to set up an altar, even in the open air if necessary, and at it to consecrate the Lord's Body and to administer the Sacraments as the occasion demands, so long as any member of the King's Chapel or any other of his servants is present in that place.

(*Liber Regie Capelle*, Dean William Say, 1449)[5]

The instruction in singing of sacred music was of great importance from the time of St Augustine onwards. In the year 635 at Dunwich on the coast of East Anglia, King Sigbert of the East Angles founded a 'school for the education of boys in the study of letters ... with teachers and masters according to the practice of Canterbury'. It was probably the first school for the education of the Chapel Royal of the East Angles. Unfortunately, in 1316, a violent storm moved millions of tons of sand and shingle which blocked the mouth of the River Blyth cutting it off from the sea. Today nothing remains but the ruins of a medieval friary and a leper chapel.

It is not known with any accuracy what happened to the existing Chapel Royal after the Norman Conquest, because William systematically replaced the English bishops with those from the continent. By 1096 the English Church was entirely governed by a French-speaking aristocracy. A remarkable document dating from the reign of Henry I, gives an evocative picture of the Chapel Royal:

Keeper of the Chapel and relics and food for two men; and four servants of the Chapel, to each of whom double rations; and two sumpter horses of the Chapel, for each one a penny a day; and 1d for serving at the table and for work in the month. For service in the Chapel, two wax tapers on Wednesdays and two on Saturdays; and at night each to have one wax taper to place before the relics; and thirty inferior candles; and one gallon of white wine to be sent to them; and one sixth part of the best wine for the day of Absolution, for use at the altar. On Easter day for communion one sixth measure of white wine and one of the most expensive. The priest's expenses for bread and wine, 2s per day, and salted cumin and one sixth part of the best wine, and one wax taper, and twenty-four inferior candles.

(*Liber Rubeus Scacarii*)[6]

A further reference is a writ dated 7 July 1316 when Edward II mentions the education of 'twelve other children of our Chapel'. From this time the Chapel flourished throughout the centuries, even travelling abroad with the monarch. There are well documented details of the arrangements for the Chapel Royal to join Henry V where they remained in France from 1417–21.

Following the execution of Charles I the Chapel was disbanded. On the Restoration of the monarch, it was re-formed, but sadly, only five of its former members – one of whom was Henry Lawes – could be found. Both Purcell brothers were appointed as 'Gentlemen' of the Chapel; Henry was also a musician for lute and voice and in addition, a 'senior singing-man' or lay-clerk and master of the choristers at Westminster Abbey. Thomas also possessed that most useful of gifts, a good tenor voice.

The Lord Chamberlain's Office was at the centre of all activities relating to the Chapel and controlled the various departments concerned; the Signet Office drew up warrants for the king's signature, the Great Wardrobe dealt with clothing and furniture, the Treasurer of the Chamber was responsible for payments of strings, musical instruments, music, special duties and other incidental expenses, the Jewel House provided trumpets and gold medals or plate to reward some servants or foreign visitors, the Greencloth dealt with diet and board-wages, the Brazier made kettle-drums and their accessories, the Surveyor General of the Works – Sir Christopher Wren – was concerned with buildings and any necessary alterations to them, the Gentlemen Ushers administered the oath of allegiance, and the Messengers of the Chamber were responsible for ensuring that the Lord Chamberlain's warrants were safely delivered and any arrests resulting from these warrants made.

A court post brought with it the special responsibilities entailed in that appointment, and unquestioning service to the monarch was demanded. All employees were expected to behave with honour and dignity and if they failed in this respect, they were reprimanded by the Lord Chamberlain, and in extreme cases could be suspended from duty for a given period. On the credit side, a court post granted them immunity from civil arrest and from certain duties and taxes. There was considerable feuding between Court and City, exacerbated by the existence of these privileges, but as we shall see, financial hardship was one of the hazards of royal employment.

The plan overleaf shows clearly how the hierarchy of royal employment worked.

However, there were degrees within this hierarchy, depending upon which instrument they played. For example, the trumpeters always appear at the head of lists of musicians – probably a legacy from their ancient establishment at Court; a dozen of them served Edward I in the late 1200s. They represented a kind of human alarm system, primed to sound whenever the monarch appeared; on ships they sounded the watches and probably did the same at Court. Within the palaces they would be stationed as required in the more public areas from the Hall to the Presence Chamber. With the drummers they led the great processions of state and accompanied the king on hunts and journeys. Trumpeters had a high profile and were well paid, so well paid by Charles II that he was obliged to move some of them into the companies of Guards so that they could be paid by the army. When called upon to accompany ambassadors, they were dressed in their finest liveries. One such trumpeter, John Christmas, was sent to Poland with Laurence Hyde to arrange a peace treaty between the Turks and Tartars. At one point the letters were carried by Christmas, a Polish-speaking Scot and a man bearing a white flag. The Tartars tore up the letters before killing both Christmas and the Scotsman; the third man was left for dead but managed to crawl to safety. So much for being one of an élite group. After the trumpeters the court

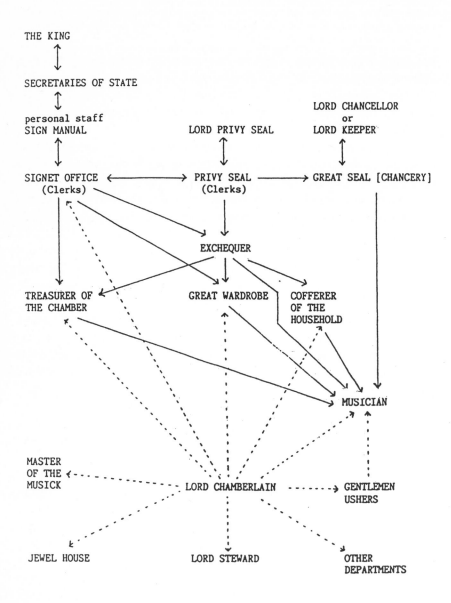

By kind permission of Andrew Ashbee

musicians were more or less equal in rank although there were variations in the wages they received. The violins, especially under Charles II, held pride of place. One of these would attend royal dancing practice in order to play the tunes; this was a semi-public affair in the hands of a dancing-master, but a full string band would play for the actual court dances. Many of these musicians would also be employed in the Cockpit Theatre just across the road from the palace.

The 'Gentlemen' and 'Children' of the Chapel Royal sang daily in the chapel and always travelled with the monarch to fulfil this duty for him. There was always a full choral service twice on Sundays and on any other days as designated by the clergy. They also were required to sing at any royal occasion such as a birth, state funeral, a marriage or a coronation.

The Master of the Children of the Chapel Royal at the Restoration was the legendary Captain Cooke. Born in Lichfield about 1615, and believed to be the son of John Cooke, a bass singer in the Chapel Royal, Henry Cooke was brought up as a boy chorister in the Chapel Royal. During the Civil War, Cooke, a confirmed Royalist, took up arms against Cromwell serving in the Duke of Northumberland's army. He was eventually promoted to a captaincy and was thereafter always known as 'Captain Cooke'.

During the Commonwealth period he had gained a reputation as a teacher of music, and it is also probable that, like so many other musicians, he took the opportunity to go to Italy to study the language and particularly voice production. In 1651, he is mentioned in Playford's *Musicall Banquet* as one of a number of 'excellent and able Masters for the voice and viol'. We know also, that he took part in one of the earliest operas performed in this country (see p 15). Evelyn, who heard him sing to his own accompaniment on the theorbo, tells us that he was 'esteemed the best singer, after the Italian manner, of any in England'.[7] Pepys considered that he had 'the best manner of singing in the world'.[8]

At the Restoration he had been appointed bass singer and Master of the Children, for which he was paid a salary of £45 per year, receiving the occasional extra sum such as £24 for: 'breeding a boy for vocall musick'.[9] As we know already, it was a difficult period in which to re-establish the pre-Commonwealth standards of church music. There were only five surviving adult members from the original choir and no boys at all. There were very few books, no surplices and, since the order of service had been so long in disuse, very few organists had

sufficient knowledge to play it correctly. So Cooke virtually started
from scratch and took to his task with energy and enthusiasm. He
immediately reinstated the press-gang warrant whereby he could go
throughout the country and remove any boys with good voices and
transfer them to London. Newark, Lincoln, Rochester, Peterborough,
Worcester, Lichfield, Canterbury, Oxford, Cambridge, Gloucester
and Hereford were his favourite hunting-grounds. His judgement was
impeccable, as a list of some of the boys in the first intake would prove;
William Turner, Michael Wise, John Blow, Thomas Tudway and
Pelham Humfrey all turned out to be accomplished musicians and fine
composers. We do not know if Cooke selected young Henry Purcell
personally, but since his father had been a member and his uncle was
still very active, there would have been no difficulty in obtaining a
place for him.

For the first year of Cooke's appointment, it had been necessary to
fill up the treble parts with cornetts (a curved wooden instrument with
a small cup-shaped 'brass-type' mouthpiece) and men singing falsetto.
Even though by 1661 Cooke had collected a sufficient number of
trebles to make the full complement of 12, we must remember they
were still in the course of training and therefore lacked the reading
ability and strength of fully trained voices. Pepys attended a service in
July 1660 and says: 'Here I heard very good Musique, the first time
that I remember ever to have heard the Organs and singing-men in
Surplices in my life.'[10] He does not mention the boys. There was
occasional criticism of the poor standard of the boys' singing:
Matthew Locke, a man of strong opinions and inclined towards
exaggeration, said that for a year after the Chapel Royal was reopened
there was 'not one Lad, for all that time, capable of Singing his Part
readily'.[11] There might have been some truth in the statement, but it
does not appear to take into account the fact that Blow, Humfrey and
Wise were among that first intake of boys. In the light of their later
accomplishments, it seems unlikely that they did not possess a
modicum of embryonic talent. None the less, Cooke seems to have
made good progress regardless of the limitations of his choristers, and
being such a good singer himself, he knew how to train his choir.
According to most people the results were generally much admired.

Cooke was a military man who brought the soldier's discipline into
his choir-training. 'The gentlemen were told that they must be
"properly surpliced, punctual and diligent, and must quit all interest in
other quires." The instrumentalists were bid "to wait in their turnes"
and rehearsals were held regularly on Saturdays.'[12]

According to some writers of the period, Cooke was extremely vain. Westrup dismisses this as 'tavern tittle-tattle'. Anthony Wood says that Cooke was eclipsed by Pelham Humfrey and as a result 'died in discontent and with greif',[13] an odd statement since Pelham Humfrey was also Cooke's son-in-law. Pepys, too, complains of Cooke's 'bragging that he doth understand tones and sounds as well as any man in the world, and better than Sir W. Davenant or anybody else'.[14] Westrup again makes the point that Cooke was a professional musician who knew what he was talking about, whereas 'Pepys, though he had self-importance enough for half a dozen men, was only an amateur'.[15]

The boys had their own livery especially made for them, and a glance at the following excerpt from the Lord Chamberlain's records gives some detail of the uniform young Henry Purcell would have worn when he joined the Chapel:

For each of them, one cloak of bastard scarlett cloth lined with velvett, one suit and coat of the same cloth made up and trimmed with silver and silk lace after the manner of our footmen's liveries, and also to the said suit, three shirts, three half-shirts, three pairs of shoes, three pair of thigh stocking, whereof one pair of silk and two pair of worsted, two hats with bands, six bands and six pairs of cuffs, whereof two laced and four plain, three handkerchers, three pairs of gloves and two pieces and a half of rebon for trimming garters and shoe strings.

And at Easter, for their summer liveries, for each boy one cloak of bastard scarlett lined with satin and one doublett of sattin with bastard scarlett trunk hose made and trimmed up as aforesaid, with three shirts, three half-shirts, three pair of shoes, three pair of thigh stockings, whereof one pair of silk and two pairs of worsted, two hats with bands, etc . . .[16]

Their livery has changed very little in style since the reign of Charles II, and certain traditions persist to the present time. For example, the juniors still wear square symmetrical buckles on their shoes, whilst seniors have the corners rounded: the head boy enjoys the privilege of wearing rectangular buckles with angled corners. The present uniforms are made of doeskin and gold trimmings have replaced the original silver.

Cooke appears to have taken his responsibilities very seriously, but his problems did not rest with uniforms or even the selection of good voices for his choir: in common with most of those in the royal employ, he had great difficulty in extricating money from the Treasury.

In 1663, Cooke had asked the Treasury for payment of arrears but received only promises. By 1666 his patience began to run out and he petitioned the king for payment presenting a list of 28 names including Thomas Purcell to whom he owed money. Cooke was owed salary dating back to 1662 and 'for teaching and apparelling two boys for 3 years ending 1666', all the others were claims for livery and services, some dating back to 1663. The King was sympathetic and informed the Lord Treasurer that he considered 'his honour concerned therein' and that there should be 'full and punctual payment' of every outstanding debt when money was next assigned to the Treasury.[17]

Unfortunately the royal wish could not command from an empty exchequer and two years later, Cooke, now at his wits' end, decided on stronger measures. He announced that he refused to allow the boys to attend the chapel. He was summoned to appear before the Lords of the Treasury who were shocked at his action, but Cooke simply retorted that the boys' clothes were in such a poor state, they were obliged to stay indoors. Even so the money was not forthcoming. The following year Cooke announced that the children should wear plain black gowns as did the boys of Westminster School, but this does not seem to have been adopted. The choristers were allowed to keep their scarlet surplices and lace cassocks but all were in tatters. It is not difficult to imagine the discomfort suffered by boys who had grown in the six years since they first donned their spectacular new robes, let alone their everyday liveries.

Cooke was still pressing for payment in 1670. This time he drew up a petition to the King himself in which he said that the children's clothes were in such a bad state that they were unfit to attend His Majesty or even walk abroad. Could he be given an order to have new liveries made? Through the Treasury the King said he wished the liveries to be made as previously, but the officers of the wardrobe were also bereft of funds. So Cooke was asked to take out a loan so that the wardrobe could place orders for the material. Incidentally, this did not hinder delivery in March 1670 of: 'three crimson damask curtains for the music room in the Chapel, the music room being enlarged'.[18] Eventually the arrears were paid, but out of the revenue from wine licences.

There are many stories of how the non-payment of salaries and liveries adversely affected many of those in royal appointments. The records show instances of debts being outstanding for up to ten years. In some cases there are petitions by the widows or executors of some creditor who died in the interim. When Cooke died, the Crown owed him £500 and only half of this was ever paid to his widow. Sometimes people would assign their arrears to a friend to whom they owed money. The friend would then take on the debt, with the dubious privilege of being a royal creditor.

References

1. Bryant, *King Charles II*, pp 183–4.
2. Bell, W.G., *The Great Fire of London in 1666*, 2nd edition, Bodley Head, 1951, p 229.
3. PD, Vol 7, p 372 (15 November 1666).
4. ED, Vol 2, pp 24–5 (23 April 1667).
5. Baldwin, David, *The Chapel Royal, Ancient & Modern*, Duckworth, 1990, pp 17–18.
6. Ibid, p 20.
7. ED, Vol 1, p 308 (28 November 1654).
8. PD, Vol 2, p 142 (27 July 1661).
9. Lafontaine, Henry Cart de, *The King's Musick*, A transcript of records relating to music and musicians, (1460–1700), Novello, 1909, p 117.
10. PD, Vol 1, p 195 (8 July 1660).
11. Westrup, *Purcell*, p 11.
12. *Grove's Dictionary of Music and Musicians*, 5th edition, ed Eric Blom, Macmillan, Vol 2, p 420.
13. Westrup, op cit, p 14.
14. PD, Vol 8, p 59 (13 February 1667).
15. Westrup, op cit, p 15.
16. AA, Vol 1, pp xiii, 136–7.
17. Westrup, op cit, p 16 fn.
18. AA, Vol 1, p 104.

5

CHILD OF THE CHAPEL ROYAL

There are no exact records of when young Henry Purcell first took his place among the Children of the Chapel Royal, but it is a fair assumption that he was about six years old. Some biographers put his age at nine or ten, but the circumstances point to him being much younger. If a boy is to have a good voice, the signs are obvious from three or four years of age – in some cases, even earlier. Purcell was obviously a gifted child and had a firm musical background. His uncle Thomas was in charge of his musical education from the age of five: if he showed interest and good vocal ability, would he not have been taken into the choir at the earliest opportunity? But at whatever age he became one of the 'Children' we know that he enrolled under Captain Cooke and in addition to tuition in singing and sight-reading, he was given lessons on the lute, theorbo, violin and harpsichord. He would also have arrived at the time when Cooke was fighting to obtain money for new liveries (see p 34), but no doubt was fitted out with a new uniform, the cost being added to the already large account outstanding. Furthermore he would have learned to abide by the strict rules governing royal service, set up some years previously, probably at the instigation of Captain Cooke. The limits of outside appearances were categorically defined in the following from the Lord Chamberlain on 12 November 1663:

An order to apprehend all musicians playing at any dumb shows, models, gamehouses, taverns, or any other places in the city of London and Westminster, without leave or licence from the Corporation of the Art and Science of Musick.[1]

Nevertheless, some musicians had disobeyed this order; on 18 June 1669, there is a list of seven musicians who have been apprehended:

for keeping playhouses and sounding trumpets, drums and fifes at dumb shows and models without paying the fee due to his Majesty's serjeant trumpeter by Letters Patent dated 24 January 13 Charles II, whereby the said serjeant trumpeter ought to receive twelve pence from every playhouse for every day they act, his Majesty's players excepted; no trumpets, drums or fifes being allowed to be sounded without his licence.[2]

The new recruit to the Children of the Chapel would not have been much concerned with what went on at the playhouses at the time, but when the opportunity to compose came his way, he would certainly have been interested. It was known that the King, always ready to foster young talent, encouraged members of the Chapel to write anthems on a regular basis. An oft-quoted example, the *Club Anthem*, was composed jointly by Humfrey, Blow and Turner to celebrate the victory by the Duke of York over the Dutch in June 1665. Charles, 'a brisk & Airy Prince',[3] liked only lively tunes to which he could beat time. Roger North tells us that Tudway, himself a chorister, accuses Humfrey, Blow and Wise of 'indulging the King's French taste so far as to introduce theatrical *corants* and dancing movements into their anthems'. He goes on to say that 'Even the great Purcell is not exempt from this charge, and many of his finest anthems are disfigured by *fiddling symphonies* invented only to tickle the ears of the wretched Charles. They are now wisely left out in performance.'[4]

It is therefore possible that Henry Purcell was composing from a very early age, and once he became one of the 'Children' of the Chapel, he lost no time in showing what he could do. The first musical composition attributed to Henry, then aged eleven, has a lengthy title: an *Address of the Children of the Chapel Royal to the King, and their Master, Captain Cooke, on his Majesties Birthday, AD 1670*. According to W.H. Cummings, a copy of this work in Pelham Humfrey's handwriting was once known to have been in the possession of Dr Rimbault, but unfortunately its whereabouts are no longer known.[5]

Henry Purcell must have been under the tutelage of Captain Cooke for about four years, and would certainly have benefited from his master's knowledge of vocal music. Cooke's leaning towards the theatrical and Italianate style of singing would not have been lost on his young pupil. When Cooke died in 1672, his place was taken by his son-in-law Pelham Humfrey, an 'enormously talented composer',[6] thus establishing a valuable continuity.

Pelham Humfrey was born in 1647, probably in London, but

nothing more is known about him until he was recruited by Cooke for the reconstituted choir of the Chapel Royal in 1660. As we know, even as a chorister he showed considerable talent in composition and five of his anthems written during this period are published in the second edition of Clifford's *Divine Services and Anthems* (1664).

Humfrey was a favourite of Charles II and in 1664 had been sent by the King to France and Italy for three years to study foreign style, his expenses being paid from the Secret Service Monies, £450 in all. On his return, Pepys notes that after this time, the music he wrote shows the influence of his contacts with composers such as Lully, Carissimi and their Italian contemporaries. But Pepys is less impressed with his behaviour and tells us that he is:

an absolute Monsieur, as full of form and confidence and vanity, and disparages everything and everybody's skill but his own. The truth is, everybody says he is very able; but to hear how he laughs at all the King's music here, as [Thomas] Blagrave and others, that they cannot keep time nor tune, nor understand anything, and that Grebus [Louis Grabu], the Frenchman, the King's Master of the Musique, how he understands nothing, nor can play on any instrument, and so cannot compose, and that he will give him a lift out of his place, and that he and the King are mighty great, and that he hath already spoke to the King of Grebus, would make a man piss.[7]

Humfrey's high opinion of himself was no doubt further inflated by the fact that in his absence he had been appointed Royal Lutenist (1666) and on 24 January the following year, a Gentleman of the Chapel Royal, being admitted on 26 October shortly after his return. In 1671 Humfrey and Thomas Purcell were appointed 'composers in ordinary to His Majesty for the violin without fee'.[8] Two years later, on 9 March 1673, this prosperous member of the Purcell family took on yet another appointment, that of 'musician in ordinary to his Majesty in the private musick in the place of John Wilson, deceased',[9] thus augmenting his already substantial income. It is not surprising that, despite the arrears which accrued over the years, he still managed to live in the Court's most fashionable residential area.

Meanwhile his 14-year-old nephew found himself promoted, and on 10 June 1673, a warrant was issued:

to swear and admit Henry Purcell in the place of keeper, mender, maker, repairer and tuner of the regals, organs, virginals, flutes and recorders and all other kind of wind instruments whatsoever, in ordinary, without fee, to his

Majesty, and assistant to John Hingston, and upon the death or other avoidance of the latter, to come in ordinary with fee.[10]

This appointment, entrusted to one so young, shows that his outstanding talent was being recognized and given scope to develop. It was also a practical advantage: not only would he have a working knowledge of the capabilities of each and every instrument, but also a familiarity with their respective sounds. This early knowledge of the instruments and their individual propensities, must have contributed to Purcell's later ability to provide colour and variety on a wider spectrum than that of any previous composer.

Hingston, too, was an admirable master: a pupil of the great Orlando Gibbons, he was an organist, composer and viol-player who had been a member of Charles I's band. During the Commonwealth he was appointed musician and keeper of the organs to Oliver Cromwell and also instructed both of his employer's daughters in music (see p 13). No doubt his young assistant accompanied him to tune the organs in the King's country residences, thus gaining valuable experience in handling a number of different instruments.

Six months after taking up this appointment, Purcell's voice broke: two further warrants were issued on 17 December 1673 from which we see how the boys were looked after even when they were no longer useful members of the choir.

To provide the usual clothing for Henry Purcell, late child of His Majesty's Chapel Royal, whose voice is changed and who is gone from the Chapel.
Warrant to pay to Henry Purcell £30 a year, beginning at Michaelmas, 1673.[11]

The 'usual clothing' would have consisted of:

two suites of playne cloth, two hatts and hattbands, four whole shirts, four half shirts, six bands, six pairs of cuffs, six handkerchiefs, four pair of stockings, four pair of shoes, and four pair of gloves.[12]

Many of the boys whose voices had broken were sent to the provinces as organists but Purcell was fortunate in that he already had his post as Hingston's assistant. He probably also studied composition under Pelham Humfrey, who would have instructed him in the style and techniques he had learned during his years in France and Italy. There was only 12 years difference in their ages: with so much in common they must have been more than just master and pupil.

It is probable that during this time, further encouraged by Humfrey, the 14-year-old Henry Purcell wrote his first surviving composition, a catch, 'Here's that will challenge all the Fair'.

Throughout Purcell's brief life he was to suffer the recurring loss of friend or mentor. In 1674, after only a year of their close association, Humfrey died suddenly at the age of 27. His place was taken by yet another fine musician and prolific composer, the 26-year-old John Blow, who had also started his career as one of Cooke's recruits in the original choir for the Chapel Royal.

Born in Newark in 1649, John Blow was a pupil of both Hingston and Christopher Gibbons, and at only 19 became organist of Westminster Abbey with an annual salary of £10. In January 1669 he was appointed a 'musician for the virginals' to Charles II, and sworn a Gentleman of the Chapel Royal in March 1674. In June he succeeded Pelham Humfrey as Master of the Children, a position he held for the rest of his life, and as such became a most important influence on succeeding generations of choristers. These included William Croft, Jeremiah Clarke and Daniel Purcell, Henry's younger brother.

Although Henry Purcell's voice had already broken when Blow took over the choristers, the two had previously become acquainted, probably when Purcell tuned the organ at the Abbey. His progress must have been swift, for he was entrusted with tuning this very important instrument only a year after his appointment as assistant, for which he received £2 in payment for one year.[13]

It is fairly conclusive that Purcell studied composition privately with Blow. Henry Hall, also a member of the Children of the Chapel Royal, writes a verse praising Blow's *Amphion Anglicus* (1700), in which the last line reads: 'And Britain's Orpheus learned his art from you'. That

Blow was proud of his young pupil's progress, is undisputed, for on his own memorial stone in Westminster Abbey we read that he was: 'Master to the famous Mr H. Purcell'.

Blow's generosity has not served him well in history. Composers rarely praise another's gifts as being greater than their own, so it has always been assumed that his was the lesser talent. The neglect of Blow's music over the centuries has hindered a true assessment of his abilities, but recent research has shown that he wrote some very powerful music. It was so highly charged that it would have been a direct inspiration for his young pupil, and we see this influence permeating Purcell's work through and through. It is because we are not familiar with Blow that we have disregarded how much Purcell is indebted to his teacher who, in turn, was indebted to the Italians. Later, when Purcell came to write semi-opera, the influence is even more apparent, but this will be discussed in the relevant chapter.

In addition to his many compositions, Blow also compiled two methods of teaching music. One was 'Rules for Playing of a Thorough Bass upon Organ and Harpsichord' which would have been invaluable for Purcell in accompanying songs and instrumental music; and the other, 'Rules for Composition', shows some of the basic principles and techniques. Zimmerman agrees with Watkins Shaw that their simplicity would point to the possibility that they were written expressly as a series of lessons for the young Purcell.[14]

Henry Purcell was only 16 when he experienced the excitement of seeing one of his own compositions in print for the first time. The song, 'When Thyrsis did the splendid eye', was published in *Choice Ayres Book I*, and with it, the young composer had become a professional.

There is in existence another example of Purcell's composition, the 'Stairre Case Overture', probably dating from 1676 when he was 17. Alan Browning, assisted by Peter Holman and Curtis Price acknowledges Nigel Fortune's initiative in drawing attention to four folio volumes of manuscript music, chiefly by Purcell, in the library of Tatton Park, Knutsford, Cheshire.[15]

There are many transcriptions from seventeenth-century manuscripts which have been carefully and accurately copied and wherever possible incorporate the original and occasionally autograph scores. The third volume is particularly interesting as it contains Purcell's early ode to St Cecilia, *Raise the Voice*, but also 'The Starr Case Overture'* ascribed to 'Hen, y Purcel'. This appears in Philip Hayes's

---

* Surely a misreading of the title given by Hayes's source?

(1738–97) hand on the last two pages of the unpaginated volume following 38 pages of Purcell's fantasias copied in by Thomas Barrow who died in 1789.

The piece is only 53 bars in all, but as Browning points out, there is ample evidence of an original mind at work. Hayes had obviously regarded it as something of a curiosity and noted it down at the end of the volume, but omitted it from his index. Therefore some doubt as to the composer might exist but for a manuscript in the Osborn Collection at Yale University where the bass viol part of the overture is again ascribed to Purcell and entitled 'The Stairre Case Overture in B me'. This version is almost identical to that by Hayes, 'the sole difference lying in the fact that Hayes has adopted the modern convention in his treatment of accidentals, substituting natural signs for the sharps of the Yale MS'. Browning suggests that Purcell, at the time, was under Matthew Locke's influence, if not actually his pupil. The running scales of the first section – which could be related to the choice of title – and the three-part treatment of the *tripla* are reminiscent of Locke's writing, but Browning considers that 'The clearest indication of Locke's guiding hand, though, lies in the uncompromising treatment of the bass line – especially in the closing section, where it strides majestically downwards to a low G flat before resolving on to the tonic of B flat.' Browning considers that this same passage predominantly foreshadows Purcell's early maturity, 'with rich, adventurous harmony which might even have surprised his mentor, and which clearly anticipates that of the fantasias of 1680'. With the two manuscripts we are fortunate in having the complete version of a work dating from Purcell's formative years.[16]

That same year we find Purcell being paid £5 for 'pricking out [copying] two bookes of organ parts'.[17] Some biographers claim that Purcell had the post of official copyist at the Abbey, but as Westrup points out, there was no such position: treasurers' accounts show that this task was carried out by a number of people. He refutes the idea that copying out Elizabethan anthems would have influenced the young composer, and asks if it does not seem odd that 16 years after the Restoration, it should be necessary to copy out Elizabethan anthems. 'In the very first year of Charles II's reign the abbey authorities bought from John Playford, the publisher, a set of Barnard's printed collection of services and anthems in addition to borrowing another set for four or five Sundays.'[18] Purcell would have been employed simply to write out the organ parts of new anthems by contemporary composers, of which there were many; an exercise that would undoubtedly have influenced his musical development.

References

1. AA, Vol 1, p 49.
2. Ibid, p 91.
3. Westrup, *Purcell*, p 199.
4. North, *Memoires*, p 104.
5. Cummings, William H., *Purcell*, Sampson Lowe, 1881, p 20.
6. Holland, A.K., *Henry Purcell, The English Musical Tradition*, Penguin, 1948, p 36.
7. PD, Vol 8, pp 529–30 (15 November 1667).
8. AA, Vol 1, p 111.
9. Ibid, p 134.
10. Ibid, p 126.
11. Ibid, pp 131–2.
12. Lafontaine, *The King's Musick*, p 251.
13. WAM 33709, fo 5.
14. Zimmerman, *Henry Purcell, 1659–1695, His Life and Times*, pp 37–8.
15. Fortune, Nigel, 'A New Purcell Source', *Music Review*, Vol 25, 1964, pp 109–13.
16. Browning, Alan, 'Purcell's Stairre Case Overture', *Musical Times*, Vol 121, December 1980, pp 768–9. A page from the Tatton Park manuscript, almost certainly in Purcell's own hand, is printed in the article.
17. WAM 33710, fo 5v.
18. WAM 33695, fo 5.

6

A BISHOP'S BOY

At the time of Queen Elizabeth, most of the musicians who attended her court were composers as well as performers, the two roles being accepted as the norm. In the early seventeenth century in England, singers, players and composers were beginning to be recognized as separate entities, a situation that had existed in Italy for some time, mainly because of their long association with the theatre and opera.

One of the composers inspired by the Italians was Matthew Locke. As an old family friend of some years standing he had exerted a marked influence on Henry Purcell in his formative years. The first mention is in Pepys's *Diary*:

After dinner I back to Westminster-hall . . . Here I met with Mr Lock[e] and Pursell, Maisters of Musique; and with them to the Coffee-house into a room next the Water by ourselfs . . . Here we had a variety of brave Italian and Spanish songs and a Canon for 8 Voc:, which Mr Lock[e] had newly made on these words: *Domine salvum fac Regem*, an admirable thing.[1]

Whether he is referring to Henry the elder or Thomas Purcell remains in question, but there is no doubt that the family were well acquainted. The entry also shows that Pepys never lost an opportunity to meet with good musicians, especially if he could take part in the music-making, as one might believe he did on this occasion.

One other interesting but as yet unsubstantiated piece of evidence is the letter from Locke to Purcell published in Cummings's biography, a copy of which was shown to him by E.F. Rimbault:

DEAR HARRY, – Some of the gentlemen of His Majesties musick will honor my poor lodgings with their company this evening, and I would have you come and join them: bring with thee, Harry, thy last anthem, and also the

canon we tried over together at our last meeting. Thine in all kindness,
          M. LOCKE

Savoy, March 16.[2]

Zimmerman, quite rightly, suggests that even if it cannot be authenticated, the letter should not be dismissed. The contents are feasible and in the style of the period. The most likely date would seem to be 1676, when Purcell was 17. Matthew Locke was born in Exeter about 1621 and trained as a chorister at Exeter Cathedral under Edward Gibbons, brother of the more famous Orlando. He spent some time in the Low Countries copying down motets by Flemish and Italian composers, which undoubtedly had an influence on his later compositions. In addition to his considerable output of songs, church, chamber and instrumental music, he wrote for a number of stage productions, which included *The Siege of Rhodes* by William Davenant in which Henry Purcell the elder appeared as a singing actor. Locke once claimed that he did more to introduce opera to the English public than anyone else. This may be an exaggeration but he did understand the importance of the dramatic element in the masque or chamber opera which would prepare the English for the full-scale Italian version when it arrived. In his preface to *The English Opera or the Vocal Musicke in Psyche* (1675), he writes:

It may fitly bear the title [Opera] though all the tragedy be not in Musick; for the authour prudently consider'd that though Italy is the great Academy of the World for that Science and way of entertainment, England is not: and therefore mix'd it with interlocutions as more proper to our genius.[3]

At the Restoration, Locke had been given three important posts; private composer-in-ordinary to the King, succeeding Coprario; composer of wind music in place of Alfonso Ferrabosco, and a new appointment as composer for the King's newly formed band of violins. He was also organist to the Queen. His music for 'His Majesty's Sagbutts and Cornetts' was probably performed during King Charles II's journey from the Tower of London to Whitehall on 22 April 1661, on the eve of his coronation.

Temperamentally, Locke was a firebrand, a caustic critic and a willing antagonist in any interesting controversy. None the less, musically, he is important as one of the most eminent of Purcell's predecessors in writing for the stage. Purcell would have inherited from Locke his Italianate style in writing for both voices and instruments. Throughout the latter part of the seventeenth century, Italian performers, composers and teachers were arriving at all the important courts of Europe. By the time Purcell was in his early twenties, the Italians and their style had been accepted as a significant fact of English musical life.

The death on 26 October 1676, of Christopher Gibbons marked the passing of another distinguished musician with a less spectacular reputation than Locke, but one who also had an influence on the young Purcell. He, like Locke, had taken part in and provided music for *The Siege of Rhodes* in 1656 and 1661, so again we have a link with the Purcell family. From 1665 onwards, he resided in Great Almonry South where the Purcells had lived until Henry the elder's death in 1664. The Fitzwilliam MS shows that young Purcell copied down a number of anthems by Gibbons from scores pre-dating the Commonwealth, presumably for study purposes.

Christopher Gibbons, Orlando's second son, was born in London and received his early training as one of the Children of the Chapel Royal. His father died when he was only ten and he was adopted by his uncle at Exeter where he first met his fellow chorister and lifelong friend, Matthew Locke.

Gibbons was one of the few remaining musicians whose careers had spanned the period from pre-Commonwealth to Restoration. He was appointed organist to the Chapel Royal and private organist to Charles II in 1660, and in the same year became organist of Westminster Abbey. Essentially a keyboard player, he would have been thoroughly proficient in polyphonic techniques and no doubt imparted these skills to the young composer. 'How important this influence may have been for Purcell's development as a keyboard artist remains a moot point, because a large share of such influence would have been reflected in improvisatory techniques, of which no contemporary descriptions have come down to us.'[4]

The death of Matthew Locke the following year would have engendered mixed feelings for young Henry Purcell. On the one hand, the sad loss of friend and mentor, on the other, joy at his appointment on 10 September 1677 as 'composer in ordinary with fee for the violin to his Majesty, in the place of Matthew Lock[e], deceased'.[5] He was barely 18.

The loss inspired Purcell to write a personal tribute: 'On the death of his worthy friend Mr Matthew Locke, musick-composer to his majesty, and organist of Her majestie's Chappel, who dyed in August 1677', opening with the moving words, 'What hope for us remains now he is gone?' This was published in *Choice Ayres* Book II in 1679.

The following year saw the departure of yet another eminent figure, the 86-year-old John Jenkins. As one of Charles I's musicians, he had formed the last remaining and most important link between the music of the pre-Commonwealth and the Court of Charles II. Born during the reign of Elizabeth, he had been a musician at a very early age, and from his youth had resided with the family of a noble patron. After the Restoration he lived with the family of Lord North and taught music to his two sons, the younger being Roger North, whose writings have left us such a vivid account of the musical world of his time. He tells us that Jenkins was 'a person of much easier temper than any of his faculty, he was neither conceited nor morose, but much a gentleman, and had a very good sort of wit, which served him in his address and conversation, wherein he did not please less than in his compositions'.[6]

Purcell was one of the many musicians acquainted with the North family, so at some time he would certainly have met Jenkins. Purcell's own musical style shows that he gleaned much from the great musical tradition that flourished from the Tudors through to the early Stuarts, so he would not have missed the opportunity to discuss with and learn from this grand old master of the fancy himself. We know that Purcell copied down a number of the compositions from this period and rearranged them for different combinations of instruments. There is in the Bodleian Library a copy of Monteverdi's 'Cruda Amarilli' arranged by Purcell for viols.

This is a significant example of how, during the Restoration, musicians were consciously trying to reconnect with the earlier ecclesiastical Tudor tradition that had been disrupted by the Civil War. Blow, Locke and Jenkins, transmitted this directly to Purcell so that almost more than any other composer of his time, he was aware of the English tradition which had been severed.

Thomas Tomkins was a composer who would also have influenced the young Purcell through his *Musica Deo Sacra* which was published in 1668. Had this work not been carried out with such care, most of the anthems and services would either have been lost or too fragmented to be restored.

Another composer who exerted a strong influence on Purcell was William Lawes, although he died long before Purcell was born. His compositions included a wide range of instrumental music including consorts of viols and unaccompanied violins, and a number of his techniques and style of writing were adopted by Purcell, especially when writing for viols.

William Lawes – younger brother of Henry – was born in Salisbury in 1602, and probably became a chorister at Salisbury Cathedral where his father was a lay vicar. He showed such early talent that Edward Seymour, Earl of Hertford, a very important patron of music from the late sixteenth century, took him into his family and had him instructed by his own music master, John Coprario. At the age of 23, Lawes became a private musician to the young Prince Charles, and continued to serve him when he ascended the throne. He had been composing music for the Court since 1633 and in 1635 was appointed 'musician-in-ordinary for lutes and voices'. His output was prolific and in addition to vocal and instrumental music he also wrote for the elaborate court masques and numerous plays performed by the King's Men at the Cockpit and Blackfriars theatres. During the Civil War he enlisted in the royalist army and was killed by a stray shot at Chester in 1645.

*   *   *   *   *

As composer for the violins, Purcell was expected to write music for social occasions, including dancing at court. We know that the King's taste was for music on the lighter side, so his young composer would doubtless have respected his wishes. Unfortunately none of the music from this period has survived.

In 1678 two important events took place in Purcell's life. The first was that he had five songs published in *New Ayres and Dialogues Composed for Voices and Viols*, therefore bringing his music before a wider public than ever before, and the second, that he took the opportunity to further his general education. It appears from the treasurer's account in Westminster Abbey that Henry Purcell became a 'Bishop's Boy' at St Peter's College, Westminster under its headmaster, Dr Richard Busby who achieved immortality through his infamous floggings. Henry's cousin Charles had been a Bishop's Boy since 1670, but in that same year we find his own name added to the records.

The 'Bishop's Boys', previously known as 'Lord's Scholars', were the recipients of scholarships founded by the Revd John Williams, Bishop of Lincoln and later Archbishop of York. In a deed dated 26 April 1624, he placed in trust farm rents which had been purchased the previous year to enable four scholarships to be awarded. The boys should be natives of Wales and Lincoln 'to be educated and

maintained in the Grammar School of St Peter's College in Westminster and there to have free education until they shall be thence
elected and transplanted into St John's Coll[ege], Camb[ridge]'.[7]
Presumably if there were no suitable candidates from these regions,
they were free to look elsewhere.

There is no information regarding the earlier part of Purcell's
schooling, but on his own admission his education was sparse. In the
preface to his trio sonatas, published in 1683, he admits his lack of
skill in the Italian language and blames it on the 'unhappiness of his
education' which, quite rightly, he cannot acknowledge as his own
fault. He would therefore have seized this opportunity to improve the
situation. Despite his strict discipline, Busby was a fine academician
and many of his charges grew up to be famous in their chosen field:
John Dryden, John Locke and Christopher Wren had all been taught
by him. The essayist and dramatist, Richard Steele, though not himself
a pupil, assessed the effect of Busby's influence by the accomplishments of his pupils: 'He had a power of raising what the lad had in him
to the utmost height.'[8]

No details are extant regarding Purcell's time with Busby, but there
is no doubt that he thought highly of his famous pupil. Frances Purcell,
Henry's widow, states in her will that there is 'a mourning ring of Dr
Busby's' among her effects.

We do not know how long Purcell availed himself of the Bishop's
Boy exhibition. It may well have been terminated when, in 1679, he
was appointed organist of Westminster Abbey, for which he was paid
£10 a year, and in addition, an allowance of £8 per annum for his
house.[9] In taking this post, he was succeeding his teacher, John Blow,
and stories abound as to why Blow resigned. The more fanciful would
have us believe that Blow was so overawed with young Purcell's talent
that he relinquished the post in favour of a greater master. Certainly
Purcell showed great promise, but had not, as yet, made his name as a
composer. It is more likely that pressure was put upon Blow to move
aside to make way for the younger man; in any case, he was fully
occupied with performing his own court duties.

Unfortunately, the records showing Purcell's declaration have been
lost, but details of the oath taken by Blow eleven years previously,
suggest that Purcell's would have been similarly worded:

I John Blow being to be admitted into the place of Mr Albertus Byrne late
organist of the Collegiate church of Westminster, doe promise due obedience,
diligent attendance and conformity to the laudable customes of the sayd

50

The contrast between these two very different catches, both by Purcell, shows the extent of his ability to write music to words, irrespective of their meaning.

5. 6. they found fo woundy great, fo wond'rous fweet, & they

ay at Four and Ten, cries come. come. come. come. come to Pray'rs. & the

arers home, but the De'il a Man will leave his Can till he

. Purcell.

Twice. Thrice. I Ju . . . LIA

and fince I can - - no better better

kifs my Ar — fo kifs my Ar — fo kifs my Ar — difdainfull

de . . . ny'd, and

a . . live, So kifs my Ar —

_ trefs now.

church; and if I shall be hereafter preferrd to any other place which may prove prejuduciall to my attendance in the sayd church; I will be content to relinquish all my right, title and interest unto the same, unto which I doe willingly subscribe, serving the first yeare upon approbation only, beginning December 3 1668

John Blow[10]

The musical establishment at the Abbey was under the authority of the dean and chapter and consisted of four petty canons (ordained choir men), 12 lay-clerks or singing-men, one of whom was master of the choristers and organist, and ten boys. All officers of the church, including members of the choir, were bound to receive Holy Communion at least three times a year (Easter, Whitsun and Christmas). These instructions date from 1679, no doubt to make sure that all members were professed Anglicans. The constant fear of Papists infiltrating even the hallowed bastions of the Abbey was not to be ruled out.

We have no first-hand accounts of life in the Abbey at this time, but there is a catch by Purcell, 'Upon Christ Church Bells in Oxford', which could give some indication of the daily routine of the organist and choir.[11]

There is also Thomas Brown's *Letters from the Dead to the Living* which, although concocted several years later, gives us an amusing imaginary insight into the pomposity and hypocrisy of the everyday occurrences. The following is supposed to be Blow's reply to a letter from Purcell after death:

I have no novelties to entertain you with relating to either the *Abbey* or *St Paul's*, for both the choirs continue just as wicked as they were when you left them; some of them come reeking hot out of the bawdy-house into the church, and others stagger out of a tavern to afternoon prayers, hick-up over a little of the *Litany*, and so back again.

Old *Claret-face* beats time still upon his cushion stoutly, and sits growling under his purple canopy, a hearty old- fashion'd bass, that deafens all about him. Beau *Bushy-wig* preserves his voice to a miracle, charms all the ladies over against him with his handsome face, and all over head with his singing. Parson *Punch* makes a very good shift still, and lyrics over his part in an anthem very handsomely.[12]

That same year the death occurred of John Banister, the court violinist who had fallen from grace some years previously. Despite his misappropriation of court funds when he was in the service of the King, Banister will always be remembered for giving what were the first-ever public concerts. Five years after he left the Court, he placed the following advertisement in the *London Gazette* of 30 December 1672:

These are to give Notice, that at Mr *John Banister's* House, now called the Musick-school, over against the *George* Tavern in White Fryers, this present Monday, will be Musick performed by Excellent Masters, beginning precisely at four of the Clock in the afternoon, and every afternoon for the future precisely at the same hour.

The concert-room was arranged with seats and small tables, alehouse-fashion, and a side box draped with curtains was provided for the musicians. He charged one shilling for admission and once the concerts became known there was seldom an empty seat. 'What is perhaps a little surprising is that a "musick school" should have existed in such a neighbourhood as Whitefriars, which at this period, by virtue of its ancient privileges of sanctuary, was still the asylum of unscrupulous debtors, here protected from arrest.'[13]

In 1678 Banister moved to larger premises at the 'Music School' in Essex Buildings in the Strand, close by the Church of St Clement Danes. He gave a concert there on 22 November of a 'consort of vocal and instrumental music' which he had himself composed. The date would suggest that it could have been one of the earliest celebrations for St Cecilia to have taken place in London.

Following closely in the steps of Banister was Thomas Britton, born in 1644 and known as the 'Musical Small-Coal Man'. Originally apprenticed to a coal-dealer, he later established his own business in Aylesbury Street in Clerkenwell, as a dealer in 'small-coal' (charcoal). He became a familiar figure walking through the streets of the City carrying the sacks upon his back. However, Britton had a thirst for learning far above his station and managed to acquire a great deal of knowledge in chemistry, rare books and the occult. He also educated himself in music from both the technical and practical aspect, and in 1678 he promoted concerts and formed a club for the practice of music. The concerts were given in a long narrow room over his shop in Jerusalem Passage and his patrons had to climb an outside stairway to gain access. At first the concerts were free but later they were given on a subscription basis of ten shillings a year. He also served his guests with coffee at a penny a dish. Despite the humble venue, the series attracted a number of famous musicians – including Handel and Pepusch – and many members of the nobility, eventually becoming one of the most important events in the musical life of London. There is no record that Purcell attended any concerts given by either Banister or Britton, but it is extremely unlikely that his curiosity would not have led him to investigate what was a completely new venture in the promotion of music outside the Church, Court or theatre. Besides which, many of his own compositions were regularly included in the programmes. In 1679 the second book of Playford's *Choice Ayres and Songs* was published. Of the seven songs by Purcell, four were light-hearted, and, according to the title page, were 'Sung at Court and Public Theatres'.

At this time Charles II needed as many light-hearted diversions as he could muster, for the previous year had seen the first rumblings of the 'Popish Plot'. Early in August 1678, he had been stopped in Windsor Park and warned of a plot to murder him so that his brother James, Duke of York – a staunch Catholic – should succeed to the throne. The man at the root of the conspiracy was Titus Oates, a renegade Jesuit novice and known troublemaker. The English fear of Catholicism in any form was so great that they needed no encouragement to believe that their lives were in danger. When Sir Edmund Berry Godfrey, a popular magistrate who had heard Oates's deposition, was found dead in a ditch on Primrose Hill – his own sword had been thrust through his body after he was strangled – there was no stopping the rumours. The cellars were said to be full of cutlasses, French ships had been seen off the coast of Kent and a massacre was imminent. Ladies who walked abroad, even in daytime, were known to carry loaded pistols concealed in their muffs.

The King tried his best to keep the situation from getting out of hand by disregarding the rumours, but when it was further alleged that his queen was planning to poison him, the public anger knew no bounds; no Catholic was safe on the streets, and a proposal for her removal was put up in the House of Lords. Fortunately it was rejected by eight votes. But eventually Charles was forced to impeach the Catholic peers and even had to forbid his brother to attend meetings of the Council. On the 22 May 1679 the Bill for changing the succession of the Crown, precluding the Duke of York from any claim, passed its second reading by a majority of 92. As a result he was quietly exiled to Flanders for his own safety.

Broadsheets were circulated to keep the public abreast of the latest news, and the catch, which had long been associated with politics, was also used to convey the latest information. Although dated 1676, and published in *A Choice Compendium* in 1681, the political catch by

Purcell, 'Now England's great council's assembled' would seem to have connotations with the Popish Plot. The final stanza makes its statement clear:

A pox on all Zealots and fools and each silly Protestant hater
Better turn cat in pan, and live like a man, than be hang'd and dye like a
traytor.

The catch was not alone in being used for propaganda purposes. Even the anthem was not above reflecting Tory policy. Since in the eyes of the Church authorities, Charles was a divinely appointed monarch, their conscience was undisturbed by using holy writings to further their cause. Under the Commonwealth, anthems were forbidden territory, along with the use of organs in church and the liturgical music that went with them. So when the anthem was restored under Charles, it was in an altogether different form from those by the early seventeenth-century composers.

Charles encouraged anthems written in the style of the Counter-Reformation motet, so popular on the Continent, and the composers of the day responded to his preferences. The anthems of Pelham Humfrey, Henry Cooke and Matthew Locke pleased all concerned by the secular and theatrical elements in their writing. This was not entirely due to the King's taste, nor the prevalent French and Italian influences. Many of the sacred songs of William Byrd and verse anthems of the Lawes brothers and Orlando Gibbons had looked forward to the post-Restoration developments.

The introduction of instrumental symphonies and solo vocal ensembles into the Church also brought a sense of theatre into the service itself, and it was this very element in Purcell's music that he later developed further than any of his predecessors and which would be the inspiration for Handel in the early eighteenth century.

References

1. PD, Vol 1, p 63 (21 February 1660).
2. Cummings, *Purcell*, p 27.
3. *Grove's*, Vol 6, p 203.
4. Zimmerman, *Henry Purcell, 1659–1695, His Life and Times*, p 41.
5. AA, Vol 1, p 173.

6. North, Roger, *Autobiography*, ed Augustus Jessopp, Nutt, 1887, p 79.

7. Zimmerman, op cit, p 50.

8. Ibid, p 51.

9. WAM 33715, fo 2, 5.

10. WAM 61228A, Precentor's Book, fo 104.

11. *The Catch Club or Merry Companion, A Collection of Favourite Catches for Three and Four Voices compos'd by Mr Henry Purcell, Dr Blow and the most eminent authors*, Book 1, London, Walsh, 1762.

12. Brown, Thomas, *Works*, 9th edition, Vol 2, 1760, p 248.

13. Elkin, Robert, *The Old Concert Rooms of London*, Arnold, 1955, p 20.

7

AYRES FOR THE THEATRE

Henry Purcell had composed his first anthem sometime in 1678 to words taken from Psalm 19, verses 12–14, 'Lord, Who Can Tell', and in the following year he set another for the anniversary of Charles I's martyrdom, 'Who hath believed our report'. Also about this time he had been working on a piece for John Gostling, the distinguished bass soloist who was then Chanter at Canterbury Cathedral. We learn this from a letter written by Thomas Purcell to Gostling on 8 February 1679:

Sir,
I have re *ed ye* favor of yours of *ye* 4th with *ye* inclosed for my sonne Henry: I am sorry wee are like to be without you soe long as yours mentions: but 'tis very likely you may have a summons to appeare among us sooner than you imagine: for my sonne is composing wherein you will be chiefly concern'd. However, your occasions and tyes where you are must be considered and your conveniences ever complyde withall; in *ye* meantime assure yourself I shall be carefull of your concern's heir by minding and refreshing our master's memory of his Gratious promis when there is occasion . . . and beleeve ever that I am, Sir, your affectionate and humble servant,
T. PURCELL[1]

This letter, originally in the possession of Cummings, appeared for the first time in his biography of the composer and is now in the Nanki Library, Japan. The piece to which Thomas Purcell refers was probably the solo anthem for bass solo and chorus, 'I Will Love Thee, O Lord', the text of which contained political allegory relating to Charles's difficulties at this time. The Duke of Monmouth, the King's natural son by Lucy Walters was a constant threat to the succession and the anti-Monmouth contingent were repeatedly pressing Charles to recall his brother James from exile in Brussels. The text of Purcell's anthem was probably inspired by Dryden's *Absalom and Achitophel* in which his allegory extends to all the main political figures, including Charles II as King David and Monmouth as Absalom. At this time Purcell also set the Latin version of Psalm 3, 'Jehovah, quam multi sunt hostes', a highly dramatic composition, the text of which could be identified as being pro the Tory, High Anglican party.[2]

Thomas Purcell obviously had prior knowledge of Gostling's forthcoming appointment, for on 25 February 1679, he was sworn 'A Gentleman Extraordinary of the Chapel Royal', and three days later was 'admitted in ordinary, on the death of William Tucker'.[3]

The Reverend John Gostling was born in East Malling in Kent *c.* 1650 and educated at Rochester School and St John's College, Cambridge. He held a number of important ecclesiastical appointments, including chaplain to the King, sub-Dean of St Paul's Cathedral in London and Prebendary of Lincoln. But posterity remembers Gostling best for the extraordinary range and volume of his bass voice which made him one of the most famous singers of his time. Purcell much admired his voice, and a number of his compositions which call for Gostling's exceptional compass and flexibility were written with him in mind.

The year 1680 was the *annus mirabilis* for the 21-year-old Henry Purcell. He wrote and completed his fantasies for viols (except for one unfinished movement), wrote his first welcome ode for Charles II and, as far as we know, made his first contribution to music for the stage. As if this were not enough, he took himself a wife, Frances Peters, probably the daughter of J.B. Peters, a noted Catholic. Little is known about the family or the date of the ceremony, which was presumably Anglican. However, the baptismal records of All Hallows the Less, London Wall have note of one Henry, son of Henry and Frances Purcell being baptized there on 9 July 1681, so we may take the year of the marriage as 1680. Sadly, the child was buried a week after his christening.

One clue to the actual date of the marriage could lie in the enigmatic entry by Purcell in the Fitzwilliam Museum autograph, 'God bless Mr Henry Purcell/1682 September the 10th' (MUMS 88). Much speculation has been put forward as to the significance of this date, which will be discussed later, but it could have been his second wedding anniversary.

The Court would have made relatively few demands on Purcell's time for much of 1680. The King was occupied with an ever-disruptive Parliament and the confrontation by Monmouth and his supporters, whose only objective was to proclaim him heir to the throne. So it is a fair assumption that Purcell spent a highly productive summer uninterrupted by court duties.

Purcell's fantasies for viols – 3 three-part and 9 four-part – plus the six-part and seven-part *In Nomines* and the Fantasy on One Note in five parts, were all written between 10 June and 31 August of that year – an incredible achievement.

The English fancy or fantasia (after the Italians), so favoured by the Elizabethans, was not popular with Charles II, who preferred more lively music. Byrd, Morley and, later, John Jenkins, William Lawes and Matthew Locke were outstanding composers of the fancy. Morley describes it as:

The most principall and chiefest kind of musicke which is made without a dittie [words] is the fantasie, that is, when a musician taketh a point [fugal subject] at his pleasure, and wresteth and turneth it as he list, making either much or little of it according as shall seeme best in his own conceit. In this may more art be showne then in any other musicke, because the composer is tide to nothing but that he may adde, deminish, and alter at his pleasure.[4]

For whom these pieces were written and why Purcell chose the fantasy form are but two more of the unanswered questions that bedevil all Purcell's biographers. As a young composer brought up on this instrumental form, naturally he would be showing his prowess in it before launching into the new Italian style of the sonatas for two Violins and Bass. They are not only undisputed masterpieces, but also show that Purcell was inspired to take a new approach to the structure of each fantasy; his inventiveness certainly matched, if not surpassed the great examples set by his predecessors.

In Purcell's fantasias we find inversions and augmentation that are rarely found in the works of Lawes, Jenkins and Locke, who tend to use direct imitation, and a technique in modulation and transition that is entirely personal. Percy Grainger describes them perfectly: they 'abound in discords, strange but lovely to the modern ear, that arise from the simultaneous sounding of major and minor forms of the same interval . . . These compositions may be regarded as standing supreme in their emotional intensity.'[5]

One of Purcell's duties as composer-in-ordinary to the King, was to write music for any occasion that called for celebration. In September of that year he was given the task of setting music to some mediocre verse for 'Welcome Vicegerent', an ode to mark the King's return from Windsor to Whitehall. This was Purcell's first instrumental and vocal work of any size and despite the banality of the words, his mastery of the form shows how fast he was developing as a composer.

Another composition which has survived from this period although in fragmentary form is the hymn 'Ah! Few and Full of Sorrows' with George Sandy's paraphrase of Job XIV:1, 'Man that is born of a woman' as the text. It is possible that Purcell intended it for part of a memorial service for a distinguished personality. If it was written in late 1680, it may well have been for the funeral of William Howard, Viscount Stafford, one of the unfortunate Catholic peers cited by Oates in the Popish Plot, who had stood an unjust and bloodthirsty trial and was subsequently executed. Someone may well have commissioned a work to mark the occasion, either the Duke of York or a member of the Howard family, and since Purcell was a close friend of the Howards, he would have felt a personal resentment at the unfairness of putting such an old man to death.

It was probably around this time that Purcell wrote his 'Chaconne' –three parts upon a ground–still wrongly catalogued as a 'Fantasia' in most reference books, including the Purcell Society Edition. It was first identified as being composed for recorders by Layton Ring in 1951 from a clue found in the title given in the unique non-autograph source in the British Library, which tells us that it is 'playd 2 notes higher for f[lutes]'. The copyist in this manuscript transcribed the work into D major for strings, but there exists a tiny fragment in Purcell's own hand of the second recorder part in the original key of F major, written on the back of a correction slip pasted over his early anthem 'Behold praise the Lord' by the composer, and first noticed by G.E. Arkwright in the *Musical Antiquary* of January 1910 (in the form of a query as to who could identify the fragment).

The work was given its first performance in modern times at the Haslemere Festival and published in 1952. But for these fortunate circumstances, recorder-players worldwide might have been deprived of a major addition to their repertoire, original pieces for three recorders with continuo being in very short supply. The Chaconne would seem to be an isolated example of Purcell's writing for this combination which, according to Ring, may date from as early as 1677–8, 'as it shows the influence of Locke and Humfrey in general style, but is *sui generis* for Purcell both in its masterful command of contrapuntal devices and in its lavish display of numerous emotive canons deployed with a youthful and exhilarating zest'.[6]

In early autumn, Purcell had the satisfaction of seeing his name on a playbill, probably for the first time. He had written the incidental music and several songs for Nathaniel Lee's tragedy *Theodosius, or the Force of Love*, of which the hitherto unpublished five-part overture (a magnificent piece in G minor) was identified in the 1950s by Layton Ring. It received its first performance in September or October at the Duke's Theatre in Dorset Garden. Downes writes:

All the Parts in't being perfectly perform'd, with several Entertainments of Singing; Compos'd by the Famous Master Mr *Henry Purcell* . . . made it a living and Gainful Play to the Company: The Court; especially the Ladies, by their daily charming presence, gave it great Encouragement.[7]

Three of the songs from *Theodosius* were published both in the play text and in the third book of Playford's *Choice Ayres* the following year; 'Now the fight's done', 'Hail to the myrtle shades', and 'Ah! Cruel bloody fate'. John Playford, in the introduction to this publication, makes some pointed remarks about the setting of text to the music. He writes of:

men that understand to make *English* Words speak their true and genuine Sence both in good humour and Ayre; which can never be performed by either *Italian* or *French*, they not so well understanding the Proprieties of our Speech . . . [having recently seen] a large Volum of *English* Songs composed by an *Italian* Master, who has lived here in *England* many Years; I confess he is a very able Master, but being not perfect in the true *Idiom* of our language, you will find the air of his Musick so much after his Country-Mode, that it would sute far better with *Italian* than *English* Words . . . [and further deploring] the Vanity of some of our *English* Gentry to admire that in a Foreigner, which they either slight, or take little notice of in one of their own Nation; for I am sure that our *English* Masters in Musick (either for Vocal or Instrumental Musick) are not in Skill and Judgement inferiour to any Foreigners whatsoever, the same Rules in this Science being generally used all over *Europe*.[8]

Here Playford was touching on a serious problem. As we know, throughout the seventeenth century, foreign composers flocked to England and were preferred to native composers, however talented. The particular foreigner to whom he was referring was Pietro Reggio who wrote a collection of 46 songs which he dedicated to the King.

In complete contrast, Henry Purcell had benefited greatly from studying the styles and devices of his eminent predecessors; as he combined this knowledge with his own genius for setting the English language to music, we see the emergence of a composer who, in the space of 15 years, would change the course of English music.

These gifts, however, were not to be recognized immediately, although what was probably Purcell's second opportunity to write for the theatre came a few months later. He was asked to set one of the lyrics in Nahum Tate's adaptation of Shakespeare's *The History of King Richard the Second*, due for production in mid-December by the King's Company at the Theatre Royal in Drury Lane. Unfortunately, the Lord Chamberlain ordered a postponement as the play contained parallels with the Exclusion Bill and the deposition of an English king. The common remedy for such problems was to rename the play – in this case, *The Sicilian Usurper* – thereby rendering the plot 'obscure and incoherent'. But the disguise was evidently too transparent and the play was taken off after only two performances.

The one song set by Purcell, 'Retir'd from any mortal's sight', for the prison scene in the final act, shows a development in his style from that in *Theodosius* only a few months earlier. Assuming that Purcell intended all the words of the song to be sung,

one can see that even the long melisma of the final phrase fits well with the corresponding lines of the second and third stanzas, though this is hardly Purcell's most characteristic way of setting the word 'sigh' ... The descending chromatics at the end of the bass part only add to the gathering gloom. With so remarkable a gift for capturing the essence of tragedy, it is a great pity that Purcell composed no other song for a serious play until nearly ten years after the abortive premiere of Tate's *King Richard the Second*.[9]

In 1680, the London stage, as Purcell would have known it, was still under the influence of the monopoly of two companies, founded originally by Sir William Davenant, already mentioned in connection with his production of *The Siege of Rhodes*, and Thomas Killigrew, an actor and playwright who had been a page to Charles I and subsequently joined the young King in exile. After the Restoration, Charles II had taken the unprecedented step of granting them *and their heirs and assigns* patents for the sole production of dramatic entertainment, which meant that they had absolute control to hire, fire and determine salaries for actors and house servants, as well as making decisions on the selection of plays. Inevitably, this situation indirectly affected the development of the British theatre until late in the nineteenth century.

Davenant was a good manager who ran a successful company. He drew up formal contracts with his actors and organized shares both for actors and outside investors. When he died in 1668, his assistant manager, Henry Harris, and the actor Thomas Betterton took over

without disruption. Killigrew was quite the reverse: he took little
interest in the business side and his grandiose ideas were far too
ambitious for his pocket. As a result the company was perpetually in
financial difficulties and remained so until the two companies finally
united in 1682. It would seem that his problems were not only
financial: he once confided to Pepys that he was obliged to 'keep a
woman on purpose, at 20s a week, to satisfy eight or ten of the young
men of his House, whom till he did so he could never keep to their
business, and now he doth'.[10]

Killigrew's company was known as the King's Players, performing
originally at the Red Bull Theatre, and Davenant's, as the Duke of
York's Players, first at the Salisbury Court Playhouse, and subsequently at Lincoln's Inn Fields Theatre, a converted tennis court. Since
the two companies also had the right to build on locations of their
choice, they were both responsible for the erection of new theatres. In
1671, Davenant's widow and her associates built the magnificent
Dorset Garden Theatre at a cost of £9000. It was ideally situated in the
gardens of the mansion belonging to the Earl of Dorset on the Thames
embankment at Salisbury Court, Fleet Street. Killigrew was the
'father' of the Theatre Royal, in Bridges (now Catherine) Street, off
Drury Lane. The original was opened in 1663 but burned to the
ground in 1672. When it was rebuilt two years later, it is believed that
Killigrew wanted Wren as his architect, but there is no evidence that
this was so. A drawing found amongst the Wren papers in the library
of All Souls College, Oxford, was possibly intended for Drury Lane,
but the plan was never executed. The new theatre also had an
additional 'scene house' in Vinegar Yard behind the main building,
where scenery was made and painted. It was in this Theatre Royal that
so much of Purcell's music would be heard over the next 20 years or so.

It is difficult for us today to realize that before the Restoration,
London had been deprived of public theatrical activity for some 18
years, and many people had grown up without having ever been to a
playhouse. Those that survived the Commonwealth such as the Red
Bull and the Cockpit in Drury Lane were built on the old Elizabethan
pattern with an open courtyard and two or three roofed-in galleries
round the sides. This was where the nobility sat whilst three or four
hundred of the common people would crowd into the courtyards,
paying a penny or twopence to stand and watch the performance. The
Cockpit (named after its previous use) was pillaged and burned by the
apprentices of London in their annual attack on houses and taverns of
ill repute in Drury Lane. When refurbished it was thenceforth known

as the Phoenix, although after the Theatre Royal was built, it fell into disuse.

The new theatres of the 1670s were all roofed in with the stage reaching back beyond the proscenium arch. There were probably two doors on either side of the stage for the actors' entrances and exits, and over these were stage boxes usually occupied by the audience but occasionally used for balcony scenes. On one side the stage boxes, known as the 'music room', were reserved for the band, but when Drury Lane opened in 1663, Killigrew placed them in front of the stage on a lower level. Pepys found this unsatisfactory: 'Only, above all, the Musique being below, and most of it sounding under the very stage, there is no hearing of the bases at all, nor well of the trebles, which sure must be mended.'[11] Evidently this criticism was shared by others, for Killigrew subsequently moved the musicians to a gallery above the proscenium arch. This was probably carried out as part of the alterations to the Theatre Royal in the spring of 1666.

The scenery consisted of wings on either side of the stage with movable backcloths or shutters, and a curtain behind the proscenium arch cut off the scenery from the apron. After the prologue, the curtain was raised to reveal the setting and it was not lowered until the end of the play. Scene-changing took place in full view of the audience, and a diversion was provided by songs or musical interludes.

The use of the singing voice in the theatre was a gradual process dating from the Middle Ages. We know that Shakespeare developed the use of music in his plays to forward the dramatic action, and the instrumental music between acts of plays was a legacy from the dumb-show dating from the mid-sixteenth century. In Purcell's time, songs were introduced as a way of opening a play, for instance when a character was asleep on stage at the raising of the curtain. A song could be useful to mark episodes within a scene or to signify the passing of time. It also heightened characterization and emphasized the emotional intensity of a scene, such as love, death or fear, or served to create a mood. From early in the seventeenth century onwards, a large proportion of plays had at least one or two songs, but as the fashion for continuous entertainment grew, more and more songs were called for. By the end of the century, audiences insisted on being amused throughout the performance, so that during the intervals they were given entr'acte entertainments which would include not only musical interludes, but also songs and dancing.

The theatre was lit by lamps and candles. Glass containers filled with coloured liquid and placed in front of oil lamps to colour the light, had been in use by the Italians since 1598; and at the court masques of Charles I a similar effect had been achieved by placing silk stretched on frames the size of a wing in front of the groups of candles and lamps which stood behind the scenes. The general lighting came from large circular chandeliers fitted with dozens of candles, which hung above the apron. There were additional candles attached to the boxes and galleries, and footlights consisting of six oil lamps at the edge of the centre stage, which could be lowered or raised to suit the action or time of the play. Night scenes were emphasized by actors carrying candles. Since the tallow candles used at the time were in need of constant attention, there were usually two 'invisible' candle-snuffers, one in the auditorium and the other on stage. Irrespective of what was happening, if a candle began to splutter, one would walk on to the stage, attend to the business in hand and quietly make his exit. This procedure was accepted as naturally as were the scene-shifters, so that the action of the play was never disrupted – unless an emergency arose: 'Far from decrying the appearance of the candle-snuffer on stage, at a most dramatic moment, perhaps, members of the audience, on seeing certain lights fail, would actually raise a shout for him, and woe betide if he was not soon forthcoming!'[12]

The audiences of the new theatres were composed mostly of people from the Court and the young gallants who just wanted to be seen. People would come and go as they pleased and held conversations without any regard for the actors. 'Sometimes there would be an argument in the pit leading to a duel: it is recorded that during a performance of *Macbeth* a young gallant met his end at the point of a sword.'[13]

Performances usually took place in the afternoon and there was always a crowd of people waiting to gain admission. The upper classes would send their footmen to keep their places in the queue, and Pepys, an enthusiastic theatre-goer who often grumbled about the difficulty in obtaining a seat, would pay a boy or poor old man to keep his place. Pepys also gives us some idea of the prices paid and the kind of people who frequented the theatre, not all of whom were to his taste:

Here a mighty company of citizens, prentices, and others; and it makes me observe that when I begin first to be able to bestow a play on myself, I do not remember that I saw so many by half of the ordinary prentices and mean people in the pit, at 2s-6d apiece, as now; I going for several years no higher than the 12d, and then the 18d places, and though I strained hard to go in then when I did – so much the vanity and prodigality of the age is to be observed in this perticular.[14]

It is strange that Pepys, who was a man of some means, did not indulge in the higher-priced seats, such as a box costing four shillings. He also tells us that on the first night of a play, the price was often doubled, so he made sure to attend on the second. He frequently took advantage of the concession whereby latecomers could see the last act free of charge, or occasionally a box for half-price at 2s. The Royal Box at Drury Lane was, by the way, the first ever, and Charles II, the first monarch who actually attended the theatre. His predecessors had enjoyed the privilege of having the theatre brought to them.

There were no printed tickets in these times, as the cost would have been prohibitive. Instead, patrons purchased small tokens which were made from brass, copper, silver or ivory. They were engraved on each side, invariably with the king's head or royal arms on the obverse and precise directions as to the seats allocated, such as; 'box', 'upper gallerie', 'first gallerie', 'for the pit', on the reverse. This was an excellent economic arrangement as the tokens were collected on arrival at the theatre, and used again and again.

In addition to those issued for public use, there were more elaborate tokens or passes beautifully engraved in silver, which were the property of the aristocracy, or their servants. There is, in the British Museum, a silver token dated 1668 with Charles II's head on the obverse and engraved on the reverse: 'For the Royal Theatre, the Pages of His Majesties Bedchamber'. Then there were the concession tokens issued to the actors for their own personal use, or for friends attending their performances. These, again, were often in silver or ivory and handsomely engraved. There were conditions for their use as we see from the following extract from Ackerman's *Microcosm of London*. The date is 1799, but, except for the salary, the same edict would have applied a century earlier. It is interesting to note that the exclusion clause contrasts greatly with our late-twentieth-century approach to the under-privileged:

All performers whose salaries are above £6 per week are entitled to four ivory tickets to Free Admission of their Friends viz: – a double or single order for the Boxes, or two double orders for the First Gallery. All performers whose salaries do not amount to £6 per week are totally excluded from any similar privilege.[15]

Theatres were then, as now, always looking for ways of obtaining extra revenue. It had often been suggested in Parliament that a tax should be imposed upon the price of seats, but it was never implemented. Theatres were closed for the whole of Lent and in summer and Christmas for at least six weeks, and a similar period on the death of a high-ranking member of the royal family. Since their main source of income was from box-office receipts, actors were paid on an 'acting-day' basis. During the Plague, for instance, the closure of the theatres would have bankrupted companies, had they been obliged to pay their actors on an annual basis. One source of steady income for the theatres was obtained by the selling of fruit under the 'Concessions' licence. Killigrew and his partners entered into an agreement with Mrs Mary Meggs, known as 'Orange Moll' who was permitted 'full, free and sole liberty, licence, power and authority to vend, utter and sell oranges, lemons, fruit, sweetmeats and all manner of fruiterers and confectioners wares and commodities' in the new Theatre Royal.[16]

She had control over all parts of the house except the upper gallery, restricted probably because they would have been more likely to use the fruit as a missile rather than eat it. Moll, who held a lease for some 39 years, engaged the girls and supplied them with their wares, which they plied at each performance: oranges were sold at sixpence a piece and the girls would also expect a tip. Moll paid to the management a retainer of £100 plus 6s 8d each acting-day as rent. Therefore a season of 200 performances would bring in a satisfying revenue for the company. An amusing sidelight on the traffic in oranges is that they were often used for conveying messages from a gallant to a lady he fancied. The orange girl would remove a tiny circle of rind from the centre, insert the tightly rolled paper on which the *billet doux* was written and replace it before delivering it to the recipient. When the orange was peeled the paper would fall out. Moll was also entrusted with verbal messages from important people; Pepys mentions her on numerous occasions. She was also not above providing first aid when a crisis arose. When Pepys was attending a performance of *Henry the Fourth* he recounts:

And it was observable how a gentleman of good habitt, sitting just before us eating of some fruit, in the midst of the play did drop down as dead, being choked; but with much ado, Orange Mall [Moll] did thrust her finger down his throat and brought him to life again.[17]

An important development which took place shortly before the Restoration, and which was taken for granted by Purcell, was the introduction of women as actresses. On the continent of Europe, women had been acting for many years but in England female roles had previously been taken by boys. One of the first women to appear on the London stage was a Mrs Coleman in Davenant's *Siege of Rhodes*. Once women were accepted, the female parts were far more realistically interpreted and a new interest was created by the young noblemen who frequented the theatre. The most famous of the actresses on the Restoration stage was Nell Gwyn (1650–87). She was born in Herefordshire, brought up in the back alleys of London, and as a teenager became an orange-seller in the pit of Drury Lane with 'Orange Moll'. She was pretty, with a vivacious personality and known for her wicked sense of humour. She attracted the attention of Charles Hart, a grand-nephew of Shakespeare, who trained her for the theatre after which she became known for her apt portrayal of comedy parts. She soon caught the lustful eye of Charles II and in 1669 left the stage to become one of his principal mistresses. The King created their son Duke of St Albans, and the line continues as such today.

One of the most important actresses of the time, and greatly admired by Purcell, was Anne Bracegirdle. She was known particularly for her performances in the plays of Congreve, with whom she was closely associated. Her greatest rival was Anne (Nance) Oldfield, whose popularity finally caused Mrs Bracegirdle to retire from the stage. A great tragic actress of the period, Elizabeth Barry, the daughter of a colonel in the Royalist army, also achieved fame by her involvement in a notorious affair with John Wilmot, Earl of Rochester.

The most outstanding male actor of the Restoration theatre was Thomas Betterton (*c* 1635–1710), the son of an under-cook to Charles I. He showed an aptitude for learning at school and was apprenticed to a bookseller who had stage connections. He was first employed in the theatre by Davenant, who recognized his talent, and was soon playing leading roles both in tragedy and comedy, excelling in both. He dominated the scene throughout the latter part of the seventeenth century, and was closely associated with Henry Purcell in numerous productions. Betterton was known for his fair dealing and natural honesty, and was equally popular with colleagues and audiences alike, a situation that placed him in a position of supremacy right through until his death early in the eighteenth century.

References

1. Cummings, *Purcell*, p 28.
2. Zimmerman, *Henry Purcell, 1659–1695, His Life and Times*, pp 64–5.
3. *Grove's*, Vol 3, p 722.
4. Morley, Thomas, *Plaine and Easie Introduction to Practicall Musicke*, Short, 1597, pp 180–1.
5. Grainger, Percy, *Programme notes on Purcell & Jenkins Fantasies*, Dolmetsch Library, Haslemere.
6. Letter to author.
7. Downes, John, *Roscius Anglicanus*, ed Judith Milhous and Robert D. Hume, Society for Theatre Research, 1987, p 38 (80).
8. Playford, John, *Choice Ayres and Songs*, to sing to the Theorbo-Lute or Bass-Viol. Most of the Newest *Ayres* and *Songs* sung at Court, And at the Publick Theatres, Book 3, 1681.
9. Price, Curtis A., *Henry Purcell and the London Stage*, Cambridge, 1984, pp 37–8.
10. PD, Vol 9, p 425 (24 January 1669).
11. Ibid, Vol 4, p 128 (8 May 1663).
12. Cleaver, James, *The Theatre Through the Ages*, Harrap, 1946, p 78.
13. Ibid, p 72.
14. PD, Vol 9, p 2 (1 January 1668).
15. Davis, W.J., and Waters, A.W., *Tickets and Passes of Great Britain and Ireland*, Spink, 1974, p 15.
16. Pope, W.J. Macqueen, *Theatre Royal Drury Lane*, Allen, 1945, p 32.
17. PD, Vol 8, pp 516–7 (2 November 1667).

8

PURCELL AND THE TEST ACT

Sometime after their marriage, Purcell and his wife moved to a house in Great St Ann's Lane, Westminster (now St Ann's Street), conveniently close to the rear entrance of Westminster Abbey. There is an observation concerning this house by W.H. Cummings, for which he is taken to task by both Westrup and Zimmerman. In the original edition of his book, Cummings says that Purcell's birthplace is St Ann's Lane, Old Pye Street, Westminster:

Some remains of the house are still standing [1881]. A sketch of it and the adjoining premises was made on the 15th of April, 1845, by R.W. Withall. The original drawing, of which a reduced copy is given, has the following note: –
Three ancient houses in Westminster; in the right-hand, one of which the great H. Purcell was born, 1658 [*sic*], and passed his early life. They are now in the last state of ruin, and have long been uninhabited. The houses adjoining that of Purcell are of modern date, and project before the others, as well as encroach somewhat on Purcell's doorway, hiding one side of the door-frame. Of the old houses the windows and doorways are nearly all boarded up in the roughest manner, under which, however, the original panelled doors are still to be partly found. The houses are of old red brick. The first door was the back way into the public-house called the 'Bell and Fish' kept by Mr Oldsworth, who lost his licence. The second door the entrance to the skittle-ground. The third was Purcell's house.

What is significant is that Cummings discovered his mistake and took pains to correct it. In his own copy of the first edition, on the page opposite, he wrote: 'This was not the birth-house of Purcell' (see plate . . .). He also deletes the four lines introducing the note by Withall.[1] This information would certainly have been incorporated into a second edition, had the opportunity arisen. But what about the description? If it is not the house where Purcell was born, could it be the house in Great St Ann's Lane where he moved with his bride? In 1845, it is just possible that some of the remains could still have been in evidence, but the matter must rest there. At least we know that Cummings fully intended to rectify his error.

Purcell's name as a resident does not appear in the rate books for the parish of St Margaret's, Westminster in 1681, but the following year it is included in a list of 'Persons entered after the assessment was made', and his payment of eight shillings is recorded. He was once again surrounded by famous neighbours: his friend, Stephen Crespion, precentor of Westminster Abbey, John Dryden's brother Erasmus in Bell Alley, John Hingston in Absey and Bowling Alley, Thomas Shadwell in Tothill Street and John Blow and others in King Street. Another neighbour was John Banister, who, sadly in character, has his name on the list of those who were 'in arrear to the assessment for relief of the poor of the parish'. Purcell's mother was probably now living with her son and daughter-in-law, as her name no longer appears.

For the first few months of 1681, the Court required virtually no music at all, a situation that would have been welcomed by Purcell. The King was now so preoccupied with political affairs that he did not even visit the theatre. Not only had he to contend with the constant threat of Monmouth and his supporters gaining power, but at the same time was negotiating secret treaties with Louis XIV, which would eventually swell his purse by £400,000.

It was not until August that Purcell was required to write a song to welcome the King back from Windsor, 'Swifter, Isis, swifter flow'. The verse itself was undistinguished, but Purcell makes memorable music out of the simple appeal of the flowing river.

In the autumn, Thomas D'Urfey's comedy, *Sir Barnaby Whigg, or No Wit like a Woman's*, had just one song by Purcell, 'Blow, Boreas blow', which is, incidentally, the only surviving music from the play. Again we see here Purcell's genius for setting words that bring to life a dramatic situation. The song describes a violent storm at sea and Price observes: 'Though the boisterous depiction of the tempest with wide melodic leaps and vigorous dotted rhythms resembles the recitatives of Purcell's mad songs and dialogues, the setting looks back to Locke, especially in adhering to the flamboyant declamatory style, even in the triple-metre sections . . .'[2]

Thomas D'Urfey (or Durfey) (1653–1723) was born in Devonshire of Huguenot extraction. He trained as a lawyer but abandoned his studies in favour of writing for the stage, at which he was highly successful. He had a facetious and licentious turn of manner which was highly fashionable at the time. 'He came into the world a few years after the Restoration when all was joy and merriment, and when to be able to drink and to sing were admirable qualities; D'Urfey could do both.' He had a talent for verse which he could adapt to any occasion, and also wrote songs. Although he 'laboured under the impediment of stammering in his speech', he had a tolerable voice and frequently sang his own songs at public feasts and meetings; 'and not seldom in the presence of King Charles II, who, laying aside all state and reserve, would lean on his shoulder and look over the paper'. The songs were often indelicate and became favourites in the whole kingdom.[3]

D'Urfey once said, 'The Town may da-da-damn me for a Poet, but they si-si-sing my Songs for all that.'[4] Hawkins also tells us that he once challenged Purcell to set to music such a song as he would write, and gave him that well-known ballad 'One Long Whitsun Holiday' which – according to Hawkins – cost the composer more pains to set to a tune than the completing of his *Te Deum*.[5]

In May 1682 Purcell was named as one of the 17 musicians who travelled to Windsor with the King. The number included several members of the Banister family, and all received £11 13s 2d, excepting John Hingston who was paid a princely £15. The total sum was £247 7s 11½d.[6]

At the end of the month Purcell had the task of setting yet another ode, this time for the return of the Duke of York from Scotland after having served for three years as High Commissioner for that country. The words have been criticized for being trite but they set well to music, a fact often overlooked by those who judge the spoken word in isolation. Whatever else they may be, they show clearly the political climate of the time:

> What shall be done on behalf of the man
> In whose honour the King is delighted,
> > Whose conduct abroad
> > Has his enemies awed
> And every proud rebel affrighted,
> > With whose absence his Prince
> > Will no longer dispense
> But home to the joys of his Court has invited?

It continues:

York, the obedient, grateful, just,
Punctual, courageous, mindful of his trust.[7]

That night, 27 May, the public celebrated with bonfires and bell-ringing. Londoners loved an excuse to celebrate, and the return of the Duke was as good a reason as any: on such occasions a blind eye was conveniently turned on his Catholicism.

On 11 July 1682, the death occurred of Edward Lowe, organist of the Chapel Royal, and three days later Purcell took his place, although he was not sworn in until 16 September.[8] The duties of the three organists in the chapel were as follows:

Two shall ever attend, one at the organ, the other in his surplice in the quire, to beare a parte in the Psalmodie and service. At solemne times they shall all three attend. The auncientest organist shall serve and play the service on the eve and daye of the solemne feastes, viz: Christmas, Easter, St George, and Whitsontide. The second organist shall serve the second day, and the third the third day. Other dayes they shall waite according to their monthes.[9]

Purcell would have had no difficulty in fulfilling all these obligations, especially when joining the choir. After his voice had broken he developed into a bass and also sang counter-tenor when required.

On the last day of July 1682, the death of Thomas Purcell deprived Henry of his uncle and surrogate father, an event that must have affected him deeply. The cause of death is unknown but Thomas had been ill for some time and, like his brother Henry the elder, might have suffered from tuberculosis, then a common disease without a cure. Since he had made his will on 4 June, he probably knew that he had not long to live. He left £5 to each of his children and bequeathed his house in Pall Mall to his wife, Katherine, together with the furniture and money owing him from the Treasury. The constant failure of this department to honour outstanding debts made no exception in the case of Thomas Purcell. Five years after his death his widow was still owed £220 12s 6d.

However, in February of the previous year, Thomas had taken the wise precaution of finding his son, Francis, royal employment as groom-in-ordinary to Charles II. After Thomas's death Francis was also promoted to his father's position of groom of the robes. Another son, Edward, had for some time held an important post as gentleman usher, so the Purcells were still assured of a court income, even if, ironically, it was not paid.

A week after Thomas's funeral, there was cause for rejoicing in

Henry's family when their second son, John Baptista, was christened at Westminster Abbey. The choice of name was unusual, and gives rise to some speculation as to whether it was with Draghi or Vitali in mind, both of whom shared the same Christian name. But the infant did not survive; two months later he, too, was laid beside his great-uncle in the cloisters at the Abbey.

This bereavement of a second child could also have had significance in the cryptic 'God Bless Mr Henry Purcell' on the Fitzwilliam manuscript already mentioned. It must have been devastating for this young man to have lost yet another son within two months of the death of his uncle. Other suggestions put forward are that it was Purcell's own birthday, or that he had some difficulty in confirming his official appointment as Edward Lowe's successor at the Abbey. It is unlikely that we shall ever know the answer to yet another tantalizing question in the annals of the Purcell family.

Despite this heavy load of work, Purcell had somehow found time to write his B-flat major service and an anthem, as the Abbey accounts for Michaelmas show that he was paid 30 shillings for this work.[10] Here we also have an insight into Purcell's stylistic development. 'On the back of a correction sheet pasted over part of the benedicite appear the first eight bars of Monteverdi's "Cruda Amarilli", the first madrigal in his famous publication of 1605, *Il quinto libro de madrigali*',[11] which when it first appeared was severely criticized for its dissonance, thus rendering it 'licentious in the extreme'. This can now be examined in some detail as the entire manuscript from which the fragment was cut has come to light.

Meanwhile, Charles II had enjoyed a relatively peaceful period in foreign relations having made agreement with both Louis XIV and the Dutch, though at home his main problem had been to control the election of the London sheriffs in July. Underlying this situation was the continual strife between Whigs and Tories. The Tories supported the Crown and the Anglican Church: the Whig party was a combination of the aristocracy and middle class determined to remove political power from the Crown, and at the same time force the country squires and the bishops to grant toleration to dissent. In order to achieve their objectives they seized on the most vulnerable target, the Catholics, who were feared by everyone.

Such a party was in some respect engendered by the social, religious and political conditions of the day, but the prime influence in the movement was Shaftesbury, who was virtually the originator of party government. Anthony Ashley Cooper, a brilliant, eloquent politician whose self-interest would stop at nothing to gain his ends, was created the first Earl of Shaftesbury in 1672. He served under the Parliamentarians but soon switched loyalties when Charles II was about to be restored. He was one of the select committee appointed to draw up the invitation to the new King, and one of the commissioners at Breda. He subsequently rose to prominence under Charles II but when he supported the Test Act in 1673, he was dismissed from office. He was not personally responsible for the 'Popish Plot' but he made full use of the two years of terror that came in its wake (1678–80), and was one of those who had tried to exclude James, Duke of York, from the succession, in favour of Monmouth. He was twice imprisoned in the Tower on charges of treason but when brought to trial at the Old Bailey in 1681, the Grand Jury ignored the charge. The following year he fled to Holland where he died a few months later.

Monmouth and his supporters had been losing sympathy month by month and their hopes were further dashed when the Tories Ralph Box and Dudley North, lawyer, author and amateur musician, and brother of Roger, were elected London sheriffs in the traditional 'Ceremony of Drinking' at the Bridgehouse Feast – discontinued in the Civil War but since revived. The Whigs protested that there had been corruption and claimed that as the result of a show of hands – of Dissenters who by the Corporation Act held, in law, no votes at all – they had a majority of between 1000 and 1200 votes. As a result the King intervened and called another election at which the Tories were somewhat dubiously re-elected.

So it was that autumn that, when it came to electing the Lord Mayor of London, the Tories had no obstacles in their way, especially when it was said that Charles discreetly brought pressure to bear for a second time that year. Sir William Pritchard was chosen and inaugurated with sumptuous municipal ceremony. Purcell's anthem, 'Blow up the Trumpet', was probably written for the twentieth Sunday after Trinity which coincided with the Lord Mayor's celebrations on 29 October. It is sad that we have neither diaries nor letters from Purcell as we know he was on intimate terms with the North family. It would have been intriguing to have some comment on these elections from one so close to the action.

After a comparatively quiet period in the political situation, new risings began in 1683. In March of that year Charles II went to Newmarket as usual for the races. On the evening of the 22nd, a groom smoking in a high wind, started a fire that spread throughout the entire estate, leaving stables, buildings, coaches and horses charred and unrecognizable. The accident proved to be a life-saver for the King, as he was obliged to return to London earlier than planned. Had this not happened, the Royal Coach would have left a few days later and, approaching the vicinity of Rye House near Ware in Hertford-shire, they would have been stopped by a hay-cart blocking the highway. Musketeers, at the ready in the ditch, were to shoot both the King and his brother dead. Horsemen waiting for the command would have galloped to London to proclaim Monmouth successor and head of a country that was either a republic or dukedom.

The discovery of a further plot involving Monmouth, Russell, Essex and the Whig grandees, to seize Whitehall and call the country to arms, was a bitter blow to Charles who loved his handsome, weak and unstable first-born son best of all his children. The conspirators were brought to trial and a Grand Jury accused 31 persons including Monmouth of complicity, and those they had managed to arrest received various sentences of hanging or beheading. Essex had cut his throat whilst imprisoned in the Tower, and Monmouth managed to escape capture. On hearing the news, Charles made no great effort to enforce the order, and when Monmouth eventually gave himself up, he was as swiftly pardoned. This caused such a furore from his fellow conspirators that he retracted his declaration. Charles was furious and threw the document in his face, telling him to go to hell.

The constant friction between the Whig and Tory factions was echoed in the Catholic vs Anglican conflict. The Test Act of 1673 meant that all persons who refused to take the Anglican sacrament and an oath against the Catholic doctrine of substantiation, were not allowed to hold public office. When the Popish Terror raged, further measures were sought. There were furious debates in Parliament, and at one point the Commons petitioned that all Papists should be disarmed, banished ten miles from London and confined to their homes. A Bill was finally introduced to exclude all Catholics from sitting in Parliament. The underlying purpose was to prevent the Duke of York coming to the throne. If this should happen the public feared for revenge and loss of property. So strong were their feelings that even moderate Protestants were following the Republican lobby.

As a result of the Act people were summoned periodically to prove their loyalty to the Anglican form of worship. In February 1683 Purcell came under scrutiny from the authorities and was asked to take the sacrament according to the Church of England service, before witnesses as required by statute. Moses Snow, a fellow musician, Robert Tanner (occupation unknown), Bartholomew Wormall, the minister, and Giles Borrowdale, a church-warden, were all witnesses, declaring that they:

hereby certify that Mr Henry Pursal, one of the [Gentlemen] of His Majesty's Chapel, upon the Lord's Day commonly [called] Sunday, being the fourth day of February instant [imme]diately after divine service and sermon, did in the parish church aforesaid receive the sacrament of the Lord's Supper according to the usage of the Church of England.[12]

Zimmerman suggests that the number of details given in the document point to possible irregularities in Purcell's religious practices. At the foot of the document, signed in February, there is an additional statement recording that Moses Snow and Robert Tanner were summoned to court at Westminster Hall on Monday 16 April to swear under oath that they had not only witnessed Purcell taking the Sacrament but also the signing of the document by the minister and the church-warden.

We know that Purcell was friendly with a number of noted Catholics including the Howard family, and much nearer home were his in-laws, the Peters. Alternatively, when Purcell succeeded Lowe in the Chapel Royal, or in view of his appointment as composer-in-ordinary to the 'King's Musicke', it might have been a routine safeguard to ascertain that all who were in public office were periodically investigated.

Purcell evidently satisfied his examiners for there is no mention of his having to make further declarations. In any case, by May of that year, he had another important matter on his mind. He had advertised in the *London Gazette* for 24–8 May, the first publication of his instrumental works.

These are to give notice to all gentlemen that have subscribed to the proposals published by Mr Henry Purcell for the printing of his sonatas of three parts for two violins and bass to the harpsichord or organ, that the said books are now completely finished, and shall be delivered to them upon the 11th June next. And if any who have not yet subscribed shall before that time subscribe, according to the said proposals (which is ten shillings the whole set), which are at Mr William Hall's house in Norfolk street, or at Mr Playford's and Mr Carr's shops in the Temple; for the said books will not after that time be sold under 15s. the set.

On 11 June 1683, a further notice appeared in the *Gazette*, advising subscribers 'to repair to his [Purcell's] house in St Ann's Lane, beyond

Westminster Abbey, or to send the proposal paper they received with the receipt to it when they subscribed . . . and they shall receive their books paying the remaining part of the money'. We do not know why he had taken it upon himself to undertake distribution. Possibly it was to save money or maybe correct errors, as suggested by J.A. Fuller-Maitland in his preface to the Purcell Society edition.[13]

Purcell would seem to have been aware of the importance of presentation as this first publication has style. The title-page describes the author as 'Composer in Ordinary to his most Sacred Majesty, and Organist of his Chappel Royall'. The first violin part is embellished with an engraved portrait which is described as the 'Vera Effigies Henrici Purcell, aetat. suae 24'. The work is dedicated to the King and Purcell makes the point that it is by his royal favour that he feels bold enough to lay his compositions at his 'sacred feet'.

The lengthy preface has been quoted extensively in every study of Purcell's music. Its importance lies in the fact that it is the first instance we have of the composer expressing himself in words, thus enabling us to learn something about his character and personality. But we must also consider the possibility that Playford may have written it. It begins:

Instead of an elaborate harangue on the beauty and the charms of Musick (which after all the learned Encomions that words can contrive) commends it Self best by the performances of a skilful hand, and an angelical voice: I shall Say but a very few things by way of Preface, concerning the following Book, and its Author: for its Author, he has faithfully endeavour'd a just imitation of the most fam'd Italian Masters; principally, to bring the seriousness and gravity of that sort of Musick into vogue, and reputation among our Country-men, whose humor, 'tis time now, should begin to loath the levity, and balladry of our neighbours: The attempt he confesses to be bold, and daring, there being Pens and Artists of more eminent abilities, much better qualify'd for the imployment than his, or himself, which he well hopes these his weak endeavours, will in due time provoke, and enflame to a more accurate undertaking.

From this we see that the writer has a dry sense of humour and knows that performance by a skilled musician is more important than all the poetic description of its charms. His statement on the 'levity and balladry of our neighbours' is clearly aimed at French music, and, as Westrup points out, is a little self-righteous. Admittedly, the French instrumental music was quite different from the Italian, but the criticism of 'levity and balladry' is strange coming from Purcell, who 'has left us a sufficient amount of frolicsome music to give a flavour of hypocrisy to his charge, and on occasion he was even capable of descending to balladry'.[14]

We should not be deluded by the self-effacing statement about his own abilities, which was obligatory at the time and surely written very much tongue-in-cheek. His admiration of the Italian masters shows his underlying confidence in his role of introducing this style to his fellow countrymen. Clearly under Purcell's hand, the Italian influence, combined with his own natural genius, gave us some of the most delightful trio sonatas of all time. One obvious difference is that he uses Italian terms, eg *Largo*, *Adagio*, etc. Purcell continues with a few confessions:

He is not asham'd to own his unskilfulness in the Italian Language; but that's the unhappiness of his Education, which cannot justly be accounted his fault, however he thinks he may warrantably affirm, that he is not mistaken in the power of the Italian Notes, or elegancy of their Compositions, which he would recommend to the English Artists.

This again shows us that he was a man with a direct approach, who even if he could not speak their tongue, had no difficulty in interpreting their musical language.

Towards the end of July Purcell was called upon to write an ode for the royal family; this time to celebrate the marriage on 28 July of George, Prince of Denmark to Princess (later Queen) Anne, daughter of the Duke of York by his first wife, Anne Hyde. The title, 'From hardy climes and dangerous toils of war', referred to the Prince's country and recent battles in which he had taken part. Evelyn met the young Prince at dinner in Whitehall and described him as being heavy in build, blond, of Danish countenance, with little conversation in poor French. He adds that he is known to be valiant since he 'bravely rescued and brought off his brother, the King of Denmark, in a battle against the Swedes, when both these Kings were engaged very smartly'.[15]

However, not all was rejoicing in royal circles that July. The day after the Prince's arrival, several of the Rye House conspirators 'of the lower form' were executed at Tyburn, and on the following day Lord Russell was beheaded in Lincoln's Inn Fields, 'the executioner giving him three butcherly strokes'.[16]

In order to distract attention from these more sombre events, the poet turns to the expectations of the marriage:

> . . . as ev'ry king that reigns
> Thro' Europe shares the blood that fills your veins,
> So shall the race from your great loins to come
> Prove future Kings and Queens of Christendom.

No prophecy could have been further from the reality. The marriage itself was a happy one, but of their 17 children, only one survived infancy, Prince William, who died at the age of eleven.

On 9 September, there was a day of public thanksgiving for Charles's delivery from the violence of the Rye House Plot, for which Purcell probably provided some music. At the end of the month he had written another ode to welcome Charles on his return to London. The words of 'Fly, bold rebellion' evoked a vivid picture of the recent events:

> The plot is displayed and the traitors, some flown
> And some to Avernus by Justice thrown down.

Here we find a typical example of Purcell giving Gostling, his bass soloist, a bottom D on the final monosyllable.

On 29 October that year, Purcell placed a further advertisement in the *London Gazette*, advising subscribers that further copies of the *Sonatas of III Parts* were now available. The demand had evidently been encouraging for they were now also to be sold by J. Playford, J. Carr and H. Rogers.

A few weeks later, in addition to all his other numerous compositions, Purcell had composed at least two odes to St Cecilia: 'Laudate Ceciliam' and 'Welcome to All the Pleasures' were written ready for the celebration on 22 November. In December the fourth book of *Choice Ayres and Songs to Sing to the Theorbo-lute or Bass-viol* was published, containing eight songs by Purcell, including the beautiful 'Sleep, Adam, Sleep' and Mad Bess's song, 'From silent shades'.

That same month, in one of the coldest winters on record, John Hingston died. Purcell would have felt the loss not only of a master who had instructed him carefully in the care and maintenance of musical instruments, but also a man who had been very close to his own family. Hingston, as Purcell's godfather, left him £5 in his will.

On 17 December, a warrant was issued

to swear and admit Henry Purcell as keeper, mender, maker, repairer and tuner of the regals, organs, virginals, flutes and recorders, and all other kinds of wind instruments, in the place of John Hingston, deceased.[17]

On 16 February 1684, there are more precise details of the conditions described in a further warrant issued to prepare a bill for the King's signature, granting the place of

'keeper, maker, repairer and mender and tuner of all and every his Majesty's musicall wind instruments; that is to say all regalls, virginalls, organs, flutes, recorders and all other kind of wind instruments whatsoever' to Henry Purcell in the place of John Hingston, deceased; wages of £60 a year, together with the money necessary for the 'workinge, labouringe, makeing and mending any of the instruments aforesaid . . . And also lycence and authority to the said Henry Purcell or his assigns to take up within ye realme of England all such mettalls, wyer, waynscote and other wood and things as shalbe necessary to be imployed about the premisses, agreeing, paying and allowing reasonable rates and prices for the same. And also in his Majesty's name and upon reasonable and lawfull prices, wages and hire, to take up such workmen, artificers, labourers, worke and store houses, land and water carriages and all other needeful things as the said Henry Purcell or his assignes shall thinke convenient to be used on ye premisses. And also power and authority to the said Henry Purcell or his assignes to take up all tymber, strings, and feathers, necessary and convenient for the premisses, agreeing, paying and allowing reasonable rates and prices for the same, in as full and ample manner as the said John Hingston . . . formerly had.'[18]

Beginning at Christmas 1683, in addition Purcell was to receive a further annual £16 2s 6d for another livery, although there was little likelihood that it would be paid. We see that in a warrant of 27 April 1683 Thomas Purcell's widow was asking for money still owed for her late husband's livery from 1679–81.

Purcell had been assistant keeper of the instruments since 1673, so these extra duties would have made little difference to his day-to-day activities. Certainly his responsibilities for the next ten years were to be formidable, but however strong the pressures, the quality of his work was never adversely affected. Whatever he undertook, whether for the Church, Court or theatre, the results continued to shine with his genius.

References

1. Cummings, *Purcell* (now in the Library of the Guildhall School of Music and Drama, London), pp 7–8.
2. Price, *Henry Purcell and the London Stage*, p 154.

3. Hawkins, J.A., *A General History of the Science and Practice of Music*, Novello, 1875, Vol 2, p 818.

4. Brown, *Works*, Vol 4, 1715, p 117.

5. Hawkins, op cit, p 818.

6. Cal Treas Books, 17 May 1682.

7. Westrup, *Purcell*, p 41.

8. Rimbault, Edward F. ed., *The Old Cheque Book, or Book of Remembrance of the Chapel Royal*, Da Capo, New York, 1966, p 17.

9. Ibid, p 83.

10. WAM 33717 (1682), fo 5.

11. Zimmerman, *Henry Purcell, 1659–95, His Life and Times*, pp 84–5.

12. *Middlesex County Records:* Sacrament Certificate, 4–13 – Zimmerman, plate 16.

13. Vol V, p iii.

14. Westrup, op cit, p 230.

15. ED, Vol 2, p 187 (25 July 1683).

16. Ibid, p 186 (20–21 July 1683).

17. AA, Vol 1, p 208.

18. Ibid, p 210.

THE KING IS DEAD! LONG LIVE THE KING!

One of the few known facts about Purcell's life is that his responsibilities never ceased until the day he died. His duties at Westminster Abbey continued as before, and now, with the added workload inherent in his taking over as Keeper of the Instruments, he would have had little spare time at his disposal. Chamberlayne gives us a detailed description of the court hierarchy: he tells us that 'The Court of the King of *England* is a *Monarchy* within a *Monarchy*, consisting of *Ecclesiastical*, *Civil* and *Military* persons and Government'. The Dean of the King's 'Chappel', usually a learned prelate, is chosen by the King and 'acknowlededgeth no *Superiour* but the King'; the Dean then chooses all other officers such as a sub-dean or praecentor capellae, the 32 'Gentlemen', 12 of whom are priests, one of whom is confessor to the King's household. His office is to read prayers every morning to the family, to visit the sick and examine and prepare communicants.

The other 20 gentlemen,

commonly called The Clerks of the Chappel, are with the aforesaid priests to perform in the Chappel the Office of Divine Service in Praying, Singing, etc. One of these being well skilled in Musick, is chosen Master of the Children, whereof there are Twelve in Ordinary, to instruct them in the Rules and Art of Musick, for the Service of the Chappel. Three other of the said Clerks are chosen to be Organists, to whom are joyned upon *Sundays*, Collar-days [the days on which knights wore the collars of their orders, such as that of the Garter] and other Holy-days, a Consort of the King's Musick to make the Chappel-Musick more full and compleat.

The three organists belonging to the Chapel were, at this time, Dr William Child, Dr John Blow, who was also Master of the Children of the Chapel, and Mr Henry Purcell, 'All eminent for their Great Compositions and skill in Musick'. Thomas Blagrave, from an old

Berkshire family who had long been in the King's service as musicians, was Clerk of the Cheque. The rest of the gentlemen are described as being

great Masters also in the Science of Musick, and most Exquisite Performers, as:

Mr William Turner	Mr Thomas Heywood
Mr James Hart	Mr Alphonso Marsh
Mr—Goslin	Mr Stephen Crispins
Mr—Abel	Mr Leonard Woodson

Then there were 62 musicians-in-ordinary who ranked in three degrees; 'Private *Musick*, Wind *Musick*, and twenty-four *Violins*, of all which, as also of the Instrumental Musick of the Chappel, Dr *Nicholas Staggins* is Master'. Then there were 16 trumpeters-in-ordinary and one kettle-drummer, 'of whom Gervas Pryce, Esq., is the Sergeant-Trumpeter, *John Maugridge* Drum-Major, four other Drummers and a Fife'.[1]

As for the workshop where Purcell would have attended to the instruments, we have a description of the building erected ten years earlier which had presumably remained the same during the intervening years. We learn that on 20 August 1663, the following warrant to the Surveyor-General was issued:

to make and erect a large organ loft by His Ma*ties* Chappell at Whitehall, in the place where formerly the great Double organ stood, and to rebuild the roomes over the bellowes roome, two stories high, as it was formerly, the lower story for the subdeane of His Ma*ties* Chappell, and the upper story with two rooms, one of them for the organist in wayting and the other for the keeper and repayrer of His Ma*ties* organs, harpsichords, virginalls and other Instruments, each room to have a Chymney, and Boxes and shelves for keeping the materials as belonging to the organ, and the organ books.[2]

Early in 1684, Purcell's 'Welcome to All the Pleasures' – performed the previous November – was published by John Playford, with a preface written by the composer. The social attitude to music and musical performance was changing, partly due to the public concerts being given by Britton and Banister: this is reflected in Purcell's dedication to the 'Gentlemen of the Musical Society' which included the stewards for the forthcoming year: William Bridgman, Esq., Dr Nicholas Staggins, Gilbert Dolben, Esq., and Mr Francis Forcer.

Gentlemen, Your kind Approbation and benign Reception of the Performance of these *Musical Compositions* on St CECILIA'S Day (by way of Gratitude) claim this DEDICATION; which likewise furnishes the Author with the opportunity of letting the World know the Obligations he lies under to you; and that he is to all Lovers of Music,
A *real Friend and Servant,*
HENRY PURCELL.

In April 1684, the Court left for its annual stay at Windsor and it is certain that Purcell would have been among the body of musicians who went with them. His name is not mentioned in the records but since on 8 April there was an important ceremony held to solemnize the installation of Prince George of Denmark as a 'Knight Companion of the Order of the Garter', Purcell would surely have participated.

Also that spring Purcell became involved with what has become known as the battle of the organ-builders. It had started in 1682 shortly after Purcell took up his appointment as keeper of the instruments. In the autumn of that year, the organ-builder Bernard Smith – known as 'Father Smith' – had been invited to set up a new organ in the Temple Church and at the same time a similar request was made to another distinguished builder, Renatus Harris. The instrument chosen for the church would be the one which, 'in the greatest number of excellencies deserved the preference', and the decision would rest with a committee set up to adjudicate.

However, the next 12 months were spent in bitter rivalry between the supporters of each builder who 'indulged in mischievous interference with the organ built by the other'.[3] Burney tells us that on the eve of the final trial of the reed stops, Harris's friends cut the bellows of Smith's organ and that both factions 'proceeded to the most mischievous and unwarrantable acts of hostilities'.[4]

Once again, religion and politics played a part. Smith was born Bernhard Schmidt, possibly in Germany and also worked in Holland before coming to England in 1666. He was an avowed Protestant who had worked under Hingston until 1683. Harris was a Roman Catholic who enjoyed firm support by the Queen and her court.

By the end of May 1684, both contestants had their instruments ready and in place in the Temple Church. Smith engaged Blow and Purcell to demonstrate the excellence of his instrument whereas Harris chose the Italian, Draghi. The organists performed on alternate days to exploit the capabilities of each instrument but no decision was reached. The controversy was to continue for several years. Only in 1688 did the matter reach a settlement, and this was brought about by calling in the famous Judge Jeffreys who was known as a man capable of dealing with difficult decisions. He declared Smith the winner.

The preference for Smith's instrument was: 'both for sweetnes and fulnes of Sound (besides the extraordinary Stopps, quarter Notes, and other Rarityes therein) ... and that the same is more ornamentall and substantiall'. The 'quarter notes' consisted of two extra notes in each octave, there being separate half-keys for G sharp and A flat and D sharp and E flat respectively, hitherto unknown in England. 'These survived until 1879 when the organ was rebuilt. Much of Smith's original work was incorporated in the new instrument and it is still in use.' Harris's organ was considered to be 'discernably too low [quiet?] and too weake';[5] and was split up and sent half to St Andrews, Holborn (where Purcell's son, Edward, would one day be organist), and the remainder to Christ Church, Dublin. Smith's instrument, for which he was paid £1000, £500 on account and 20 shillings for setting it up, was regarded as one of the most modern yet constructed in England.

In the late spring of 1684, Charles had sent the actor Thomas Betterton to France to investigate the possibilities of introducing opera to England. He had left with high hopes but in Paris managed only to contact Grabu, who formerly had been Master of the King's Musicke from 1666 to 1674 and had offended both Banister and Humfrey by his lack of musical ability. None the less, a company of players arrived in England and proceeded to Windsor to perform for the King, whose preference for everything French would have assured them at least minimal success. However, the royal patronage did little to endear them to the British theatre-goer, for after a short season at Whitehall in London later that year, they were to depart in December never to return. Grabu was to remain in London but failed to bring any influence to bear on the promotion of French opera in that city.

In September of that same year (1684) Purcell was again composing a welcome ode, 'From those serene and rapturous joys', to words by Thomas Flatman to celebrate Charles's return from Windsor, the last he was to write for that monarch. In the Calendar of Treasury Books for 13 August, 'To Mr Purcell, one of the King's musicians' a sum of £8 19s 4d is recorded but unspecified. Since the sum is unusual, it probably represents remuneration for some special service such as this.[6]

One of the catches that Purcell composed around this time, 'Come My Hearts', shows how it could be used politically, in this case, for the King and Tory policy, with direct reference to the Test Act:

> Come, my hearts, play your parts
> With your quarts, see none starts,
> For the King's health is a drinking;
>
> Then to His Highness see, see there wine is,
> That has past the test above the rest,
> For those healths deserve the best.
>
> They that shrink for their chink,
> From their drink,
> We will think, we will think
> That of treasons they are thinking.

Another famous catch by Purcell, 'My Wife Has a Tongue as Good as E'er Twang'd' (see overleaf), was written for the revival of Ravenscroft's *The English Lawyer* by George Ruggles, probably in 1685.

The catch was generally written for three or more male voices and enjoyed great popularity in the sixteenth and seventeenth centuries. The earliest catches, rounds and canons, celebrated the sorrows and simple pleasures of life, and could also be inspired by religious subjects, but were always unsophisticated. In contrast, the Restoration catches were mostly bawdy, often satirical, with political implications, and invariably sophisticated. The trick (or catch) was to place unexpected rests between the words so that a double meaning could be suggested when the next voice entered to take up the disconnected text. The best description comes from notes 'To the Reader' in John Playford's *Catch that Catch Can*, published in 1658.

For the Information of such as know not the Nature or manner of singing Catches or Canons, which are, Three parts in one; They are to observe that the first man begins and sings alone to the signature and so forward. The second man observes that when the first is at that Note which has this signature over or under it (which is thus marked . . or thus :S:) then he begins and sings it round as the first did. The third observing that when the second is at the same Note with the signature over or under it, he begins also and sings as the other, each man singing his part round four or five times. Vale J.P.

The catch was intended to give as much pleasure to the singers as to any audience which may have gathered to hear them. Men from all

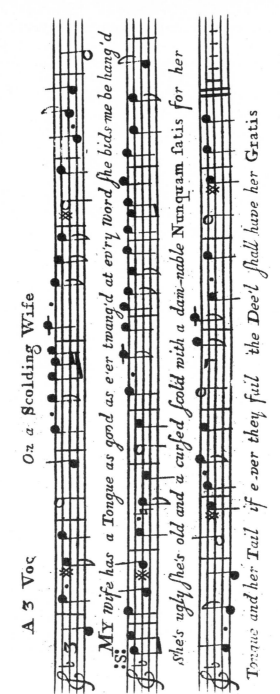

A 3 Voc   On a Scolding Wife

MY wife has a Tongue as good as e'er twang'd at ev'ry Word she bids me be hang'd

She's ugly she's old and a curfed fcold with a dam-nable Nunquam fatis for her

Tongue and her Tail if e-ver they fail the Dee'l fhall have her Gratis

walks of life would meet in the taverns for drinking and good company, and Pepys records how he and Mr Spong of the Six Clerks' Office had done some business transactions and dined 'at a club at the next door, where we had three voices to sing catches'.[7]

The Restoration catch favoured an easy melody. 'The kind of tune thus established was simple, bold, shapely, mainly monosyllabic; in short "Old English".' And in this Purcell, who wrote over 60 catches, was immensely superior to his contemporaries in that he had a unique and sure touch which they often lacked: 'This was not just because he could write better tunes, but because of his amazing versatility, due in part to his responsiveness to the words he was setting ... The incomparable advantage Purcell possessed over his fellow-composers, as regards these anecdotal catches, was his genius for hitting off character and emotion.'[8] Purcell's great gift for combining words and melody made him a master of the catch, and for this reason the words must not be tampered with. In the nineteenth century, the Purcell Society, on moral grounds, bowdlerized the bawdy texts; in so doing they destroyed not only the meaning, but the musical entirety. Fortunately today we are less inhibited and in a recent publication, *The Catch Book*,[9] there are 153 unbowdlerized catches including the complete [*sic*] catches of Henry Purcell.

The next important event in which Purcell was concerned was the celebration of the Queen's birthday in November, preparations for which had begun five days earlier. The celebrations are described by Luttrell:

The 15th, being Her Majesty's birth day, was kept at Whitehall, and in the evening were very fine fireworks on the water before Whitehall, which lasted for about two hours; and at night was a great ball at Whitehall, where the Court appeared in much splendour and bravery.[10]

It has been suggested that Charles had an ulterior motive in staging a gala affair as a camouflage to cover Monmouth's secret return to England, which occurred at the same time.[11]

A week after the birthday celebrations Purcell was involved in the preparations for the St Cecilia's Day celebrations for 21 and 22 November. This year, since he now had entire responsibility for all the instruments, he would have been organizing their removal to and from the Stationers' Hall, first making sure they were in good repair, and, once installed, that they were tuned ready for the concerts. The musical offering of that year, 'Begin the Song', was entrusted to Blow.

In the autumn, Purcell and his wife moved from Great St Ann's Lane to Bowling Alley East, as we see from the entries in the St Margaret's, Westminster, churchwarden's accounts for 1684 and 1685. The rates still remained at 14 shillings per annum which indicates that his position was respectable though not as yet affluent. No doubt he would have found the move a tiresome hindrance to his daily working routine but there were also possible advantages. It was certainly nearer to the Abbey, and the move may well have been engineered through Stephen Crespion, precentor of the Abbey and one of Purcell's closest friends.

Purcell's capacity for work showed no sign of diminishing. During this time we see his music developing in individual style and expression, alongside a technical facility that becomes increasingly innovative. From late 1684 to early 1685 are listed no fewer than 21 works consisting of songs, dialogues and catches.

An anthem dating from this time and commissioned by Gostling was 'They that go down to the sea', set to verses from Psalm 107. Hawkins recounts the incident that led to its composition. Charles II had recently launched a new yacht which he had called *Fubbs** after his mistress the Duchess of Portsmouth who had grown rather fat of late. The King had made a party to sail her down the river and round the Kentish coast, and to assist in keeping up the mirth and good humour, the Revd Gostling had been invited to join them. When they were approaching the North Foreland, a violent storm arose and the King and Duke of York

were necessitated, in order to preserve the vessel, to hand the sails, and work like common seamen; by good providence however, they escaped to land; but the distress they were in made an impression on the mind of Mr Gostling, which was never effaced. Struck with a just sense of the deliverance, and the horror of the scene which he had but lately viewed, upon his return to London he selected from the psalms those passages which declare the wonders and terrors of the deep, and gave them to Purcell to compose an anthem, which he did.[12]

The composer adapted it so peculiarly to the compass of Gostling's deep bass voice, that for many years scarcely anyone but himself was able to sing it. The first two verses are taken from the twenty-third and twenty-fourth of the psalm: 'They that go down to the sea in ships, and

---

* A term often used to describe children or ladies who were plump

occupy business in great waters. These men see the works of the Lord, and his wonders in the deep.' It is doubtful if Charles ever heard the anthem as it was not performed until after 7 February, 1685.

The New Year of 1685 was beginning to show for the English people the effects of the prosperity that had been growing for the last 12 months. Evelyn criticized the King for his libertine ways and many complained at the tardy settlement of long-outstanding accounts. But Charles II, for all his faults and excesses, had a profound love for his people and took an unfailing interest in the way they lived. He had an insatiable curiosity and a breadth of view on so many different subjects, his enthusiasm for which contributed in many ways to make life better for his subjects. He certainly encouraged people to seek a more spacious and satisfying way of life than they had known in the past.

The very luxury of his Court had served to bring this about. Even the wild Buckingham took out a patent for extracting glass and crystals from flint and founded a factory at Lambeth. Evelyn saw it and praised the huge vases of metal, clear and thick as crystal, and the looking glasses better than any from Venice . . . The glories of Windsor and Greenwich, the new faubourg of St James, and the London which arose from the ashes of the fire, posterity owes primarily to him. Everywhere his subjects followed his example, building those commodious and classical houses which in the next age were to give a park and palace to every village in England, encompassing gardens with walls to catch the sunlight, making fountains and parterres and grottoes, and planting walks of ash and sycamore.[13]

His concern was not confined to his immediate subjects. Even when Louis XIV of France rescinded the rule of religious toleration given by their mutual grandfather, Henry IV, Charles immediately invited the Huguenot silk-weavers to settle in England.

In the 24 years of his reign Charles, despite all his financial problems, had somehow managed to restore all the arts to their former glory, and music in particular had attained such a high standard that it commanded respect throughout Europe. He also patronized scientific research and granted the first charter to the Royal Society in 1662. Another encouraging sign was that now the King was solvent for the first time during his reign, he saw to it that salaries were maintained on a current basis and even settled some of the oldest outstanding debts.

It was thus as a loved and respected monarch that he departed from his people on 6 February 1685. His illness remains undiagnosable, but according to Hutton the symptoms resemble 'chronic glandular kidney disease with uraemic convulsions'.[14] He took four days to die and during this time was subjected to unthinkable blisterings and bleedings that could only have added to his suffering. But even in this intolerable state, his wit remained as sharp as ever. He looked at his courtiers standing round his bed and said: 'I am sorry to take so long a-dying. I hope you gentlemen will pardon me?'

On the night before his death, Charles was finally received into the Catholic Church. The rites were given by the King's old friend, Father Huddleston, whom he had sheltered at Whitehall during the Popish Terror. Since the King was surrounded by his Protestant courtiers, the priest had to be smuggled into the bedchamber, disguised in cassock and wig. Charles made full confession of his sins and received the sacrament. He also made peace with his brother, asking forgiveness for the way he had treated him in the past. Within a few hours England was faced with the private burial of one secretly converted Catholic king and the proclamation of another as James II. The Protestants would have had some cause for concern, but they need not have worried, for James II was to prove to be the worst manager of all the Stuarts and would reign for only four uneasy years.

For lack of information, all we know is that for Purcell, the death of his monarch meant writing an elegy, 'If Pray'rs and Tears', to the words of an anonymous poet. But over the years he would certainly have had regular communication with the King. Charles would have approved of Purcell's lively and colourful writing, and could easily tap his feet to the compelling rhythms in which it abounds. It is also probable that he detected in Purcell some of the wit that was so much an integral part of his own personality.

James moved to St James's Palace in April in readiness for his coronation on the 23rd of the month. The anti-Catholic brigade were soon at work, with rumours that Charles II had died of unnatural causes and that his ghost frequently appeared at Whitehall. It was evidently sufficiently disturbing to give rise to an official denial being issued at Court: 'April 27 1685. There is a common report about town of some apparition that walks at Whitehall; and the Kings removal to St James's hath given many credulous persons the occasion to believe the same, tho' it was onely for a little while, that the lodgings at Whitehall might be fitted up.'[15]

The Coronation itself was a splendidly colourful affair. Fifers, drummers and a kettle-drummer, in liveries of scarlet cloth, richly laced with gold and silver, led the procession of musicians. They were followed by eight trumpeters, in crimson velvet also laced with gold and silver. Their silver trumpets were adorned with banners of crimson damask, again fringed with gold and silver. These were followed by court dignitaries and then the Children and Gentlemen of the Chapel Royal together with the Westminster Choir and 'two sackbuts and a double curtall'. They were then joined by the entire English nobility, court and Abbey employees and, protected by His Majesty's Horse and Footguards, moved from Westminster Hall through the New Palace Yard into King Street and through the Great Sanctuary to the west door of the Abbey. Two breadths of 'blue broad-cloth' were spread from the Hall to the Choir, 'strewed with nine baskets full of sweet herbs and flowers by Mary Dowle, a Strewer of Herbs in Ordinary to His Majesty'.[16]

Charles II had not been married at the time of his coronation, but this time the Queen, Mary of Modena, was also to be crowned. Purcell's anthem, 'My Heart is Inditing of a good Matter', set to words from Psalm 45 was chosen for the anointing of the Queen. There were altogether nine anthems, which began with Purcell's 'I was Glad When They Said' and included Henry Lawes's 'Zadok the Priest' and Blow's 'Let Thy Hand be Strengthened', but the climax was Purcell's 'My Heart is Inditing' performed by the entire consort of voices and instruments It must have been a thrilling performance with a string band, hautbois, trumpets, drums and other instruments accompanying the eight-part solo and choral ensembles. Most likely the following would also have applied to the same anthem:

November 1686.
These are to pray and require you to pay or cause to be paid unto Dr Nicholas Staggins, Master of His Mats Musick, the sum of £19 11s 6d [written in words] for faire writeing of a composition for his Majesty's coronation day from the originall in score the 6 parts, for drawing ye said composition into forty severall parts, for trumpetts, hautboyes, violins, tennors, bases, prickers' dyett included, for ruled paper, penns, inke and chamber rent, and disburst in providing severall musitians for ye coronation day who were not His Majesty's servants.[17]

Only two unusual incidents occurred. One, that the ceremony was completed in every sense according to tradition, except that the holy sacrament was omitted, and when the crown was placed upon the new King's head, it toppled and almost fell off. Some regarded this as a bad omen, and when James fled the country only four years later, the more superstitious of his erstwhile subjects were convinced they had been right.

The festivities continued the following day with fireworks on the water at Whitehall and a splendid ball afterwards. There is no account of the music performed but the musicians would of course have been in attendance. Two days after this celebration the theatres were re-opened.

In March 1685, Purcell had been commissioned to set up a second organ in Westminster Abbey specifically for the Coronation, and had incurred expenses of £34 12s. in the process. Not surprisingly, he had to wait for payment until March 1686:

To Henry Purcell, for So much money by him disbursed and craved for providing and Setting up an Organ in the Abbey Church of Westm*ster* for the Solemnity of the Coronation, and for the removing the Same, and other Services performed in His said M*aties* Chapell since March 1685 according to a Bill signed by the Bishop of London . . .[18]

Also in June, John Dryden's opera *Albion and Albanius* was performed. This piece had had a somewhat chequered career. The poet had chosen the unpopular Grabu to write the music and in a letter to the Countess of Rutland in January, Edward Bedingfield had declared that it was 'so well performed at the repetition that has been made before His Majesty at the Duchess of Portsmouth's, pleaseth mightily, but the rates proposed will not take so well, for they have set the boxes at a guinea a place and the pit at half. They advance £4,000 on the opera, and therefore must tax high to reimburse themselves.' Ward suggests that the members of the company may well have been forced to contribute towards the cost of 'stunning scenes and devices' employed.[19]

The production was halted by the death of Charles II and finally presented, not at Whitehall as originally intended, but at Dorset Garden. The intention had been to pay tribute to Charles II as Albion and James as Albanius. The libretto therefore had to be revised to allow Albion to be transported to heaven by angels and cherubims whilst Albanius is left to mourn below. The opera received only six performances, for on 9 June the Duke of Argyll launched an attack in Scotland, and Monmouth, one at Lyme Regis in Dorset. Clearly, the piece could not survive its symbolism becoming irrelevant, and died a natural death. A few weeks later, Monmouth was defeated at the Battle of Sedgemoor, taken prisoner on 8 July and brought to London where he was beheaded a week later. Evelyn tells us that the executioner 'made five chops before he had his head off; which so incensed the people, that had he not been guarded and got away, they would have torn him to pieces'.

John Evelyn was one of Monmouth's sternest critics but this brutal inefficiency so touched him that he wrote:

Thus ended this quondam Duke, darling of his father and the ladies, being extremely handsome and adroit; an excellent soldier and dancer, a favourite of the people, of an easy nature, debauched by lust; seduced by crafty knaves, who would have set him up only to make a property, and taken the opportunity of the King being of another religion, to gather a party of discontented men. He failed, and perished.[20]

References

1. Chamberlayne, E., *Angliae Notitia, or the Present State of England*, 15th edition, Sawbridge, 1684, pp 142, 143, 147, 180.
2. AA, Vol 1, p 48.
3. *The New Grove Dictionary of Music and Musicians*, ed Stanley Sadie, Macmillan, 1980, Vol 17, p 413.
4. Burney, Charles, *A General History of Music*, Beckett, 1789, Vol 3, p 439.
5. Westrup, *Purcell*, pp 52–3.
6. Zimmerman, *Henry Purcell, 1659–1695, His Life and Times*, p 407.
7. PD, Vol 1, p 205 (21 July 1660).
8. Hart, Eric Ford, 'The Restoration Catch', *Music & Letters*, Vol 34, no 4, October 1953, pp 302–4.
9. Oxford Song Books, ed Paul Hillier, Oxford University Press, 1987
10. Luttrell, Narcissus, *A Brief Historical Relation of State Affairs from September 1678 to April 1714*, Oxford University Press, 1857, Vol 1, p 320.
11. Zimmerman, op cit, p 110.
12. Hawkins, *A General History of the Science and Practice of Music*, pp 744, 693, 693n.
13. Bryant, *King Charles II*, 346–7.
14. Hutton, Ronald, *Charles II, King of England, Scotland and Ireland*, Oxford University Press, 1989, p 443.
15. Lutt, op cit, Vol 1, p 338.
16. Zimmerman, op cit, pp 122–3.
17. AA, Vol 2, p 12.
18. Bodleian, Rawl MS D 872, fo 99.
19. Ward, Charles E., *Life of John Dryden*, University of North Carolina Press, Chapel Hill, 1961, p 209.
20. ED, Vol 2, p 232 (15 July 1685).

10

PURCELL AND THE CATHOLIC COURT

The new King and Queen were not much in favour of the services of English composers, nor their compositions, so for Purcell, times were far from easy. It was not only the King's Catholicism that stood in the way of continuing traditions set down by his brother during his reign, but also the fanatical approach of the royal pair to anything threatening their beliefs.

James, Duke of York and Albany, was born on 14 October 1633, the third of the six children of Charles I and Henrietta Maria, and junior to his brother Charles by three years. He was far more attracted to 'quick and nimble recreations, as running, leaping, riding',[1] than to his general education, and hunting amounted to an obsession. James was, in fact, probably one of the earliest of the aristocracy to pursue fox-hunting. When he ascended the throne, his lack of education held him at a disadvantage. He showed scant interest in the arts and science, although he did have some interest in music. As a young man he learnt the guitar and once obtained access to a young lady's boudoir through the exploitation of this talent. He was also said to accompany his brother when singing duets with the famous bass singer, John Gostling.

James also had an instinctive eye for the ladies. His attachment and promise of marriage to Anne Hyde, daughter of Sir Edward Hyde, later the Duke of Clarendon, brought him into trouble when he was in exile. The marriage finally took place in secret in September 1660, but was registered only in February the following year.

In 1668, James, influenced greatly by his mother, converted to the Church of Rome. The event coincided with the fall of Clarendon, and James's support for his father-in-law earned him many enemies. From this time, moves were made to exclude him from the succession (see p 54).

When Anne Hyde – who had also been converted to Catholicism the previous year – died in March 1671, Charles was determined to get his brother remarried to someone of the right blood and religion. Eventually, the choice was made secretly by Louis XIV of France, and fell on the 15-year-old Maria Beatrice, sister of the young Duke of Modena, who saw her future only as a nun. As a devout Catholic her main fears were that in a Protestant country she would not be allowed to worship God in the manner to which she was accustomed, but she was given assurance that a chapel would be provided where she could arrange everything as she wished. Finally she reluctantly agreed to the marriage and arrived at Dover on 21 November 1673, taking part in a proxy ceremony conducted by Nathaniel Crewe, the Bishop of Oxford, with Peterborough representing the Duke. It was described as 'surely the most casual ceremony that has ever been dignified by the title of marriage service under the laws of England'.[2]

The marriage caused great distress throughout England. Not only was Maria Beatrice a Catholic, but when it became known that Louis XIV had had a hand in arranging the match, it naturally followed that he had probably supplied the dowry as well. Louis had a genius for striking bargains that put the other party in a weaker position.

Although Purcell and the other members of the court musicians were not pleased at the way in which the King and Queen favoured foreign composers, they had no option but to obey their royal master. Purcell, in fact, contributed to the protagonists by writing a two-part setting of D'Urfey's 'A Grasshopper and a Fly', which clearly was outrageous in its references to the defeated Monmouth:

> So rebel Jemmy Scot
> That did to Empire soar;
> His father might be the Lord knows what,
> But his mother we knew a whore.

This song was published with several others in the Third Book of *The Theater of Music* in 1686. The First Book, dedicated to 'Dr John Blow, Master of the Children, and one of the Organists of His Majesty's Chapel Royal. And to Mr Henry Purcell, Composer-in-Ordinary to his Sacred Majesty and one of the Organists of his Chapel Royal', shows that although Purcell had now attained an important place as a composer and his achievements were being recognized, the King was not disposed to ask him or any other English composer to mark the fall of Monmouth. Instead he employed the Italian, G.B.

Vitali, a musician in the service of Duke Francisco II, the Queen's brother, to celebrate the defeat and execution by writing an oratorio, *L'Ambizione debellata; ouvero, La Caduta di Monmouth* (Ambition brought low; or the Downfall of Monmouth): it was never presented in England although it may have been performed in Italy. So the English Henry Purcell of the Chapel Royal simply continued to write for church and stage. About this time he provided a duet to be performed between Acts II and III of Tate's 1685 adaptation of *Eastward Ho* called *Cuckold's-Haven* at the Theatre Royal, the same theatre where he had supplied music for four previous productions. Purcell's 'How great are the blessings of government grown' was inserted as a gesture to James II who happened to be attending the performance. It is not an integral part of the music written for the play, and this particular performance probably took place around the time of the public thanksgiving ordered by James for 28 July. Two more compositions by Purcell were possibly written that year: the music for Charles Davenant's *Circe*, originally set by Banister, and the 'Mad' song for Lee's tragedy, *Sophonisba, or Hannibal's Overthrow*, published later in *Orpheus Britannicus*. However, Zimmerman suggests the florid and echo passages reflect the later style of Purcell's writing.

By the end of the summer of 1685, James turned his attention to organizing his court musicians. The unpopular Nicholas Staggins, who had succeeded Grabu as Master of the King's Musick in 1674, had his position confirmed as such. On 31 August, Henry Purcell's name appears on a long list of those who have been sworn in as His Majesty's musicians-in-ordinary. Dr Blow is described as composer and Henry Brockwell is Keeper of the Instruments. Purcell is simply 'harpsicall'. It is clear that Purcell had lost the two important positions he had filled under Charles II, those of composer and organist to the Chapel Royal, which is a powerful argument that Purcell was not a Catholic.

The celebrations for the Queen's birthday on 25 September (1685), held at Windsor with a ball at night, employed only about half of the sum total of the court musicians; Purcell's name is absent from the list, although we know that on 9 October he was 'sworn and admitted in the private music in ordinary'.[3] But in any case, he would almost certainly have been working on an ode for the King's fifty-second birthday on 14 October, just three weeks later. It is interesting that although Blow officially remained the court composer, the demoted Purcell was still expected to provide music for royal occasions.

The resulting ode was 'Why Are All the Muses Mute?' Evelyn writes in his diary the following day: 'Being the King's birth-day, there was a solemn ball at Court, and before it music of instruments and voices. I happened by accident to stand the very next to the Queen and the King, who talked with me about the music.'[4]

However, the music on this occasion did little to deter James II in his zealous pursuit of all whom he considered to be enemies of himself or his church. Anyone who could be found guilty of persecuting papist plotters, even for several years back, was brought to trial and hung, drawn and quartered, often with little or no substantial evidence.

So pale was James's interest in court music that St Cecilia's Day was barely noticed. Nahum Tate wrote words which William Turner set to music for the occasion but the event was evidently so unremarkable as not to be celebrated at all the following year (1686).

Meanwhile there was an announcement in the *London Gazette* for 19–23 November (1685) which showed a new development in the relationship between music publishers and the sponsorship of concerts in London:

Several sonatas, composed after the Italian way, for one and two Bass Viols, with a Thorough-Basse, being on the Request of several Lovers of music (who have already Subscribed) to be Engraven upon Copper Plates, are to be perform'd on Thursday next, and every Thursday following, at Six of the Clock in the Evening, at the Dancing School in Walbrook, next door to the Bell Inn, and on Saturday next, and every Saturday following, at the Dancing School in York Buildings. At which places will be also some performances upon the Barritone [baryton], by Mr August Keenell [Kuhnel], the Author of this Musick. Such who do not subscribe are to pay their Half Crown towards the discharge of performing it.[5]

We know that this kind of concert was always well attended. And the close proximity of the Dancing School to the Bell Inn would have been an added attraction.

Meanwhile, the King continued frequently to invite foreign dignitaries to court; Evelyn gives us a graphic description of the splendour of a dinner given in honour of two Venetian ambassadors and ten nobles who had come to congratulate James on his accession to the throne:

The dinner was most magnificent and plentiful, at four tables, with music, kettle-drums, and trumpets, which sounded upon a whistle at every health. The banquet [dessert] was twelve vast chargers piled up so high that those who sat one against another could hardly see each other. Of these sweetmeats, which doubtless were some days piling up in that exquisite manner, the Ambassadors touched not, but leaving them to the spectators who came out of curiosity to see the dinner, were exceedingly pleased to see in what a moment of time all that curious work was demolished, the comfitures voided, and the tables cleared. Thus his Majesty entertained them three days, which (for the table only) cost him £600, as the Clerk of the Green Cloth (Sir William Boreman) assured me. Dinner ended, I saw their procession, or cavalcade, to Whitehall, innumerable coaches attending. The two Ambassadors had four coaches of their own, and fifty footmen (as I remember), besides other equipage as splendid as the occasion would permit, the Court being still in mourning.[6]

In February 1686, the French Opera Company was invited back to London, possibly to compensate for the previous failure of Grabu's *Albion and Albanius* to Dryden's text.[7] This time they were presenting Lully's *Cadmus et Hermione*, but it seems that the performances were postponed several times and, according to a letter from Peregrine Bertie to the Countess of Rutland, dated 11 February: 'Today was the French opera. The King and Queen were there, the musicke was indeed very fine, but all the dresses the most wretched I ever saw; 'twas acted by none but French.' But despite the poor wardrobe, the company would appear to have made exorbitant charges for admission: 'The King & Queen & a Box for ye Maydes of honour at ye French Opera £25.'[8]

It is probable that Purcell may have gone to Windsor in May, but must have returned before the other musicians in order to arrange for the burial of his son, Thomas, the third child who had not survived infancy. This is confirmed by the fact that Purcell's name is not included in the list in the warrants presented on 15 October and 9 November for riding charges to attend on the King at Windsor Castle for 141 days from 14 May to 1 October 1686. Nicholas Staggins received £35 5s, and each musician, £21 3s with riding charges of 5s per day for everybody.[9]

Purcell was also occupied at this time with the installation of the organ which had been commissioned from Bernard Smith for the Church of St Katherine Cree in London. The church records tell us that

The organ being now finished, it is ordered that Mr Joseph Cox do procure Mr Purcell, Mr Barkwell, and Mr Moses, masters in music, and Mr White, organ master, or such others competent judges in music as may be prevailed with to be at our church on Thursday next the 30th of this instant September, at two of the clock in the afternoon to give their judgements upon the organ.

On 30 September we learn that

Dr Blow, Mr Purcell, Mr Mosses, Mr Fforcell this day appeared at our church, Mr Purcell was desired to play and did play upon the organ, and after he had done playing they all reported to the vestry that in their judgements the organ was a good organ, and was performed and completed according to contract.

Purcell then heard the four contestants for the post of organist. From these the judges voted 'by scratch of pen or scrutiny' and the votes

fell upon Mr Snowe who had eight hands and Mr Beach but five hands, and Mr Nicholls and Mr Heath but one hand apiece. And the said Mr Snowe being afterwards made acquainted with the said choice, gratefully accepted of the said place.[10]

Despite Purcell and his colleagues finding the organ to be eminently suitable, poor Bernard Smith did not receive his payment of £250 until 28 May 1687. Purcell and Smith received 14s each for the undertaking and Blow and Purcell received 5s each for the hire of a coach. In addition to the sum of 10s to Mr Snow for two quarters for playing the organ, there is another significant account: 'Paid and spent at the Crowne Taverne upon Dr Blow and others when they approved of an organ and chose an organist £8.13s.0d.'[11] One trusts that this was for services after the event rather than before.

However depressed the musicians might have felt at James II's constant foreign importations, they must have been gladdened by his decision to clear up the arrears in salaries which had bedevilled the court musicians since the beginning of the Restoration. For two centuries the musicians' annual wages had ranged between £200 and as little as £18. James gave his musicians all the same – £40 – abolished the many plural posts, and set up a scheme to pay all the arrears, which was to take seven years to complete. On 21 September 1686, a warrant was issued from the Lord Chamberlain to the Master of his Majesty's Great Wardrobe for the payment of the following sums:

Whereas it appears that £2,484.16.3d. remains due to the respective musicians to his late Majesty whose names follow, for the arrears of their liveries incurred during his late Majesty's reign: – after making such

retrenchment throughout as was intended by his late Majesty and is
commanded by his present Majesty to be observed in cases of arrears of this
nature, these are to desire your Lordship, out of the money which is or shall be
imprested to you at the receipt of the Exchequer of the new imposition on
tobacco and sugar, to pay all the sums due to the said musicians.[12]

There then follows a long list with many familiar names including
Nicholas Staggins, John Gamble, John Clements, Charles Coleman,
Thomas Lanier, Edward Hooten, William Turner, John Blow and
William Child, but Purcell's name is not on the list, so we can assume
either that he received his payments on a more regular basis, or was
not due for remuneration at this time (1686). But what is so striking is
that although most of the debts are in the 1670s, some go back as far as
1660.

For the King's birthday celebrations on 14 October (1686), Purcell
composed another ode, 'Ye Tuneful Muses, Raise Your Heads'. The
anonymous poet takes care to pay suitable respect to the Queen as well
as the King with the words, 'Happy in a mutual love'. The day was a
splendid affair with four troupes of guards 'all new clothed very finely'
assembled in Hyde Park. Westrup reminds us that instrumental effects
were then in their infancy, and yet to illustrate the words, 'Tune all
your instruments', he makes the violins 'scrub' over all four strings; a
very advanced technique at the time.[13]

One of the additional excitements, out of which the gossips made
capital was that the King also brought his mistress, Mrs Sedley, out of
retirement in Ireland. Could Purcell have introduced the ballad tune
'Hey, then up go we' as the bass to the chorus 'Be lively then and gay',
with tongue in cheek?[14]

A problem besetting Purcell at this time was yet a further instance of
the financial hazards of musicians. In a letter to the Dean of Exeter
regarding an outstanding debt owed by one of his pupils, he writes:

Westminster, November the 2nd. 1686

I have wrote severall times to Mr Webber concerning what was due to me on
Hodg's account and recd no answer, which has occassion'd this presumption
in giving you the trouble of a few lines relating to the matter; It is ever since ye
beginning of June last that the Money has been due: the sum is £27, *viz*, £20
for half a years teaching and boarding the other a Bill of £7 for nessecary's
wch I laid out for him, the Bill Mr Webber has; Compassion Moves me to
acquaint you of a great many debts Mr Hodg contracted whilst in London
and to some who are so poor 'twere an act of charity as well as Justice to pay

'em. I hope you will be so kind to take it into Your consideration and also pardon this boldness from

> Sr,
>> Yr most obliged
>>> humble sert
>> Henry Purcell[15]

The outcome of this matter is unknown. We can only assume that Purcell instructed his pupil in music in general, maybe including composition and improvisation. He might also have taught him how to keep and tune instruments. We know that Purcell was a perfectionist and that every task he undertook was executed to a very high standard, so whatever he imparted to his pupil would have been of value. Obviously the relationship was uncongenial and certainly Purcell has a low opinion of the pupil's character. It must have been all the more frustrating to have provided so much over a period for such an undesirable person, and still be left out of pocket. Sadly, it is yet one more example of the way in which musicians were at the mercy of their creditors. It would have been interesting if the said Hodg had turned out to be a famous musician, but unfortunately his name has never since been mentioned. None the less, Purcell would have been grateful for one extra payment that year, £10 for providing service books for Westminster Abbey.[16] Financially, it had been a bad year. Even the money for the rent of Purcell's house, due at Christmas, did not arrive until Michaelmas of the following year.

It is possible that Purcell might have received payment for some duets and catches which appeared in Playford's *Pleasant Musical Companion* Book II, but unlikely. Certainly in *The Theater of Music*, a similar publication,

the preface to Book I implies that the composers received no payment for the printing of their songs, nor were many of them consulted about what pieces were included; they were simply requested in future to leave copies of their new songs at either Playford's or Carr's shop to ensure 'perfect and exact' printed versions, which were apparently regarded as sufficient recompense.[17]

Two of the catches from the *Pleasant Musical Companion*, 'He that drinks is immortal' and 'Full bags, a brisk bottle', are in praise of drinking, and the text of the latter, which appeared anonymously in 1686, was later bowdlerized in the Purcell Society edition. A glance at the original text, as printed overleaf, makes it easy to see why.

On 9 June 1687, a fourth son was born to Frances and Henry Purcell

A. 3. Voc.

A Catch the words by Cob. Alliftree   Set by H. Purcell

Full Bags, a brifk Bottle, and a Beautifull Face, are the three greatest Bleffings poor

Mortals embrace, but a-lafs we grow Muckworms if Bags do but full, is a bonny gay

Dame of-ten ends in a Pill: then hey for brifk Claret, whofe Plea-fures ne'er wafte,

by a Bumper we're rich, and by two we are chaft.

and baptized Henry after his father; but, like his brothers, he did not survive, and was buried on 23 September only three months later.

Clearly Purcell was experiencing real difficulties under the new regime from every quarter. He had already been demoted from his post as composer and now he also found that he was not being paid for his work as keeper of the king's organs; furthermore there is no evidence that he was required to continue in this capacity. He pointed out to the authorities that the office was most necessary and at the same time petitioned for money owing to him. He also asked that provision should be made for the future. On 10 June (1687) the Treasury referred the petition to Edward Griffin who held on to it for six months before handing the document to the Bishop of Durham who was also Dean of the Chapel Royal. After another two months' delay, the Bishop wrote to say he deemed the request very reasonable and that the matter would receive attention. However, it took until March 1688 until the matter was finally settled. The accounts submitted by Purcell give an interesting glimpse into the dire state in which music had fallen under the reign of James II:

The organ at present is so out of repair that to cleanse, tune and put in good order will cost £40 and then to keep it so will cost £20 per an. at the least.   £20.0.0

For the loan of a harpsichord, portage and tuning to three practices and performances of each song to the King at £4 per song for four several songs at least.   £16.0.0

Whereas the salary of the place in the late King's time was £60 per an. for any care and trouble which will unavoidably occur.   £20.0.0

                                                                          £56.0.0

Wherefore I humbly pray that I may be established at the yearly salary of £56 to commence from Christmas 1687.
And whereas it will cost to put the organ in repair as is above mentioned about   £40.0.0

and my bill already delivered in, which ended at New Year's Day 1686 [i.e. 1687] amounts to   £20.10.0

since which the service performed amounts to about the like sum of £20.10.0

                                                                  Total £81.0.0

I humbly pray that order may be given for the present payment of the said sum of eighty-one pounds.

Hen. Purcell[18]

Westrup points out that one George Wyatt, the Chapel organ-blower, an indispensable but lower-ranking royal servant, was dependent on Purcell for his annual salary of £10 a year. He petitioned also, drawing attention to the fact that he had been in the royal service since the Restoration, but, unlike Purcell, received acknowledgement within three weeks of submission. The Board of Greencloth were instructed to make provision for the annual £10, the 'petitioner being certified by the Dean of the Chapel Royal as an object of charity and necessary in the attendance there'.[19]

The neglect of the Chapel Royal was intentional, and it did not take the Catholic James long to establish his own private chapel in Whitehall. It had been opened in 1686, and Evelyn, as usual, can be relied upon for an emotive description of the occasion. After going into raptures over the architecture, he tells us about the 'Popish Service' itself:

Here we saw the Bishop in his mitre and rich copes, with six or seven Jesuits and others in rich copes, sumptuously habited . . . the crosier, which was of silver, wa: put into his [the Bishop's] hand with a world of mysterious ceremony, the music playing, with singing. I could not have believed I should ever have seen such things in the King of England's palace, after it had pleased God to enlighten this nation; but our great sin has, for the present, eclipsed the blessing, which I hope He will in mercy and His good time restore to its purity.[20]

The establishment of the chapel must have caused considerable rancour among the regular court musicians. It was quite independent and consisted of an organist, an assistant organist, seven or eight choristers, singing-men, instrumentalists and several officials including a chaplain, a master and a housekeeper for the boys. There was also a man to tune the harpsichords and another to look after the music, and the organ-blower was paid twice as much as poor George Wyatt at the Chapel Royal. The singing-men and instrumentalists alone cost £1500 a year and when the King moved to Windsor it was his own royal chapel who attended him. The singing-men included several followers: Bartolomeo Albrici who had served under Charles II and was music-master to Evelyn's sister, Mary, and the few English singers employed were John Abell, the famous counter-tenor and Mr Pordage, a well-known singer in London society.

A colourful character also associated briefly with the private chapel was the Italian castrato singer, Siface, born near Pescia in 1653, as Giovanni Francesco Grossi. It was his performance in the part of Siface in Cavalli's *Scipione affricano* in Rome in 1671 that earned him the nickname by which he was known thereafter. He had achieved early fame as a soprano castrato and sang for four years in the papal chapel. In 1679 he entered the service of Francesco II d'Este, Duke of Modena, with whom he remained for the rest of his life.

It was Siface's association with the Duke which prompted his visit to London in 1687, where he was sent to entertain the Duke's sister, now Queen of England. It was in the 'Popish' chapel of James II that Evelyn first heard Siface sing and was shocked at the absence of the devotional atmosphere proper to a sacred building, which he described as 'Much crowding – little devotion'.[21]

Evelyn heard Siface again when 'a select number of particular persons' were invited to the house of Mr Pepys, who had obtained his services with much difficulty: 'the Signor much disdaining to show his talent to any but princes'. Evelyn admitted that his 'holding out and delicateness in extending and loosing a note with incomparable softness and sweetness was admirable', but he had reservations: 'for the rest I found him a mere wanton, effeminate child, very coy, and proudly conceited, to my apprehension. He touched the harpsichord to his voice rarely well.'[22] It seems that Siface also continually complained that the English climate affected his voice and finally departed for Modena barely six months after his arrival.

It is not known if Purcell was personally acquainted with Siface, although he must have heard him sing. He would certainly have shared his fellow court musicians' resentment at the display of temperament by this foreign visitor, and perhaps it was with some relief that Purcell wrote a harpsichord piece called 'Sefauchi's Farewell', to commemorate his departure. It was published in Part II of *Musick's Handmaid* in 1689.

Despite the fact that Purcell was no longer organist to the Chapel Royal, he was kept busy writing anthems: the Gostling family have a manuscript book in which seven have been assigned to the years 1687–8.

On 14 October 1687, the King's birthday was again celebrated with an ode by Purcell, *Sound the Trumpet*, the last he would write for the monarch, who within the year would be living in retirement in France.

After Purcell's death, this rousing music was to be resuscitated and the words changed to welcome William III home from Flanders. But Purcell also must have thought the music too good to be left alone as four years later he used it for the Chaconne in *King Arthur*.

Meanwhile, James II was obviously having trouble with Nicholas Staggins and used very plain language to show his displeasure. On 21 October a warrant was sent to him as 'master of his Majesty's Musick':

Whereas you have neglected to give Order to ye Violins to attend at ye Chappell at Whitehall where Her Royal Highnesse ye Princesse Ann of Denmarke is present. These are therefore to give notice to them that they give theire attendance there upon Sunday next & soe continue to doe soe as formerly they did.[23]

Sometime in late 1686 the publisher and bookseller, John Playford, had died. The association between a composer and his publisher is important, and it was known that Playford and Purcell had a most congenial business relationship, besides being close friends. There are no details of when the funeral took place, but we do know that in early 1687, Purcell wrote an *Elegy on the Death of John Playford*, setting the verse by Nahum Tate.

Some confusion exists as to the identity of the two John Playfords who ran the publishing house of the same name. John Playford (the elder) was born in Norwich in 1623, the son of a mercer who came from a long line of stationers or scriveners. He was probably educated at a choir school attached to the Cathedral where he received a good musical education and a 'love of Divine Service'. At 16 he was apprenticed for seven years to John Benson, a London publisher, after which he became a member of the Yeomanry of the Stationers' Company, which entitled him to trade as a publisher on his own account. He rented a shop in the porch of the Temple Church and it was from this address that all his publications were issued right up to his retirement, and for over 30 years he dominated the music-publishing trade which was then virtually confined to London. His books were printed by Thomas Harper, William Godbid and his own nephew, also named John. Playford (the elder) was a Royalist by nature and in 1649 a warrant was issued for his arrest, but nothing more is known of him until the following year when he published *The English Dancing Master*, probably his first publication. He became a highly respected local figure and served as a clerk to the Temple

Church where he devoted himself to the repair and maintenance of the building. He was also vicar-choral of St Paul's Cathedral.

Playford's son, Henry, born in London about 1657, and godson of Henry Lawes, was called to the livery of the Stationers' Company in 1680, and entered the business around this time. On his father's death he took over the firm and for a short while joined with Robert Carr. Later, he continued independently in Fleet Street, in Arundel Street where his father had lived, and at the old shop by the Temple Church. Henry Playford did not approach the trade with the same dedication as his father. Much of what he published was simply an updated version of what his father had started, and his own interest was in supplying the requirements of public entertainments and pleasure-garden concerts which created a market for 'favourite songs'.

John Playford, the younger, born about 1655, was apprenticed to the printer William Godbid. After Godbid's death in 1679, his widow, Anne, took John into partnership, and he acquired ownership in 1682, the same year in which his name appears in the livery list of the Stationers' Company. He died in 1685, bequeathing the business to his sister Eleanor, who advertised it in the *London Gazette*. The royal printers purchased only part of the material so that Eleanor was obliged to ask permission from the King to continue to print music as it was her only means of existence.

James II was not well disposed to the Playfords for their known Protestant sympathies, and the petition was dismissed. The royal printers, having bought much of the petitioner's materials, purchased the rest, and in so doing, a firm that had enjoyed some 40 years of prominence was destroyed.

On 7 November (1687), the publication was advertised of the first book of Playford's *Harmonia Sacra, or Divine Hymns and Dialogues*, 'composed by the Best Masters of the Last and Present Age', the words being 'by several Learned and Pious Persons'. Purcell had contributed several pieces, including the celebrated 'Evening Hymn' on a ground, 'Now that the Sun hath veil'd his light', and also what Westrup terms 'a remarkable' setting of Herbert's 'With sick and famish'd eyes'. In addition to his own contributions Purcell was employed as editor, and in his introduction to the reader, Playford tells us:

As for the musical part, it was compos'd by the most skilful masters of this age; and though some of them are now dead, yet their composures have been reviewed by Mr Henry Purcell, whose tender regard for the reputation of those great men made him careful that nothing should be published, which, through the negligence of transcribers, might reflect upon their memory.

We also are informed by an advertisement at the back of the volume that the *Sonatas of III Parts* are still on sale.

On 18 November (1687) the *London Gazette* announced the publication of the first volume in a new songbook series *Comes Amoris: Or, the Companion of Love*, published by John Carr, who had compiled a 'choice collection of the newest scores now in use'. Purcell supplied five songs, one of which, 'When first Amintas Sued for a kiss', is printed anonymously. Another song by Purcell, 'Catch by Way of Epistle: To All Lovers of Music', is virtually the publisher's advertisement set to music. This is probably the first example of a publisher advertising by way of a piece of music, and therefore a forerunner of the 'theme' tune of the twentieth century.[24]

November was an important month for Purcell. The *London Gazette* for 21–5 November 1687 announces the publication of the fourth book of *The Theater of Music*, the last in the series brought out by Playford after he and his partner Robert Carr had fallen out and parted. Playford suggests that his ex-colleague may well try to disparage the collection but that 'when it comes into the hands of judicious gentlemen and understanders of music', they will not be put off. Purcell had ten songs in the collection, and his musical integrity is again underlined by Playford:

First, That most of these Songs and Dialogues were Composed by the Eminent Dr *John Blow*, and Mr *Henry Purcell*, my ever kind Friends, and several other able Masters, from whom I received true Copies, which were by them perused, before they were put to the press.[25]

Playford immediately brought out a new series of his own, called *The Banquet of Music* and provided a variety of songs, catches, dialogues and a small pastoral cantata, 'How Pleasant Is This Flow'ry Plain', by Purcell. Included among the other contributors were Moses Snow, mentioned earlier as one of the judges in the organ competition, John Banister, John Blow and Purcell's brother, Daniel.

After the omission of any celebration of St Cecilia's Day in 1686, the members of the London Society invited John Dryden to write the poem and Draghi to supply the music. Zimmerman asks: 'Was Purcell too busy composing and editing pieces for the first book of *Harmonia Sacra* and other collections? Or was he, perhaps, out of favour under a Catholic monarch, whose "papist" policy at court may have been reflected in the choice of these two prominent Catholics to provide the poetry and music for the celebration of 1687?'[26] There is no evidence to provide an answer to these questions, but obviously Draghi's musical powers were not up to the opportunity Dryden had provided with the lyrics of the ode, 'From Harmony, from Heavenly Harmony'. This would have to wait for half a century for Handel to immortalize.

References

1. Turner, F.C., *James II*, Eyre & Spottiswoode, 1948, p 13.
2. Ibid, p 111.
3. AA, Vol 2, p 4.
4. ED, Vol 2, p 243 (15 October 1685).
5. Tilmouth, Michael, *Royal Musical Association, Research Chronicle*, no 1, p 7.
6. ED, Vol 2, p 249 (18 December 1685).
7. Lawrence, W.J., 'The French Opera in London', *Times Literary Supplement*, 28 March 1936, p 268.
8. *The London Stage*, Part 1 (1660–1700), ed William van Lennep, Emmett L. Avery and Arthur H. Scouten, Southern Illinois University Press, Carbondale, 1965, p 347.
9. AA, Vol 2, p 12.
10. Vestry minutes St Katherine Cree, quoted in Zimmerman, p 135.
11. Guildhall MS 1198/1.
12. AA, Vol 1, p 289.
13. Westrup, *Purcell*, p 178.
14. Zimmerman, *Henry Purcell, 1659–1695, His Life and Times* p 136.
15. Westrup, op cit, illustration facing p 21.
16. WAM 33722, fo 5v.
17. Spencer, Robert, Introduction, *The Theater of Music*, Richard Macnutt, 1983, p x.
18. Cal Treas Books, 10 June, 12 December 1687, 18 February, 5 March 1688.
19. Ibid, 7, 26 February, quoted in Westrup, pp 57–8.
20. ED, Vol 2, pp 263–4 (29 December 1686).
21. Ibid, p 265 (30 January 1687).
22. Ibid, p 268 (19 April 1687).
23. AA, Vol 2, p 16.
24. Zimmerman, op cit, p 145.
25. *The Theater of Music*, or A Choice Collection of the newest and best Songs, Sung at the Court and Public Theaters. The *Words* composed by the most ingenious *Wits* of the Age, and set to Music by the greatest Masters in that Science . . . Fourth and last book, for Henry Playford, 1687.
26. Zimmerman, op cit, pp 146–7.

11

THE GLORIOUS REVOLUTION

In the autumn of 1687 there were rumours that the Queen was pregnant, but it was not until January 1688 that the signs were positive. She had already suffered four miscarriages and given birth to a daughter who died in infancy, so this apparent certainty gave rise to much rejoicing within the royal family. Evelyn tells us that 'There was a solemn and particular office used at our, and all the churches of London and ten miles round, for a thanksgiving to God, for her Majesty being with child.'[1]

This celebration was subsequently carried out in churches all over the country. Purcell came briefly back into favour with the commission to write an anthem for the thanksgiving ceremony: 'Blessed are they that fear the Lord'. 'The text of this anthem can be construed as special pleading for the maintenance of the established monarchial house, just as the annual celebration of the martyrdom of Charles I, observed on the following day, can be interpreted as both a caveat on the dangers of Protestant revolution and a plea for loyalty to the House of Stuart.'[2] Evelyn seems to have come to the same conclusion: 'Being the Martyrdom-day of King Charles the First, our curate made a florid oration against the murder of that excellent Prince, with an exhortation to obedience from the example of David, I Samuel xxvi.6.'[3]

There was more rejoicing on the evening of 6 February, when a performance by the United Players of *The Double Marriage* by Fletcher and Massinger was held at Court. Luttrell tells us that 'The 6th, was observed as a festival of joy for the king's comeing to the crown; there was musick at the chapell, cannons discharged at the Tower, and at night was a play at Court.'[4]

The incidental music for this play was believed to be by Purcell, but Zimmerman considers the music 'awkward, unpolished' and doubts that it was composed in 1688. He suggests, either it dates from a much earlier period, or is not, in fact, written by Purcell.

A few weeks later, it was Purcell's turn to rejoice. He received the good news that the Treasury had finally agreed to pay the expenses and stipend listed in his petition of the previous year. The warrant to the Board of the Greencloth – who actually paid the money – did not appear in the accounts until early in March, by which time costs had increased. 'And whereas it hath been represented unto us by the Bishop of Durham that £81 is due to Henry Purcell for repairing the organ and furnishing the harpsichords Christmas last and that it is necessary for that service to allow the sum of £56 per an.; these are to require you that the same be passed, allowed and paid accordingly.'[5] On 6 April he also received £32 for the provision of an organ and sundry necessities, so Purcell would have been happier with his financial situation than he had been for some time.

In late March or early April, Purcell's music was again heard in the theatre. He had set eight of the songs in D'Urfey's adaptation of Fletcher's *Noble Gentleman*, performed under the title of *A Fool's Preferment, or the Three Dukes of Dunstable*. The play, 'a smutty comedy', was produced at Dorset Garden by the United Company, and enjoyed only a few performances. The songs were printed separately later that year. All Purcell's songs were sung by the tenor William Mountfort, and 'I'll sail upon the dog-star' is still attempted by those who can meet the musical challenge it offers. Price believes that Purcell's mature style of writing begins to emerge in the songs he wrote for this play, and eventually 'led to the creation of other important singing roles'.[6]

Two further collections of songs appeared in May. The first, announced in the *London Gazette* (7–10 May), was Henry Playford's second book of *The Banquet of Music* which comprised the 'newest and best songs sung at Court and at public theatres'. Four of these were Purcell's. There were another four songs in John Carr's *Vinculum Societatis, or The Tie of Good Company*, also advertised in the *London Gazette*. This collection was to satisfy common rather than fashionable taste, and Carr's second book of *Comes Amoris; or the Companion of Love* was also aimed at this wider 'popular' section of the community. Purcell's contributions are in the form of three bawdy catches with a separate title-page, *A Small Collection of the Newest Catches for 3 Voices*. Here again, we have a glimpse of a man who could write superb ceremonial music and church anthems, yet no doubt derived pleasure from a little salacious humour which shows what a very rounded human being he must have been.

This, too, was a happy time for Purcell in his domestic life. On 30 May, his wife gave birth to a daughter, baptized at St Margaret's, Westminster on 1 June and named Frances after her mother. She was the first of Purcell's children to survive and live to marry and have a child of her own.

By the summer of 1688, the undercurrents of revolution were rife. Since his accession to the throne, there had been increasing evidence of James II's intention to bring back the Catholic faith to a nation fanatically opposed to popery. In 1687, James issued the first of his Declarations of Indulgence, when thousands walked free from the prisons and public worship was resumed by Catholic congregations who have never since had any restraint put upon them. It can truly be said that from this time there was religious freedom in England. But James, insensitive as always as to the mood of his people, decided to go one better. On 27 April 1688, he issued a Second Declaration of Indulgence, confirming some of the provisions of the first but differing in that it announced the appointment of Catholics to civil and military command on the grounds that no one should be employed in the public service 'who will not contribute towards the peace and greatness of their country'.[7] Moreover, he issued an order that the Declaration should be read twice in every church throughout the kingdom.

Discussion among the leading churchmen led to a petition to the King against the reading of the Declaration, presented to the monarch by seven bishops: the archbishop Sancroft, and bishops Lloyd, Turner, Lake, Ken, White and Trelawny. James reacted violently, turning on them in a fit of temper, accusing them of rebellion. He then refused flatly to return the paper to the bishops.

There then follows one of the best unsolved mysteries in British history. That same evening, as if by magic, the petition was printed and distributed throughout London. No one has ever discovered the identity of the person who 'leaked' this document to the press. At the time, there were only two newspapers, *Mercurius Publicus* – in which Charles II advertised for a missing dog – and the *London Gazette*, but broadsides and ballads on events such as murder, robbery, scandal or politics had been circulated ever since the early days of printing. These could generally be bought at the north door of St Paul's. The central aisle of old St Paul's, known as 'Paul's Walk', was the popular haunt of the gossip-writers; these were virtually the first English journalists who also supplied court and foreign news to noblemen and country squires for a regular fee.

It is not difficult to imagine the effect of the news upon the people and the already explosive situation was inflamed to the point of rebellion. As a result, the seven bishops were brought to trial, accused of seditious libel and committed to the Tower. A week later the bishops were released, and on 15 June, when they were brought again from the Tower to Westminster Hall, the banks and the roadways were swarming with people. Their acquittal caused an enormous outburst of cheering and at night there were bonfires which James tried in vain to check. The rejoicing could not have been greater if they were celebrating a victory over a foreign enemy.

Five days before the bishops were released, on 10 June 1688, a son, James Francis Edward, afterwards known as the Pretender, was born to Queen Mary in the Old Bedchamber at St James's Palace. The room was situated at the east end of the south front, the unusual position giving rise to the reports that the Prince was not the true son of the King and Queen. There had been much gossip about the Queen's 'false belly' and the fact that none of her ladies of the bedchamber ever saw her undressing. The birth was premature and took everyone by surprise. It was immediately rumoured that, acting on instructions from the Jesuits, a substitute infant had been smuggled into the palace in a warming-pan. There had been a sudden suspicious move from Windsor to St James's, where the Queen's room had three doors, one leading to a private staircase at the head of the bed, and two windows opposite the bed. In 1822 when extensive alterations were made to the palace, this room was demolished. In any case, however much the 'warming-pan plot' is denied, from this time it was customary for several 'Privy Councellors and Ladies in Waiting to be in attendance, in an adjoining room, at Royal births'. 'Queen Victoria in 1894 instructed for the birth of the future King Edward VIII, that the presence of only one Cabinet minister would be sufficient, and from then on the Home Secretary was summoned to attend. The birth of Princess Alexandra of Kent in 1936 was the last occasion on which the Home Secretary was present. In 1948, before the birth of Prince Charles, an official announcement stated that, as the attendance of a minister of the Crown at the birth in the Royal Family was neither a statutory requirement nor a constitutional necessity, the practice would be discontinued.'[8]

The birth of a Catholic male heir brought about a situation that necessitated action. Until this time, Mary and Anne, the two Protestant daughters of Anne Hyde were the immediate successors to the throne. Mary could no longer peacefully succeed her father for her husband, William of Orange, Stadholder of Holland, championed the

Protestant cause against the papal enemies in Europe. In France, the Protestant Huguenots, were subjected to horrific torture with an entire army let loose on them. Many thousands managed to escape to England, but thousands more were forbidden to emigrate. The roads and ports were watched for families trying to escape by night and they were forced 'to worship idols' whilst their children were torn from them to be educated in the Catholic religion. It is believed that about 400,000 managed to escape to England, Brandenburg and Holland and with this exodus the bulk of the Protestant population disappeared from France for ever.

On 18 June, there were more celebrations at Court, although there is no mention of the King being present. This time, the festivities were held on the water before Whitehall in a barge borrowed from

one of the Companies of London richly decorated and illuminated by numerous torches . . . the performers, vocal and instrumental, amounted to one hundred and thirty selected as the greatest proficients in the science. The musicke being ended, all the nobility and company that were upon the water gave three shouts to express their joy and satisfaction; and all the gentlemen of the musick went to Mr [John] Abell's house, which was nobly illuminated and honoured with the presence of a great company of the nobility.[9]

There is no record of the music performed nor if Purcell was among the musicians, but it is quite likely that he did attend, if only on account of the large number quoted. John Abell, a Gentleman of the Chapel Royal since 1679, was also a fine counter-tenor, composer, lutenist and violinist. Between 1679 and 1688 he was paid £740 'bounty money' for 'undisclosed services to the king while travelling abroad, ostensibly to study'.[10] He was obviously a talented musician who, as a Catholic, was making the most of his popularity under James, but he, like so many others of his religion, was soon destined to flee the country when his monarch would also take his leave.

Meanwhile the Queen was making extra demands upon the royal musicians, which cannot have been greeted with enthusiasm. On 19 August the Lord Chamberlain sent out the following message:

I do hereby order that a number of his Majesty's musicians shall attend the Queen's Majesty's maids of honour to play whensoever they shall be sent to, at the homes of dancing, at such homes and such a number of them as they shall desire. And hereof the master of the musick and the musicians are to take notice that they observe this order.[11]

Such orders would soon be of no significance since on the day the bishops were acquitted, a written invitation to invade had been sent to

William of Orange: it was signed by Shrewsbury, Devonshire, Danby, Lumley, Russell, Sidney and Compton, Bishop of London. On 5 November 1688, William landed at Torbay with a force that could not be overpowered. James refused to call a free parliament with the result that many of his supporters deserted him, the most prominent of these being Marlborough. Meanwhile, as William advanced, the English army disintegrated and there were risings among the civilian population all over the country. William met with no resistance. By December the 'Glorious Revolution' had forced the unhappy James to flee to France.

William III, Prince of Orange, was born on 4 November 1650, to the 19-year-old Mary Stuart, the Princess Royal and Princess of Orange, sister of the future Charles II, eight days after his father had died of smallpox. Mary, his future wife was born at St James's Palace on 30 April 1662, daughter of the Duke and Duchess of York, the former Anne Hyde. The baby was named Mary after her great-great-grandmother, the Queen of Scots, but was brought up as a strict Protestant.

The solution to Charles II's never-ending problems with both the Dutch and the French depended much on the line of succession in England. He had reckoned that if he could arrange a marriage between William and Princess Mary, heir to the throne after her father, James, it would suit everyone. But William had been in no hurry to make a match with the daughter of a commoner, who had also been one of his mother's ladies-in-waiting. However, in 1677 the Prince had paid a visit to his uncles Charles and James, ostensibly to discuss the political situation and in particular the way to secure a peace with France. When the subject of the marriage had been broached, William took them aback by declaring he 'was resolved to see the young princess before he entered into affairs'. He need not have feared. She was both charming and beautiful and William was delighted with 'her person and all those signs of such a humour as had been described to him upon former enquiries'.[12]

The betrothal did not meet with the approval of the Catholic Duke of York, nor of the French. When the young bride herself was told the news, it is said that she wept for a day and a half. After all, she was only 15, engaged to a man she scarcely knew and would soon be separated from family and friends to live in a foreign country. Her cause for concern was justified.

At first sight they must have been an ill-matched pair. Mary was 5 feet 11 inches in height and fashionably dressed. William was a head shorter at 5 feet 6 inches, thin and stooping due to a congenital weakness of the lungs caused through chronic asthma, added to which a youthful attack of smallpox had left him with a permanent cough. His clothes were undistinguished, and even though periwigs had been in fashion for some ten years, to the astonishment of the elegant English Court, he preferred his own hair. In personality too, they were opposites. William was reserved and cold in his manner whereas Mary was a high-spirited, outgoing girl who loved to chatter.

The marriage took place privately in Mary's apartments at St James's Palace on Sunday 4 November 1677. The somewhat staid ceremony was said to be enlivened by some coarse jokes by Charles II which were not appreciated by the austere William. When the couple were put to bed according to custom, and the company had departed, Charles is reputed to have closed the bed-curtains with the words: 'Now nephew to your work. Hey! St George for England!'[13]

When Louis XIV heard the news he was shattered, and privately bemoaned the event 'as if it had been the loss of an army'. Publicly, he made the vicious comment that 'Two beggars are well-matched', but wrote to James: 'You have given your daughter to my mortal enemy.'[14] For once, William of Orange had scored a major victory over the Sun King.

All in all, William and Mary turned out to be a reasonably happy pair. Mary's style and sunny nature made her popular with the Dutch, and she seemed to understand her dour and often short-tempered husband. She knew she could never take part in his working life, mostly spent away from home, but she provided a tranquil haven in their beautiful Dutch Renaissance-style house, Honselaersdijk, which always remained her favourite residence. She and William shared an interest in their gardens and both appreciated fine paintings; unfortunately her husband did not share her taste in music. Over the years there were the usual problems with mistresses, and a somewhat excessive devotion to his male favourites at Court, but it was clear that the couple were bound by love rather than duty, and when a difficult situation arose, of which there were many, they managed to survive unscathed. Sadly, they had no children. There had been two miscarriages and several phantom pregnancies, but Mary remained childless.

*   *   *   *   *

The arrival of the new King gave cause for much speculation, especially among musicians. In the revolution itself the music consisted solely of that concerned with trumpets, drums and other instruments which make up the military band. 'Lillibulero' became a favourite tune, especially when the Whig Thomas Wharton provided an anti-Jacobite text, for which Purcell provided the harmonization. His version, anonymously listed as 'A New Irish Tune', had been included in Playford's publication, *The Delightful Companion or Choice New Lessons for the Recorder or Flute* in 1686. It only came to be associated with Purcell with its anti-Jacobite text, intended to 'whistle King James out of three Kingdoms'.[15]

We know nothing of Purcell's political views, but it probably made not the slightest difference which monarch was on the throne, as long as he required musicians, and, better still, paid their salaries. As we know already from the Restoration onwards, this would seem to be a continuing problem. Purcell's duties did not change when William ascended the throne.

In December 1688 Henry Playford's third book of *The Banquet of Music* was published. Purcell contributed two compositions, a catch, 'If All be True That I do Think', and a duet, 'Were I to Choose the Greatest Bliss'.

Soon after the New Year there were many manifestations of the people's joy at being freed from their popish king, and in early January there was a formal announcement to that effect. Luttrell tells us:

The 22nd, the lords spiritual and temporal assembled at Westminster, and proceeded to businesse without taking the oaths ... lords and commons unanimously agreed on an address of thanks to the prince for what he has done and to desire him to continue the further administration of publick affairs till farther application be made to him; they also ordered the 31st for a day of publick thanksgiveing in London and Westminster, and 10 miles round, for haveing made the prince the glorious instrument of the great deliverance of this kingdom from popery and arbitrary government; and the 14th of February be a day of publick thanksgiveing for the same throughout the kingdom.[16]

In early February the Catholics were being counted with a vengeance. A census was taken of papists who had not been resident for three years in the wards of St Ann's, Soho and Gerrard Street and 24 were found. Ironically, that same month the Act of Toleration was passed allowing only Protestant Dissenters to worship as they pleased: neither Catholics nor Unitarians were allowed this freedom, but as

William was disinclined to persecute Catholics openly, unless they acted overtly against the established Church, they remained un-molested.

However, during the early months of 1689, religious controversy became relatively unimportant. The forthcoming Coronation was the main topic of conversation and preparations were soon in full swing. On 13 February

The lords and commons assembled at Westminster came both houses to the banquetting House at Whitehal, and there presented the prince and princess of Orange with the instrument agreed on for declaring them king and queen ... and the night ended with bonefires, ringing of bells, and great acclamations of joy.[17]

There is no record of any music written for such an occasion – and music there must have been – but no doubt William III's trumpets and drums would have had prominence. There is, however, an entry in the Jewel House records on 12 February 1689, showing that William was making sure traditions were upheld.

Delivered unto [the] serjt Trumpeter for the proclaimeing of ye Prince and Princess of Orange King & Queene & as soon as the service is over to bee returned vizt One Large Mace [weight] 342 [oz.] 1[dwt.]. And Recd by mee Wm Bull [signature].

William was no less diligent where liveries were concerned, especially for his beloved trumpeters and drummers. On 16 March a warrant from the Lord Chamberlain to the Great Wardrobe was issued:

to provide liveries with their Majesties' cyphers embroidered thereon (a) for the serjeant-trumpeter, 16 trumpeters and a kettle-drummer; (b) for his Majesty's drum-major, four drummers and a fife, in all particulars as was provided unto them at the last coronation, for the coronation of William and Mary.[18]

Six days later a similar warrant was issued to provide scarlet mantles for the Master of the Musick and 38 musicians who were to attend the Coronation.

Later in the month a list was published showing the King's servants who received their salaries in the Treasury of the Chamber's Office. It also has an account of what was owing and in arrears to each of them at Lady Day 1689. Purcell's name does not appear on this list, but the omission is of no real significance. Zimmerman suggests this may have been due to the suspicion that Purcell had Catholic tendencies. But surely if this had been so, he would have fared better than he had done under James. Could it have been that for once Purcell had already received payment to date?

William III's preference for his drums and trumpets is reflected in two bills presented by John Mawgridge, drum-major, and Mathias Shore, serjeant-trumpeter, to the Great Wardrobe for £40 and £60, respectively. Matthew Shore also received a salary of £80, only £20 less than that paid to Nicholas Staggins, Master of the Musick.[19]

On April 5, there appeared a 'Lyst of the Musick who are to attend at their Maties Coronation' including Purcell. It continued: 'I doe hereby appoynt the persons above named for the private musick to attend as their Maties Musick at their Mats Coronation and to have the Liverys allowed being thirty-six [sic] in Number.' There were 37.[20]

The coronation took place on 11 April and was described by Evelyn:

I saw the procession to and from the Abbey-Church of Westminster, with the great feast in Westminster-Hall ... What was different from former coronations, was some alteration in the coronation oath. Dr Burnet, now made Bishop of Sarum, preached with great applause. The Parliament-men had scaffolds and places which took up the one whole side of the Hall. When the King and Queen had dined, the ceremony of the Champion, and other services by tenure were performed. The Parliament-men were feasted in the Exchequer-chamber, and had each of them a gold medal given them, worth five-and-forty shillings. On one side were the effigies of the King and Queen inclining one to the other; on the reverse was Jupiter throwing a bolt at Phaeton, the words, 'Ne totus absumatur:' which was but dull, seeing they might have had out of the poet something as apposite. The sculpture was very mean.

Much of the splendour of the proceeding was abated by the absence of divers who should have contributed to it, there being but five Bishops, four Judges (no more being yet sworn), and several noblemen and great ladies wanting; the feast, however, was magnificent. The next day the House of Commons went and kissed their new Majesties' hands in the Banqueting-house.[21]

However, for Purcell there were difficulties. The Abbey records have details of what has gone down in history as the 'Organ Loft' incident. In retrospect it would seem to have arisen due to a misunderstanding, but even so, it is yet a further indication of the dubious privilege of serving in the royal establishment.

At previous coronations, former organists had always sold tickets to spectators for places in the organ loft, said to be the best viewing-point in the Abbey. And people were prepared to pay well for the privilege. Never had there been any dispute as to who pocketed the gains. So Purcell and his friend Stephen Crespion took advantage of what they presumed to be their right, and sold seats accordingly.

It would seem that there had long been confusion regarding perquisites relating to royal occasions. An entry in the Precentor's Book at the Abbey concerning the coronation of Charles II gives us some idea of the way the dues were calculated:

In April 1661 a Warrant was granted by the Reverend Dean to the Chanter and the rest of the Choir for the erecting of scaffolds in the Churchyard in respect of His Maties Coronation solemnized on St George's Day, for which purpose agreement was made between the Quire and the Carpenter, that the profits thereof should be equally divided betweene them, the Carpenter receiving the one half, he being at the whole charge of the scaffolds; excepting only, that the Quire payd for sayle-cloathes 0.15s.0. and the Carpenter but 0.5s.0. and that the Quire payd also for watching and other expenses equally with the Carpenter 0.14s.0. and given by the Quire to the poore of St Margaret's Parish 0.16s.0. The sums received for the Quire was 17.9s.0. out of which deducting [as above] . . . there remained to be divided into 16 equall parts 15.4s.0. which was to every part 0.19s 0, but the Vergers who should have had a part being left out, they had betweene them 0.19s.0. out of the mony collected for the monuments. The organist being a good gainer by his Organ loft and scaffolds thereon erected, had no share with the rest of the Quire.[22]

According to this, the organist's right to funds collected from seating in the organ loft is plainly stated. Purcell and Crespion would therefore have considered themselves eligible. There are no details of the arrangements for the Coronation of James II, except retrospectively in a much later account which refers to the coronations of James II, William and Mary and Queen Anne, mentioning scaffolds built for the families and friends of the Dean and Chapter and some unscrupulous possession of these by someone who pretended he had an order from the Earl Marshal. It shows clearly that no real policy had been defined.

However, on 25 March, just over two weeks before the Coronation, there was clearly an attempt to ensure that these somewhat loose privileges should be curtailed. Surely this notice arrived too late? Purcell must have already ordered the scaffolding and almost certainly would have disposed of the seats.

It is Order'd that all such Money as shall be raised for Seates at the Coronation within the Church Organ Loft or Churchyard shall be paid into the hands of the Treasurer & distributed as the Dean & Chapter shall think fit. And that all vacant Places both in the Church & Churchyard which are not taken up and imployed for the King's use be disposed of by the Dean & Chapter of Westm as they shall think fit.

It is more than likely that Purcell never knew of this order. If he had, it is highly improbable that he would have defied his royal employers.

On 18 April, a week after the Coronation, a stiff reminder was sent out:

It is Order'd that Mr Purcell the Organist to Ye Dean & Chapter of Westm. do pay to the hand of Mr John Needham (Treasurer) of the College All such money as was received by him for places in the Organ Loft at ye Coronation of King William and Queen Mary by or before Saturday next being ye 20th day of this inst. Aprill. And in default thereof his place declared to be null & void. And it is further Order'd that his Stipend or Salarie due at our Lady Day last past be detayned in the hands of the Treasurer untill further Order.[23]

We know that within a few days Purcell handed over the money keeping only the amount authorized and acknowledged by Needham:

The account of the monies received at the coronation of King William and Queen Mary (and the payments thereof). The account of such monies as I have received from Mr Crispyn and Mr Purcell of the money received by them at the Coronation.

Of Mr Crispyn	£423.16s 7d
Of Mr Purcell his poundage and other expenses being deducted	£78.04s 6d
Total	£492.01s 1d
[Even this was incorrect. The total should have been	£502 1s 1d]

The 'poundage' was probably a percentage earned on the sale of seats, but the 'other expenses' were most likely to have been incurred in the organization of the setting up of the seats and the payment for scaffolding and suchlike. As to what happened to the £10 deficit it is anyone's guess, but such discrepancies are rife in so many of these accounts where no auditor seems to have been employed to check their faulty arithmetic.

Perhaps in the end, Purcell did not fare so badly. A further account details the payments Mr Needham was to make to those who had given their services at the Coronation. These included chanters and petty canons at £24 each, choirmen, seniors at £15, 'the next choirmen' at £10 and £8 each and 'To the two that supply the 12th place in the choir at £5 each'. Two vergers received £14 each and four bell-ringers £5 each. The college butler and gardener received £2 a head and three sweepers 10s each and the cloister porter, £1 10s. Mr Purcell received £35.[24]

Even though this account seems to have been settled, it is ironic that at the time Purcell's half-yearly stipend was several weeks overdue. Furthermore, as we already know, Purcell had to wait for over a year before receiving his dues for keeping and repairing the organs and instruments of the Chapel Royal (see p 94). In April 1689 he had presented an account for £32, for 'providing an organ and other necessaries for the use of the Chapel Choir at their Majesties Coronation, April 11th 1689'. This was not to be settled until 1 August 1690.

All these money matters might have been tiresome and time-wasting, not to mention the possible hardship they engendered, but they did not affect Purcell's output, which seems to have been uninterrupted. On 30 April the Queen's birthday was celebrated by an ode, 'Now Does the Glorious Day Appear', the music by Purcell to words by Thomas Shadwell.

Two weeks later, strong measures were being taken to make life difficult for the Catholics. Luttrell tells us that on 14 May 'A proclamation by their majesties has been published, requireing all papists forthwith to depart the cities of London and Westminster, and ten miles adjacent, pursuant to the late act of parliament.'[25]

The first meeting between Henry Purcell and the poet and dramatist John Dryden probably took place early in the year 1689. It was a meeting that would result in the fusion of two of the most remarkable talents of the time, and a close friendship during the last six years of the composer's life. Dryden had asked Purcell to provide a new setting for 'Whilst I with grief did on you look' for the revival of his play, *The Spanish Fryar*, presented on 28 May either at Drury Lane or Dorset

Garden. One of Dryden's most successful comedies, it had first been produced in 1679 and was published in 1681. Curiously enough, coming from the Catholic Dryden, it had a strong Protestant bias. It concerns the pimping services of the disreputable Friar Dominic who tries to arrange an affair between Lorenzo and Elvira (who turns out to be his sister), the wife of the elderly Gomez. It had been permitted by Charles II, but James II had refused to allow it to be performed. It seems that Queen Mary attended, but, understandably, did not find it all to her liking:

The only day Her Majesty gave herself the diversion of a play, and that on which she designed to see another, has furnished the town with discourse for a month. The choice of the play was the Spanish Fryar, the only play forbid by the late K—. Some unhappy expressions, among which those that follow, put her in some disorder, and forc'd her to hold up her fan, and often look behind her and call for her palatine and hood, and any thing she could next think of, while those who were in the pit before her, whenever their fancy led them to make any application of what was said. (Sir John Dalrymple, *Memoirs of Great Britain*, Vol II, Appendix, Part II, pp 78–80)[26]

Since the play had been permitted by Charles II and banned by James, William and Mary would naturally have been curious to see it for themselves. It soon became painfully obvious that they had not read the text. The speech which caused such embarrassment was spoken in the first act by a character named Pedro: 'Very good: She usurps the Throne; keeps the old King in Prison; and, at the same time, is praying for a Blessing: Oh Religion and Roguery, how they go together!'[27]

With the accession to the throne of William and Mary, royal musicians were soon to discover that music was not of prime importance and they were forced to look elsewhere to supplement their incomes. It was to the theatre that they turned, where many changes were taking place; and, for the first time, the English were beginning to look at that most Italian of enterprises – opera.

References

1. ED, Vol 2, p 273 (15 January 1688).
2. Zimmerman, *Henry Purcell, 1659–1695, His Life and Times*, p 148.

3. ED, Vol 2, p 273 (30 January 1688).
4. Lutt, Vol 1, p 431.
5. Cal Treas Books 5 March 1687/8.
6. Price, *Henry Purcell and the London Stage*, p 160.
7. Turner, *James II*, pp 395–6.
8. *Royal Encyclopaedia*, Macmillan, 1991, pp 50–2.
9. Pulver, Jeffrey, *A Biographical Dictionary of Old English Music*, Novello, 1927, pp 2–3.
10. NG, Vol 1, p 15.
11. AA, Vol 2, p 20.
12. van der Zee, Henri and Barbara, *William and Mary*, Macmillan, 1973, p 115.
13. Ibid, p 121.
14. Ibid, p 122.
15. Westrup, *Purcell*, p 65.
16. Lutt, Vol 1, pp 498–9.
17. Ibid, p 501.
18. AA, Vol 2, pp 22–3.
19. Ibid, pp 23–4.
20. Ibid, p 25.
21. ED, Vol 2, pp 297–8 (11 April 1689).
22. WAM 61228A, Precentor's Book 1660–71, fo 15.
23. WAM 51125, Coronation Papers, 1689.
24. WAM 51126, Coronation Papers, 1689.
25. Lutt, Vol 1, p 533.
26. LS, Part I, p 371.
27. Price, *Henry Purcell and the London Stage*, p 293.

12

NEW LIGHT ON *DIDO*

Although persistent attempts had been made to introduce Italian opera in some form to England, no one had found the right means of expression acceptable to the English character.

At the moment when Italian poets and composers brought opera to birth in Florence, music in England was at its highest level. It was an age when the English mind was peculiarly susceptible to the influence of all Italian ideas, literary as well as musical. How was it that we did not at that wonderful moment develop an English form of opera in which Jonson and Shakespeare might have collaborated with Douland [*sic*] and Wilbye?[1]

Dent suggests that the answer lies simply in our national attitude to music. To the Italian, music is a means of self-expression whilst to the Englishman it is 'a thing apart, a message from another world . . . Music for the Italian is the exaggeration of personality – for the Englishman its annihilation.'

In England the spoken drama was already far too highly developed and far too deeply rooted in the heart of the people for its musical counterpart to be accepted as an equivalent, much less as a transfiguration of its most powerful emotional workings. It was only when the Puritans succeeded in suppressing the drama that masques were able to assume a more definitely dramatic form, and that a real systematic attempt at English opera could be made.[2]

Therefore, by far the strongest formative influence on Restoration dramatic opera was the Stuart court masque; it 'reveals in full clarity the English reluctance to go all the way in uniting words and music – in other words, their reluctance to create genuine opera'. These masques were forms of entertainment in which the passion for ceremonial behaviour found its ideal; songs, dances and dialogues set to an allegorical drama, 'appealed to the court taste because it not only gave almost limitless scope to the designer of scenery, machines and costumes, but also allowed the courtiers themselves to enter towards the end of the spectacle as dancers'.[3]

The masque plot was always the triumph of good over evil, the good being portrayed as the reigning monarch or the goddesses of Peace or Concord, whilst evil was characterized by witches or monsters, often representing the opposition in the current government. These productions were not subject to financial control so they were lavish in every respect with splendid costumes and scenery, the players often wearing real jewels. The professional theatres of the time could not hope to achieve anything like this magnificence.

Two of the most significant early influences on opera in England were Inigo Jones and Ben Jonson: Jones had seen the new Italian operas and was responsible for introducing Italian scenery into England, and Jonson had worked closely with him on a number of occasions.

The most important link between the Caroline and Restoration theatre was Sir William Davenant, who had strong personal associations with Shakespeare. The poet was known to pay frequent visits to the Crown Inn at Oxford where his friends the Davenants were the innkeepers. They were both devoted to the theatre, and the relationship between the innkeeper's beautiful wife and Shakespeare was said to be rather more than friendship. When she gave birth to a son in 1606, he was called William with the poet as his godfather. In later years Davenant never denied that Shakespeare was his natural father.

Davenant was granted a licence by Charles I to build a theatre of his own but the worsening political situation caused these plans to be delayed. Had Davenant succeeded in this venture, 'England would have been the first country outside Italy to see public opera, and that only two years after the building of the first Italian public opera-house'.[4]

James Shirley – who wrote the text for William Lawes's *The Triumph of Peace* in 1634 – must not be overlooked, but undoubtedly Davenant was the last important playwright and producer before the closing of the theatres during the Commonwealth. When the Civil War broke out, he was manager of the Phoenix Theatre (also known as the Cockpit), but fled the country on more than one occasion to avoid being arrested by Parliamentary soldiers. During his exile he lived mainly in Paris where he was in touch with Henrietta Maria and her son, the future Charles II. It was here that he became interested in the performances of Italian opera at the Théâtre du Marais, supported by Cardinal Mazarin. When Davenant returned to England, he was arrested and imprisoned in the Tower, but was freed, possibly by the intervention of Milton.

Davenant knew that for the Puritans it was the spoken word that offended, not the theatre *per se*. The music – by way of the masque – was not, in itself, capable of corrupting the audience. A good example was Milton's *Masque of Comus* with music by Henry Lawes, where both drama and words were important. So it was through the masque that the Puritans allowed the operatic element to creep surreptitiously into the theatre. The astute Davenant clearly realized that if he appealed to their love of music and called the piece an 'entertainment' instead of a play, he might win them over. But Dennis Arundell disagrees with Dent. He maintains that Davenant had been trying to put on opera in England for some 17 years and that this was a natural development in his scheme of things. Whatever his motive, in 1656 Davenant put on a semi-private performance of *The First Day's Entertainment* in a hall at the back of his own house. It was so well received that he produced another, *The Siege of Rhodes*, described as an opera with scenery by John Webb, given 'At the back part of Rutland House in the upper end of Aldersgate Street, London' (programme). On this occasion – and possibly at a further performance – the role of Mustapha was taken by Henry Purcell the elder. Others who took part, either as actors or singers, were the composers Matthew Locke and Henry Lawes together with Captain Cooke, who with the Restoration had become bass singer and Master of the Children of the Chapel Royal and teacher of the six-year-old Henry Purcell.

When Davenant's theatre was finally opened in Dorset Garden by his widow in 1671 (see p 63), the first 'opera' to be produced there was a Davenant–Shakespeare adaptation of *Macbeth*, the music of which is a continuing argument for scholars, as to whether it was written by Locke or Purcell. It was 'tricked out with all the latest inventions of French stagecraft and long sung scenes complete with dancing'.[5] An adaptation of *The Tempest* followed in 1674, a production so expensive that in the Epilogue an apology was made as to the need to charge double prices for the seats.

About the same time – the exact date is unknown – Matthew Locke's *Psyche*, with libretto by Shadwell, was produced. This was 'an important landmark in our musical history, because it is the first systematized attempt at a musical and dramatic scheme which for a long period was characteristic of English opera'.[6] The principal characters do not sing but Dent applauds the attempt to bring them into contact with the music. Another play in which music played an important part was *Circe*, by Charles Davenant, son of Sir William. The story is that of Iphigenia in Tauris with a suitable love-interest in true seventeenth-century manner. It had first appeared in 1677 with music by John Banister, but Purcell wrote music for the first act in the revival of 1685.

Dent tells us that in *Circe* there is no reason why anyone should sing *anything* as the poet has not planned sufficient action. Nevertheless

It is powerful and beautiful music; if a stage action can be fitted to it so much the better – if not, it does not make any very great difference . . . we can still see that Purcell intended the general effect to rise to a climax in the last section . . . The final *arioso* is in fact one of the best declamatory solos to be found anywhere in Purcell's works . . . The declamation of the voice is natural and free from exaggerations; the upper strings have parts of very independent character, and develop the salient themes of the voice part in effective imitations.[7]

Someone who had considerable influence on the promotion of Italian opera in London was the beautiful Hortense Mancini, better known as the Duchess de Mazarin, niece of Cardinal Mazarin. During his exile, Charles II had wanted to marry her but the Cardinal refused his consent. In 1675 she had abandoned a husband 'insufficiently exciting for her tastes'[8] and come to England. Charles had lost no time in installing her as one of his mistresses at St James's Palace with an allowance of £4000 a year. Hortense had an attractive and passionate personality with a taste for gambling, shooting and swimming and was said to entertain her friends by performing a Spanish dance whilst accompanying herself on the guitar. It was her taste in music that prompted her to make strong efforts to introduce Italian opera to London.

Until recently, by far the most important event known in the development of opera in England was the private performance in 1689 of Purcell's *Dido and Aeneas*, with the libretto by Nahum Tate. At the time, the general public were unaware it existed, whereas today it is regarded as being the first English opera.

However, it would seem that we will have to do some rethinking as to the date of the composition itself. There have been doubts in the minds of scholars for some time, but since no concrete evidence has presented itself, the question has remained in a state of animated suspension. Over the last two years, Bruce Wood and Andrew Pinnock have undertaken extensive research on the subject and their argument in favour of a date earlier than 1689 is convincing.[9]

It is generally believed that *Dido and Aeneas* was written expressly for a performance at the boarding-school for young gentlewomen run by Mrs Priest – assisted by her husband Josias – at Gorges House in Chelsea, the parts being taken by their pupils. No doubt they were well trained in deportment, singing and dancing, for there are no fewer than 17 dances in *Dido*. The most likely date for the performance is sometime in April, either on the 23rd as a tribute to William and Mary on their coronation day, or the 30th, Queen Mary's birthday. Certainly it would have been before the autumn when an Epilogue to the opera, by D'Urfey, appeared in print. We have no idea who took the part of Aeneas nor of the bass, tenor and counter-tenor parts in the choruses. It is possible that Purcell might have brought in some of his friends for the occasion, but there is no evidence to support this theory.

Mrs Priest's boarding-school was originally set up in Leicester Fields and in 1680 moved to Chelsea, then a 'leafy, Thames-side suburb west of London'.[10] Josias Priest was a choreographer at the Theatre Royal and had been an important dancer appearing at the London playhouses since the 1660s. He was arrested in 1669 for 'teaching, practising and exercising music in companies or otherwise, without the approbation or license of the Marshall and Corporation of musick, in contempt of his Majesty's authority and the power granted to the Marshall and Corporation'.[11] This misdemeanour does not appear to have affected his career adversely.

The plot of *Dido and Aeneas* is taken from Virgil's epic the *Aeneid*. Aeneas with a band of devoted followers has left the city of Troy in total destruction, with the intention of founding a new state in Italy. After seven years of storm and tempest the somewhat battered fleet takes to harbour at Carthage where the widowed queen Dido welcomes them. Dido and Aeneas fall in love but Dido has sworn to remain chaste after her husband's death, and has already turned down an offer of marriage from Iarbas, king of a neighbouring state. She is also uncertain as to whether Aeneas will be faithful. However, the gods decide to take a hand. Juno supports Dido, and Venus, her son, Aeneas. Ascanius, Aeneas's young son, disguised as Cupid, is sent to Dido and she keeps him in her palace. Juno then conjures up a storm during a hunting-party so that the couple must take shelter in a cave. It is here that Dido succumbs to her lover's charms and all appears to be well. But Jove, disapproving of Aeneas's preoccupation with Dido, sends Mercury to remind him that he still has the task of founding a kingdom at Rome. Although Aeneas is not happy at the idea of parting from his mistress, he appears also to have a strong desire to return to battle. Dido threatens and pleads without success and after Aeneas has departed she thrusts a sword through her heart and dies.

Nahum Tate (1652–1715) was a minor playwright who had made several adaptations of Shakespeare, including a *King Lear* with a happy ending. He was to succeed Thomas Shadwell as Poet Laureate in 1692. Tate's libretto makes many changes from Virgil. He reduces the number of characters and the goddesses are replaced by witches who plot the fall of Dido. In Tate's version, Dido and Aeneas do not consummate their love, no doubt in deference to the morals of the young gentlewomen of the boarding-school. The witches, with their attendants, plan the downfall to take place in a darkened cave and here the libretto and Purcell's music are perfectly matched. The hunt takes place as in Virgil and the party hurry back to town. Aeneas is intercepted by a false vision of Mercury conjured up by the witches – who tells him that Jove commands him to leave Dido and return to restore Troy. Aeneas accepts his command with rather too little resistance but is none the less upset by Dido's refusal to accept his departure. There is considerable argument; Aeneas agrees to stay but Dido will have no more dealings with him. She sends him away but does not take her own life. She simply dies of grief.

The differences between Virgil and Tate's libretto are for a number of reasons. In the first instance, as already mentioned, the piece was for performance by young ladies at a boarding-school and would therefore not show explicit love-scenes: the mention of 'One night enjoy'd, the next forsook' is poetic rather than actual. In Tate's version Dido pays the price of a single indiscretion and is penalized by loss of reputation, love, and eventually her life. She refuses to allow her lover to stay and finally dies.

The moral, of course, is that young girls should not accept the advances of young men however ardent their wooing or however persistent their promises. Perhaps this is best expressed in the blatant callousness of the departing sailors:

> Take a boozy short leave of your nymphs on the shore
> And silence their mourning with vows of returning,
> But never intending to visit them more.[12]

Tate's libretto for *Dido* has been criticized as 'banal' by some scholars who adhere to nineteenth-century criteria: Westrup says that 'As a poet he deserves all the unkind things that have been said about him, but whatever the literary quality of *Dido* – and it is on the whole very poor – there is no doubt that the text is thoroughly suitable for musical setting.'[13] Later opinions are less harsh. Layton Ring, whose researches on Purcell and William Lawes have been singularly fruitful, says: 'It is a model libretto. Tate may not be a great poet – though he is a good hymn-writer – but Dryden himself could have done no better. Furthermore, the words, lines and rhymes considered "banal", are common currency in all late-seventeenth-century writers.'[14]

Imogen Holst also defends Tate. She maintains that he knew what was wanted in the libretto for *Dido*, having learnt that 'music was the exaltation of poetry'. She quotes the lines for Aeneas's first entry, criticized so often as being prosaic:

> *Belinda.* See, your Royal Guest appears
> How God-like is the Form he bears.
> *Aeneas.* When, Royal Fair, shall I be blest,
> With cares of Love and State distrest?
> *Dido.* Fate forbids what you Ensue.
> *Aeneas.* Aeneas has no Fate but you.
> Let Dido smile, and I'le defie
> The Feeble Stroke of Destiny.

She agrees that in these eight lines the music exalts the libretto, but reminds us it is the libretto that has brought the music into being. On a professional stage, a flourish of trumpets would seem to be the natural choice, but at the Priests' school there would have been neither money nor space for the trumpeters. It is Purcell's extraordinary power of dramatic characterization that brings the story to life. Holst gives, as an example, Aeneas' opening lines:

There is the gesture of a drawn sword in his rising phrase: it is strengthened by the wide-mouthed, bright insistence of the repeated vowel 'i' in the line

> Let Dido smile and I'le defie

where Purcell seizes on what would be considered a weakness in poetry and triumphantly turns it to musical advantage. The phrase is a wonderful example of Purcell's 'genius for expressing the energy of English words'; after the climax of 'defie', the word 'feeble' sinks down with no strength left in its curving spinelessness; the 'k' of 'stroke' cuts across the cadence like a knife; while in the final word 'destiny' the hero conveys his scorn in the low level of his voice, yet, at the same time the harmonic resolution makes it quite clear to the listener that Fate is going to have the last word in the tragedy that is beginning to unfold.[15]

Tate has been much criticized for the seeming bathos of Dido's mocking:

> Thus on the fatal Banks of Nile,
> Weeps the deceitful crocodile.
> Thus hypocrites that murder act,
> Make heaven and gods the authors of the fact.

But Holst maintains it is brilliant characterization because Dido is obviously working herself into a state and she quotes Cleopatra and other queens who have behaved similarly. She maintains that the 'remember me' of the Lament owes 'some of its poignancy to the way in which Dido's creators, throughout the opera, have made her unforgettable as a person. Every detail has helped, including that much-maligned crocodile. And Tate must have his share of the glory.'[16]

Another aspect of the libretto which has caused a great deal of controversy is whether it was meant to be allegorical in respect of William and Mary and the ever-recurrent danger of a new 'popish plot'? Harris considers it unlikely whereas Buttrey and Price think it is possible.

John Buttrey reminds us that this was the period when determined efforts to re-establish a Catholic monarchy had failed. William and Mary were Protestant but there was always a danger that the papists would make renewed attempts to overthrow the monarchy. In the theatre, allegory was often used to press home a political or topical point, as we know from Dryden's *Albion and Albanius* which had failed in 1685 because the timing was wrong, coinciding as it did with the death of Charles II. Tate had previously tackled the subject of *Dido* in his *Brutus of Alba*, produced in 1678 during the reign of Charles II, a fact which has considerable bearing on the true dating of *Dido and Aeneas*. At the time, the King was trying to get the better of the Earl of Shaftesbury who, aided by the Duke of Monmouth, was trying to dethrone Charles. The story is basically the same as Virgil's except that Tate introduces a scheming Syracusan noble (Monmouth) who is intent on possessing the crown himself and enlists the help of a sorceress (Shaftesbury). With magic potions, the couple (Brutus and Dido) are defeated and both commit suicide. As Buttrey says, we can see 'the legend was adapted, not to portray, but to reflect the events of the time when it was written'. The new opera, produced in the reign of William and Mary, 'reflects the position of the new English queen whose reign depended upon the support she could claim from her foreign husband'.

In Tate's *Dido*, the courtiers encourage the uniting of the two nations:

> ... The greatest blessing fate can give,
> Our Carthage to secure and Troy revive.
> When monarchs unite, how happy their state,
> They triumph at once on their foes and their fate ...

'Thinking of the two new monarchs on the English throne, he [Tate] seems to have been pointing out, by means of an allegory, the possible fate of the British nation should Dutch William fail in his responsibilities to his English queen.'[17]

He further stresses the tremendous upheaval that came about after the deposition of James II, so he was merely reflecting the political unrest that must have been the main preoccupation of many people in 1689. We must remember that Buttrey views Tate's dramatization as a cautionary tale rather than a direct allegory depicting actual events.

Curtis Price makes the point that the story according to the original Virgil was likely to be misconstrued in the aftermath of the Bloodless Revolution, therefore Tate was forced to 'adapt the classical tale already deeply entwined with the supposed origins of the British monarchy, to disengage Queen Mary from a symbolic link with Queen Dido'. For this reason the major changes of plot and characterization were necessary. Price considers that the 'gaping ambiguities' in the libretto are due to the potentially sensitive nature of the allegory. Had Tate followed Virgil as he did in *Brutus of Alba*, 'faithfully depicting the queen's obsessive love for Aeneas, their winter of debauchery, her paralyzing guilt, extreme bitterness, and blazing anger at his departure, eyebrows would have been raised from Chelsea to Whitehall'. By the same token, Price postulates that the enchantresses in *Dido* symbolize a new popish plot, their destruction of the lovers representing the outcome if James II were restored to the throne.[18]

In most of the plays of this period, the plots were based on Greek mythological figures. In the seventeenth century a study of the classics was compulsory, so that whether the plot was taken directly from mythology or presented in allegorical terms, everyone would understand the meaning. This is in contrast to our twentieth-century education where the classics are taught only as a specially selected subject.

At this point it is necessary to examine the reappraisal of Wood and Pinnock. In January 1989, Bruce Wood was involved in the planning of a concert in Westminster Abbey, in which all the surviving music from the Coronation of William and Mary would be played. At the same time, he started work on a new Purcell Society volume which included the Queen Mary birthday ode for 1689. It suddenly occurred to him that Purcell must have been very busy that spring:

William and Mary accepted the throne only in mid-February; yet by late April Purcell had composed and rehearsed an elaborate coronation anthem with strings, *Praise the Lord, O Jerusalem*, and an ode of unprecedented magnificence, *Now does the glorious day appear*. Texts for these had to be prepared before he could begin work; and he had to find time to compose their settings while he was also busy with his duties at the Chapel Royal and the Abbey – duties which, at both institutions, would have been made heavier by an impending coronation.

So even a fluent composer would have had his work cut out to manage these two big pieces. But an opera as well? Three acts and a sung prologue, lasting well over an hour altogether? An opera that had to be choreographed, and learnt – by a cast of schoolgirls, not professionals – and rehearsed until it was safe enough to offer as a tribute to the King and Queen? All this in ten weeks?[19]

Also in 1989, Richard Luckett announced his discovery of a printed libretto for Blow's *Venus and Adonis* from a performance in April 1684 at Josias Priest's school.[20] Until this document appeared, no one imagined that Blow's court masque had been revived as a school opera. This raised the possibility that a similar case may apply to *Dido*. Strangely enough, the much-criticized W.H. Cummings had written to Barclay Squire pointing out that there was no evidence to support his date of 1689 as the premiere and suggested the Epilogue might have been written for a revival. Squire reported this in an article in the *Musical Times*,[21] but it failed to raise any comment.

Once we begin to revise our concept of the 1689 performance, everything takes on a new significance. In their excellent paper, Wood and Pinnock give full explanations for their thesis. Here it is possible only to extract a few relevant points. Of considerable importance is D'Urfey's Epilogue which is generally accepted as being added later. It

clearly aims to inform the audience that the actors are young ladies
who live a sheltered life:

> Great Providence has still more bounteous been
> To save us from those grand deceivers, men.
> Here blest with Innocence, and peace of Mind,
> Not only bred to virtue, but inclin'd;
> We flourish, and defy all human kind . . .
>
> Besides, to show we live with strictest Rules,
> Our nunnery-door is charm'd to shut out fools;

And furthermore, have as yet no understanding of politics:

> Rome may allow strange Tricks to please her sons,
> But we are Protestants and English nuns;
> Like nimble fawns, and birds that bless the spring
> Unscarr'd by turning times we dance and sing;
> We hope to please, but if some critic here
> Fond of his wit, designs to be severe,
> Let not his patience be worn out too soon,
> For in few years we shall be all in tune.

Wood and Pinnock also point to how the 'turning times' affected the
girl who spoke the Epilogue, Lady Dorothy Burk. She was the
daughter of the Catholic 8th Earl of Clanricarde who had fled to
Ireland with James II in 1689, and commanded a regiment in James's
Irish Army. He also served as a privy counsellor and two years later
would be responsible for the surrender of Galway after the Battle of
Augrim. Lady Dorothy was able to stay on at Priest's school only by
virtue of a pension from Queen Mary, her parents being bitterly
opposed to the idea of an English education. Consequently 'She
brought to her part all the authority of a real-life Protestant heroine,
and gave D'Urfey's playful words an ironic twist they might not have
had if Priest had chosen one of her classmates instead'.[22]

We must also look at similarities in the Epilogue to a masque by
Thomas Duffett, *Beauties Triumph*, the music by Banister, performed
at Chelsea in 1676 under the previous school management. In this we
read of 'cloister'd Nuns with virtuous zeal inspir'd', whilst in *Dido*
D'Urfey writes: 'Nuns . . . blest with Innocence and peace of Mind'.

Beauties Triumph had been available in print for some time, and
clearly D'Urfey had seen it. In order not to make a political point in
1689, his nuns are safely Protestant. 'Roman nuns serve a celibate

clergy who will try all manner of "strange Tricks" to win the sisters' favour – but none of that goes on here . . . "strictest Rules" apply at Josias Priest's school, to "shut out" men and safeguard the ladies' honour.'[23]

The Prologue, for which no music has survived, begins with Phoebus rising in his chariot over the sea, with the Nereids emerging from it, shortly after which Venus descends, also in her chariot. Wood and Pinnock suggest that the Prologue 'was evidently planned for performance on a stage equipped with trapdoors, but later adapted to another one without them, where only the "flyings" were possible'. They certainly refute the idea that the rising star was meant to be 'William crossing the Channel in allegorical guise'.[24]

Take, for instance, the first lines of the Prologue:

> From *Aurora's* Spicy Bed
> *Phoebus* rears his Sacred Head

This would have been a painfully tactless opening. According to the legend, Phoebus had seduced Aurora, and everyone knew of William's affair with Betty Villiers, which was a constant torture to Mary until she died. Therefore any reference to it in an opera would have been unthinkable. Similarly the lines from Act III:

> No faithless Man thy course pursue,
> I'm now resolved as well as you.
> No Repentance shall reclaim
> The Injured Dido['s] slighted [Fame].

Curtis Price's theory that even the danger of political allegory would have prevented *Dido* from being performed on the professional stage at the time is confirmed by Wood and Pinnock. And also his view that 'after Mary's death in December 1694, it would have been unthinkable, since the tragic ending would have implied that William's neglect was in some way responsible for his wife's passing'.[25]

Tate could not have foreseen all the events of the 1690s when he wrote the *Dido* libretto. But even in 1689 it must have appeared a tactless piece of work. Purcell, a royal musician, would never have gone along with it; and it would surely have put Tate out of the running for Poet Laureate, which he became only three years later.

But what if the words and the music were written *before* William and Mary came to the throne? Then the problem disappears.[26]

As for the music of *Dido and Aeneas* the earliest score (the Tenbury MS (1266), is now in the Bodleian Library at Oxford and it dates from more than 50 years after the first performance, and disagrees with Tate's 1689 libretto in that it lacks the French-style allegorical Prologue and the chorus 'Then since our Charms have Sped' at the end of Act II. These differences have bedevilled scholars for almost three hundred years. Price poses the questions: 'If Purcell originally set the prologue and verse at the end of Act II, why are they not preserved in Tenbury? Does the score in fact bear any resemblance to the one used for the Chelsea premiere, or is it thoroughly corrupt both in detail and dramatic outline, like many mid-18th century manuscripts of Purcell's other stage works?'[27]

There are many interesting arguments put forward in scholarly writings on the subject but for our purposes, the most helpful explanation is from Curtis Price. Bearing in mind that *Dido* never received a second performance in Purcell's lifetime, and appeared in 1700 only as a kind of masque within a play – a 'revised' version of Shakespeare's *Measure for Measure* – he hypothesizes that Purcell set the libretto virtually as it stood, 'changing a word here and there, dividing a few choruses into solos and ensembles . . . the kinds of alterations that opera composers from Monteverdi on made to their librettos as a matter of course'.[28]

Price suggests that after the first performance the score was put away and forgotten until Purcell's widow made his papers available to the editors of *Orpheus Britannicus* who, incidentally, selected only one aria from the opera. Later, Betterton acquired the manuscript and had John Eccles adapt the score for performing within *Measure for Measure*. Eccles set the additional verses sandwiched between Aeneas's soliloquy and the witches' chorus in Act II and wrote a grand finale for the Prologue. It was successful enough to be revived twice in 1704 when it was attached in an abridged form to two different plays. Price considers that the Tenbury score was copied from a manuscript dating from about 1700 and suggests that an outstanding clue is that the minimal bass figuring was limited to essentials. 'Continuo figuring was undergoing significant change about the time Purcell died.' For example, *Orpheus Britannicus* (1698) is profusely figured in comparison to the pre-1695 prints from which most of its contents were copied. 'Purcell's own figuring in the few extant autographs of theatre music is also very simple, often petering out altogether after a line or two.'[29] Is this, perhaps, because it was aimed at amateurs rather than professional musicians? Furthermore, in the Tenbury score sharps and flats rather than natural signs are used to cancel accidentals, the natural sign not being in common use in England before 1710.

It has been said that as far as Purcell was concerned, *Dido and Aeneas* had no precedent; but surely Blow's *Venus and Adonis* is a precedent and certainly would have been known to Purcell? The fact is that it lay outside the kind of music that Purcell's official duties commanded. Furthermore it had no real place on the professional stage at the time. A.K. Holland aptly says:

It is the genius of the man and not the uniqueness of the form that is surprising. Purcell had already shown his ability to organise a sequence of movements into one continuous whole in his Odes, anthems and dramatic scenes and the composition of this little work . . . could have given him no trouble from the purely formal point of view once the character of the libretto was settled. In fact, it may be said that it was the very nature of the performance which gave to the opera many of the qualities for which it has been most praised, its concentration, its directness, its swift and vivid presentment of the drama . . . The style is variegated, like all Purcell's work, but that does not prevent it from having a dramatic consistency. It is full of personal mannerisms, yet nowhere did Purcell write with more spontaneous feeling. It is at once simple, sincere, unaffected, technically sophisticated and intensely human.[30]

Dido's 'Lament' has come to be regarded as one of the great moments in music. Westrup gives the perfect description:

Here Purcell rises within narrow limits to monumental grandeur. The brief aria has a Miltonic dignity; in that last repeated 'Remember me' it is almost as though the musician, tearing himself away from the artificiality of court and theatre, had written his own epitaph. It is succeeded by a little chorus that rounds off the work with the same tragic finality as the last chorus in the St Matthew Passion. And having sung it once the chorus must sing it again so that the drooping cadences may linger in the memory.[31]

We must now return to the latest research and see where it fits into the jigsaw. As we know, Barclay Squire considered the style mature Purcell and so plumped for the date of 1689, but he gave no reasons for thinking so. Cummings, editor of the Purcell Society *Dido* – ironically, published in 1889 – was always under the impression that it was early Purcell, but also gave no explanation. Wood and Pinnock quote the Norwegian scholar, Dag Schjelderup-Ebbe, who has made a detailed study of Purcell's cadences and finds that certain 'Sturm und Drang' tendencies of the earliest period (*c* 1676–85) contrast with a more simplified style of stronger tonal direction in his latest period (*c* 1691–5). A very interesting discovery is the choral spacing:

A striking feature of 4-part choral writing earlier in the Restoration period is the wide gap often found between the treble part and the other three, which tend to cluster together. In the music of Humfrey, and in early works by both Blow and Purcell, the gap can be as much as an eleventh or even more. By the late 1670s this is becoming rare, and a more uniform spacing is preferred – but the gap between treble and counter-tenor parts lingers on into the early 1680s. At several points in *Dido* the gap is fully two octaves. At the beginning of 'Haste, haste to town', for instance, the alto part is so low that the Purcell Society editors suggest the tenors sing it instead. Such spacing is very rare in Purcell's music after about 1683: in the whole of *The Fairy Queen*, for example, the gap between treble and counter-tenor parts seldom exceeds an octave, and then only briefly.[32]

Another musical clue is the way in which Purcell uses instruments to accompany the choral sections in *Dido*. The string parts, except for a few short phrases, do nothing but double the voices in unison. One of the most important features of Purcell's later writing is the rich sonority he obtains from using the strings 'either to add at least one independent part, usually above the vocal treble, or consistently to double voices at the *octave*',[33] a technique he began using in the mid-1680s. A striking example of this is in the 1685 coronation anthem, 'My heart is inditing', where at certain thrilling moments, all three upper string parts are an octave above the corresponding voice. Purcell never completely abandoned unison doubling but from 1685 onwards he made very little use of it, except in some of the more modest of his Chapel Royal anthems.

The overture in *Dido* suggests an early date of composition. It has a simplicity common to the French overtures of Humfrey and Blow, but is scarcely ever found in Purcell after 1685. After that, his writing invariably used more elaborate semiquaver patterns, often starting and ending mid-bar (anacrustic).[34]

One of the glories of *Dido* is its declamatory writing, descended directly from that in the theatrical works of Locke. But if we trace Purcell's development in that style as far as *Dioclesian* in 1690, *Dido* seems out of place in 1689. In his mature declamatory writing Purcell frequently deploys with ease and confidence an important technique which in *Dido* scarcely figures at all: he makes the declamation more melodic, and gives it clear overall structures by primarily melodic means, rather than through the *direction* of the vocal line and through the cadential structure as in *Dido*. The declamatory writing in *Dido* is typical of Purcell's music not in 1689 but in the early 1680s.[35]

The sheer volume of declamatory writing in *Dido* is another aspect: there is far more than in any of Purcell's stage works of the 1690s. *Dioclesian, King Arthur* and *The Fairy Queen* contain very little, whereas *Dido* is

full of arioso, with a slow-moving, purely harmonic bass line: it amounts to nearly half of all the solo writing in the opera. This is far more than would be necessary simply to propel the drama along. . . The high proportion of arioso in *Dido* seems in itself to point to a date well before 1689. Moreover, subtle declamatory writing is about the last thing one would expect to predominate had the piece really been written for schoolgirls. (*Beauties Triumph*, the 1676 school masque, had avoided it altogether and used spoken dialogue instead.) What one would expect is tunes: precisely what Purcell so generously provided in his stage works of the 1690s.[36]

Why all the arioso in *Dido*? It would seem the answer is a simple one: Purcell took as his model, Blow's court masque *Venus and Adonis*. It is similar in structure, the tonal plan, the hunting elements, the tragic final act, a mourning chorus, the importance of the dance movements, and the declamatory writing in both prominence and style. Wood and Pinnock give us a clear comparison:

Purcell and Blow were constantly borrowing from each other, right through from the late 1670s to the end of Purcell's life. There are dozens of specific examples, involving all sorts of musical ideas: melodic, harmonic, tonal, textural; vocal and instrumental scoring; even structural planning, whether of a movement or of a complete piece. In all this traffic there are two clear patterns. First, the two composers borrowed almost exclusively from each other's *recent* music: often the two works concerned were written so close together that we cannot be sure which was the model and which the derivative. I do not know of a single instance where the two are separated by more than a year, and usually it is only a few months or even weeks. Second, although the borrowings went both ways for a whole decade, by the late 1680s Purcell had come to be the pioneering partner.[37]

In the light of this assumption it is unlikely that Purcell would be borrowing in 1689 from Blow's *Venus and Adonis*, written six or seven years earlier. Yet he certainly did borrow and there are many examples quoted by Wood and Pinnock, which concern not only the text but also the music and the casting. We know for certain that

Purcell and Blow collaborated in preparing the *Theater of Music*, also in 1684.[38]

Anthony Rooley also confirms that there are in *Venus and Adonis* several pointers to *Dido*, the most outstanding of which is Venus's 'Lament'. He considers that Purcell was very much aware of what his master had achieved:

The works ends with one of the most amazing laments in the history of English music. When Venus realizes that Adonis is dead, her lament is a wonderful dirge. It sounds almost like an Indian rag in the extraordinary harmonies created by those melodic minor intervals. It is unmistakably the predecessor of Dido's 'Lament'. It even ends with a chorus which is a funeral march where the body is carried out through the audience.[39]

It is important to remember that Tate's *Brutus of Alba*, written under the name of *Dido and Aeneas*, was first presented and published in 1678. 'Friends' advised him to rename the principal characters 'for modesty's sake', but 'more likely to discourage point-by-point comparison' with Virgil. The significance of this, according to Wood and Pinnock, is that 'wherever Tate strayed far from the Virgilian storyline in *Dido*, he had already done so in *Brutus of Alba*, in the same direction, and probably with the same dramatic ends in view'. There are countless similarities detailed in Wood and Pinnock, and they all show that none of the adaptations in *Dido* was made 'in deference to the sensibilities of a schoolgirl cast: all originated in *Brutus of Alba*, a professional play'.[40] There are also distinct signs that the same scenery – kept in stock at Dorset Garden – would also be used for *Dido*.

We know that in April 1683, John Blow and Nicholas Staggins had approached the King 'praying his Majties Royall Grant & License for the creating an Academy or Opera of Musick, & performing or causing to be performed therein their Musicall compositions'.[41] These attempts have a legacy in a similar move by Grabu and Cambert some ten years earlier to found a 'Royal Academy' in London.

Was the new plan to present all-sung English opera in a public theatre? Was *Dido* designed as an addition to the company repertoire? The link with *Venus and Adonis*, through Venus herself – Aeneas's mother – could have been deliberate, making *Dido* a sequel of sorts; the *Venus* model would have to be followed if there were known resources to keep within (a company with fixed personnel, perhaps?); and the stock scenery and costumes would provide popular 'operatic' spectacle for the smallest possible outlay. It was, after all, the costumes and scenery which contributed most to the expense of putting on opera in this period.[42]

Dido was clearly designed for the professional stage – one with a trapdoor for Venus to rise through, and with scenic facilities and flying machinery; but there is no record of a public performance taking place. Was the show kept in reserve until a court performance opportunity came along, in the Hall Theatre at Whitehall? There may not have been a trapdoor handy for use there – though there was certainly a 'cellar' beneath the stage where music of some sort was presented during a performance in November 1683 . . .[43]

'flying ropes' were fixed up specially in October 1684 more likely for a French acting troupe than for *Dido*[44]

but some such arrangement might explain the strange descent of Venus. Our best guess is that one or two performances were fitted in during the autumn of 1684: 'there was a numerous Court at Whitehall' from 26 September, according to Evelyn, looking forward eagerly to the Queen's birthday (15 November) which they planned to celebrate on a lavish scale. '. . . the court appeared in much splendor and bravery', reports Luttrell. 'The Court, had not ben seene so brave and rich in apparel since his Majesty's Restauration.'[45]

Finally, there may be a clue in a most unlikely element – the weather. Evelyn's diary would appear to match the Prologue in several instances. Evelyn was a keen gardener and throughout his entries there is regular comment on the weather. Tate also had 'a meteorological turn of mind', and 'One of the most remarkable features of *Brutus of Alba* [is] that the weather appears in metaphors on nearly every page'.[46] So let us compare the notes made by these two weathermen.

See the Spring in all her Glory
Welcomes Venus to the Shore . . .
The Sun has been to Court our Queen,
And Tired the Spring with wooing.
[Read 'Tired' as 'tired out', 'exhausted'.]

(Tate)

The weather began now onely to be more mild & tollerable, but there was not the least appearance of any Spring.

(Evelyn, 28 March 1684)

. . . hardly the least appearance of any Spring.

(4 April 1684)

Henry Purcell: a portrait attributed to Johann Baptist Closterman.
(National Portrait Gallery)

Commonwealth catch singers

Right: W.
Cummi
refutation of
own statem
that this
Purcell's ho
From
privately prir
and edited c
of his biogra
of *Purcell*(18
(See page
(Guild
School of M.
& Dra
Libra

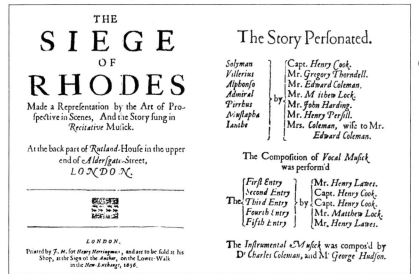

Programme of *The Siege of Rhodes* in 1656, first produced by Sir William Davenant during the Commonwealth. 'Mr Henry Persill' was the father of the composer

Right:
Chapel Roya
it was in 16
(British Muse

Below R
London Bur
by Day. (Fro
German pri
the G
Collect

Tokens purchased for seats in the theatre in the 17th and 18th centuries prior to the introduction of printed tickets. (See page 66)

The original drawing, of which a reduced copy is
given, has the following note:—

"Three ancient houses in Westminster; in the
right-hand one of which the great H. Purcell was
born, 1658, and passed his early life. They are now
in the last state of ruin, and have long been uninhabited.   The houses adjoining that of Purcell are
of modern date, and project before the others, as well
as encroach somewhat on Purcell's doorway, hiding

This was not the birth-house of Purcell

PURCELL'S HOUSE.

one side of the door-frame. Of the old houses the
windows and doorways are nearly all boarded up in the
roughest manner, under which, however, the original
panelled doors are still to be partly found.   The
houses are of old red brick. The first door was the
back way into the public-house called the 'Bell and
Fish,' kept by Mr. Oldsworth, who lost his licence.
The second door the entrance to the skittle-ground.
The third was Purcell's house."

John Dryden, poet and playwright; collaborator and close friend of Henry Purcell, by G. Kneller, 1693. *(National Portrait Gallery)*

Samuel Pepys, by J. Hayls, 1666. *(National Portrait Gallery)*

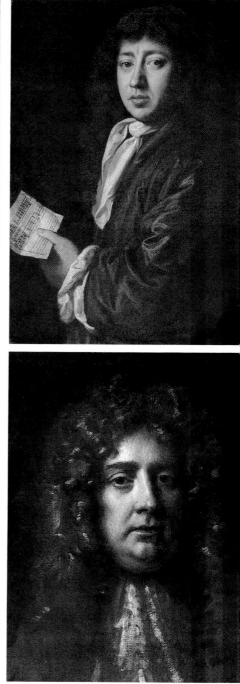

John Evelyn, diarist and contemporary of Purcell, by Robert Nanteuil, 1650. *(National Portrait Gallery)*

John Blow, the celebrated composer and 'Master of the Children' of the Chapel Royal, and teacher to Purcell. *(Reproduced by kind permission of Anthony Rooley)*

Thomas D'Urfey, scurrilous but highly successful writer of songs and verse for the stage. Purcell wrote music for many of his plays and songs. *(Mander & Mitchenson)*

Sir William Davenant, one of the first producers of opera during the Commonwealth. *(Victoria and Albert Museum)*

Purcell's pupil, Annabella, Lady Howard, who was also responsible for the monument in Westminster Abbey. *(By kind permission of Dr Richard Luckett, Magdalene College, Cambridge)*

Purcell's signature dated Jan 9 1691 – the text reads:
Received from Dr Peter Birch (JM) for one quarters allowance for my house
ending at Christmas last past. £02.0 0
Henry Purcell   *(Westminster Abbey Archives)*

The cover of *Orpheus Britannicus*, 1718 edition

ORPHEUS BRITANNICUS.

A

COLLECTION

OF ALL

The Choiceſt SONGS

FOR

One, Two, and Three Voices,

COMPOS'D

By Mr. Henry Purcell.

TOGETHER,

With ſuch Symphonies for *Violins* or *Flutes*,

As were by Him deſign'd for any of them :

AND

A *THROUGH-BASS* to each Song;

Figur'd for the *Organ, Harpſichord*, or *Theorbo-Lute*.

All which are placed in their ſeveral Keys according to the Order of the *Gamut*.

LONDON,

Printed by *J. Heptinſtall*, for *Henry Playford*, in the *Temple-Change*, in *Fleet-ſtreet*, MDCXCVIII.

A letter written by Henry Purcell to the Dean of Exeter.
(By kind permission of Dean & Chapter of Exeter Cathedral)

Charles I, after A. Van Dyck.
(National Portrait Gallery)

Charles II, from the studio of J. M. Wright.
(National Portrait Gallery)

James II, by an unknown artist c. 1690.
(National Portrait Gallery)

William III, by an unknown artist
c. 1690 – 1700. *(National Portrait Gallery)*

A flat trumpet built by Frank Tomes (1988), following John Talbot's description of the original (c. 1690). (See page 217, 249). *(By kind permission of Andrew Pinnock and Bruce Wood)*

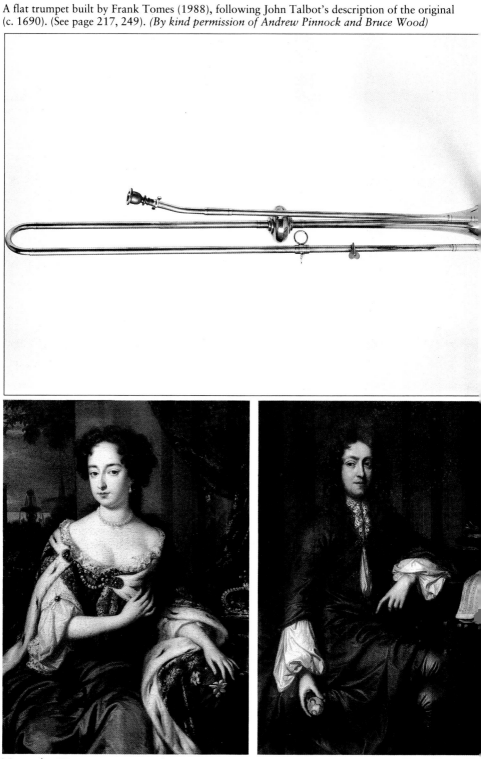

Mary, after W. Wissing. *(National Portrait Gallery)*

Generally believed to be Daniel Purcell, younger brother of Henry. An organist and competent composer, he lacked his brother's imagination. By J. Closterman. *(National Portrait Gallery)*

An excessive hot & dry Spring after so severe a Winter.

(19 May 1684)

[But by 2 July:]
So greate a drought still continu'd, as never was since my memorie.

Look down ye Orbs and See
    A New Divinity.
Whose Lustre does Out-Shine
Your fainter Beams, and half Eclipses mine . . .

(Tate)

I went to the Observatorie at Greenewich, where Mr Flamstead tooke his observations of the Ecclipse of the sun, now hapning to be almost 3 parts obscur'd.

(Evelyn, 2 July 1684)

But the Jolly Nymph Thitis that long his Love sought . . .

(Tate)

In what condition would Thetis – the Sea – seek the Sun's love for a long time and in vain? When frozen solid. That happens very rarely, but in Evelyn:

The Weather continuing intollerably severe, so as streetes of booths were set up upon the Thames &c: and the aire was so very cold & thick, as of many yeares there had not ben the like.

(1 January 1684)

The frost still continuing more & more severe . . . the very seas so lock'd up with yce, that no vessells could stirr out, or come in.

(24 January)[47]

Could these freak weather conditions in 1683/4 provide the key to Tate's 'seasonal allegory' in the Prologue to *Dido*, and help to date it? The evidence of musical style already discussed seems to point in the same direction. The literary evidence has no contra-indications, and the theatrical politics of 1683/4 'offer a context into which *Dido* fits neatly'. Even the 'much-maligned crocodile' cannot be ignored. In 1678 he had taken a brief part in *Brutus of Alba*, but in 1684 he hit the headlines. Evelyn visited him in October: 'went to see a crocodile, brought from some of the West India Islands, resembling the Egyptian Crocodile'.[48]

In the *London Stage* we learn that in September of that year: 'A Crocodile was this weeke brought over from the East Indies & showed in the faire the like haveing never been seen before it is a young one abt 4 ffoot long.'[49]

'There, in the theatrical calendar for 1684, we can imagine him lurking with gently smiling jaws, ready to welcome in Dido and Aeneas.'[50]

By a strange coincidence the weather could also have had some bearing on the 1689 performance. We know that it took place at Gorges House in Chelsea, but did it take place indoors or outdoors? Dennis Arundell thinks it could be the latter. A sketch of what the house looked like in 1892 suggests that no room was large enough for an opera and audience.[51] Arundell points out that each scene, excepting the Palace scene at the opening, is an exterior, including that of the witches who assemble *outside* their cave before performing 'too dreadful a practice for this open air'. An aerial view of the house drawn by L. Knyff, reproduced in Joannes Kip's engraving of several houses in the vicinity (*Britannia Illustrata* 1720), shows the garden of Gorges House as ornamental, and it probably had changed little since 1689. The engraving shows that the garden joined the back of Lindsey House, built in 1674 by Robert, Earl of Lindsey, the King's Lord Great Chamberlain.

When William and Mary ascended the throne, many Italian Catholics left London, including that colourful character, the Duchess de Mazarin. She had moved from St James's Palace to Paradise Row in Chelsea, and 'her house there became a kind of academy with highbrow discussions, gambling games, and musical representations which were chiefly dramatic and celebrated for their magnificence'. The singers were women from the theatres and the instrumentalists 'the most eminent masters of the time'.[52] But despite this lavish entertaining, or perhaps because of it, the rate books state that the Duchess was usually behind with her payments.

Her house was not large enough to have mounted magnificent musical dramatic entertainments. But it was rumoured that she had connections with the owner of the much larger Lindsey House through her association with the former King. Presumably she would also have been on good terms with her neighbours, the Priests, who would certainly have tried to cultivate an acquaintance with a lady of such influence in the arts.

Dennis Arundell, who conducted some researches in the Chelsea Library, presents some interesting speculation. In a map made in 1706

(Chelsea no 70) concerning legal difficulties over the water supply through pipes from Kensington (which had been organized since the reign of Henry VIII), we see that at the back of Lindsey House adjoining the Priests' garden was a Wood Yard leading to the Stable Yard on one side and an ornamental garden on the other. Arundell suggests this would have been a fine setting for both the royal and the rough opera scenes with Aeneas's ships clearly in view on the River Thames. The Wood Yard could also have had ropes and pulleys to enable the witches to 'fly up' according to the stage directions of the libretto.

Arundell's second discovery was that all round the neighbourhood were many underground passages and rooms which were too large to have been made simply to accommodate the water-pipes from Kensington. Among several water-colours depicting these underground structures, there is one (227c) which shows a narrow arched passage some 10–12 ft high with rising steps at the end. If there was one of these at the time in Lindsey House running from the cellar into the Stable Yard, it would have been the ideal 'deep vaulted cell' (an odd phrase unless specifically exact), admirably suited for an echo chorus.

There still remain many unanswered questions. For instance, who took the leading parts in the opera? Were they professionals brought in by the Duchess? Or by Betterton who certainly would have known about the production? Was Purcell himself consulted? This latest research opens so many avenues that could be explored. Surely it must make us take a fresh look at *Dido* and all the exciting possibilities that now exist?

References

1. Dent, E.J., *Foundations of English Opera*, Cambridge University Press, 1928, p 2.
2. Ibid, pp 2–3.
3. Moore, Robert Etheridge, *Henry Purcell and the Restoration Theatre*, Heinemann, 1961, pp 24–5.
4. Arundell, Dennis, *The Critic at the Opera*, Benn, 1957, p 42.
5. Ibid, p 100.
6. Dent, op cit, p 120.
7. Ibid, pp 155–6.
8. Hutton, *Charles II, King of England, Scotland and Ireland*, p 336.

9. Wood, Bruce, and Pinnock, Andrew, 'The Dating of Purcell's *Dido and Aeneas*' Royal Musical Association.* 5 April, 1991.
10. Price, Curtis A. ed *Henry Purcell: Dido and Aeneas, An Opera*, Norton, New York, 1986, p ix.
11. AA, Vol 1, p 92.
12. Harris, Ellen T., *Henry Purcell's Dido and Aeneas*, Clarendon, 1987, p 17.
13. Westrup, *Purcell*, pp 115–16.
14. Letter to author.
15. Holst, Imogen ed *Henry Purcell 1659–1695, Essays on His Music*, Oxford University Press, 1959, pp 38–9.
16. Ibid, p 41.
17. Price, *Dido*, pp 234–5.
18. Ibid, pp 8–9.
19. Wood and Pinnock, op cit, pp 1–2.
20. Luckett, Richard, 'A new source for "Venus and Adonis" ', *Musical Times*, Vol 130, February 1989, p 76.
21. Squire, Barclay, 'Purcell's Dido and Aeneas', *Musical Times*, Vol 59, 1918, pp 252–4.
22. Wood and Pinnock, op cit, p 3.
23. Ibid, p 4.
24. Ibid, p 5; see also Buttrey, J., 'Dating Purcell's *Dido and Aeneas*', *Proceedings of the Royal Musical Association*, 94 (1967–8), p 61.
25. Price, *Henry Purcell and the London Stage*, p 262.
26. Wood and Pinnock, op cit, p 8.
27. Price, *Dido*, p 15.
28. Price, *Henry Purcell and the London Stage*, p 242.
29. Ibid, p 243.
30. Holland, *Henry Purcell, the English Musical Tradition*, pp 137–8.
31. Westrup, op cit, pp 123–4.
32. Wood and Pinnock, op cit, p 9.
33. Ibid, p 8.
34. Ibid, pp 8–9.
35. Ibid, pp 9–10.
36. Ibid, pp 10–11.
37. Ibid, p 11.
38. Ibid, p 11.
39. Interview with author.
40. Wood and Pinnock, op cit, p 14.
41. Ibid, p 20.

* The above is an edited transcript of a paper read by the authors at the London conference of the Royal Musical Association, on 5 April 1991, with musical illustrations sung by Meinir Wyn Thomas and Ian Caddy. Published in *Early Music*, August 1992.

42. Ibid, p 20; Milhous, Judith, 'Opera Finances in London, 1674–1738', *Journal of the American Musicological Society*, Vol 37 (1984), p 570.

43. Ibid, p 21; Boswell, Eleanore, *The Restoration Court Stage*, Harvard University Press, Cambridge, Mass, 1932, p 53.

44. Ibid, p 126.

45. Wood and Pinnock, op cit, p 21; *The Diary of John Evelyn*, ed E.S. de Beer, Vol 4, Clarendon, 1955, p 395; Lutt, Vol 1, p 320.

46. Craven, Robert R., 'Nahum Tate's Third *Dido and Aeneas*: The Sources of the Libretto to Purcell's Opera', *World of Opera*, Vol 1 (1966), p 70.

47. Wood and Pinnock, op cit, pp 21–2.

48. ED, Vol 2, p 203.

49. LS, Part 1, p 329.

50. Wood and Pinnock, op cit, p 23.

51. Beaver, Alfred, *Memorials of Old Chelsea*, Elliott Stock, 1892, p 32.

52. Arundell, Dennis, 'New Light on Dido', *Opera*, Vol 13 (July 1962), p 445.

13

DIOCLESIAN

By July 1689, William and Mary would seem to be reorganizing their royal music, for a warrant was issued to admit Henry Purcell, along with John Banister, Robert Carr, Robert Strong and others, as musicians for the private musick. Presumably this meant that Purcell was gradually being reinstated into the royal fold, now listed as 'Composer' under the Master, Dr Nicholas Staggins.[1]

Later that summer, on 5 August, Purcell was again featured in music performed at a girls' school, this time for a Mr Maidwell's. The words to the song, 'Celestial music did the gods inspire', were written by one of the pupils, and music for the Symphony was borrowed from the coronation anthem, 'My heart is inditing'.

In September, Purcell and his wife had much cause for rejoicing, with the birth of another son, Edward. He was the second child to survive infancy, marry and have children of his own. He was also to follow in his father's footsteps and become an organist, though not approaching his father in talent.*

During late October or early November, *The Massacre of Paris*, by Nathaniel Lee, was produced by the United Company at Drury Lane. This particularly gruesome tragedy concerning the extermination of the Huguenots during the reign of Charles IX, contains only one song by Purcell, 'Thy genius, lo!', which as usual, makes a compelling contribution to the dramatic atmosphere. The weak-willed King tries unsuccessfully to prevent the massacre in which his mother is the prime mover, and is ridden with guilt. An apparition appears, a genius who assures Charles that if he repents, a divine power will intervene to save him. The apparition will plead his case before the angels, but warns: '*Charles* beware, oh dally not with Heav'n/for after this no

---

* Edward had a granddaughter, Frances b 1761.

Pardon shall be giv'n.' Price calls it 'a grand "set piece" for baritone [Bowman], which opens with an expansive recitative in C major, an appropriate key in which to address a king'. For an analysis of the modulation and brilliant use of keys and rhythms to provide the dramatic developments of the act, as well as Purcell's treatment of another version for the treble Jemmy Bowen in a later revival, see Price.[2]

Meanwhile, concert life in London, pioneered by Banister and Britton, was gradually becoming established. Roger North mentions a society of gentlemen (whom he cannot name as some were still living) who met weekly to perform upon the Bass violins (probably early cellos without a spike, held between the legs). Their performances were so successful that they began to attract an audience. To prevent overcrowding they hired a room in a tavern in Fleet Street where formal seating arrangements were made by the taverner for which he made a charge. When the society disbanded, the taverner, 'finding the sweets of vinting wine and taking money, hired masters to play, and made a pecuniary consort of it, to which for the reputation of the musick, numbers of people of good fashion and quallity repaired'.[3]

About 1680 a number of professional musicians had built a concert room on the east side of Villiers Street in between the Strand and the river, near the York Watergate. At the time it was a fashionable area known as York Buildings (so named because it had formerly been York House, residence of the Archbishop of York). It was customary for members of society to rent houses there for the winter: John Evelyn chose one very near the concert room.

The concerts were referred to as the 'Musick Meeting (or Consort) in York Buildings'. Little is known about the room itself except that it had a beautiful ceiling, painted by Verrio, which had been salvaged from York House before its demolition. Sadly, it was destined to be pulled down in 1768 to make way for two smaller houses.

According to Roger North, the concerts which took place in the earlier years of its existence were not very well organized:

All the quallity and *beau mond* repaired to it, but the plan of this project was not so well layd as ought to have bin, for the time of their beginning was inconsistent with the park and the playhouses, which had a stronger attraction. And what was wors, the masters undertakers were a rope of sand, not under the rule or order of any person, and every one foreward to advance his owne talents, and spightfull to each other, and out of emulation substracting their skill in performing; all which together scandalized the company, and poysoned the entertainment. Besides the whole was without designe or order; for one master brings a consort with fuges, another shews his guifts in a solo upon the violin, another sings, and then a famous lutinist comes foreward, and in this manner changes followed each other, with a full cessation of the musick between every one, and a gabble and bustle while they changed places; whereas all entertainments of this kind ought to be projected as a drama, so as all the members shall uninteruptedly follow in order, and having a true connexion, set off each other. It is no wonder that the playhouses got ground, and as they ordered the matter, soon routed this Musick-meeting.[4]

The situation had improved considerably by 1689. In November of that year the *London Gazette* reported that a merger had taken place between the concert series given at Bow Street (possibly at the Two Golden Balls) and York Buildings. The Bow Street concerts later moved to Charles (now Wellington) Street and were known as the 'Vendue' because sales of pictures were also held there. Concerts took place there from 1689–95. On December 25 1689, a special licence was granted to Robert King for the Vendue concerts:

W.R. Whereas we do well approve of the Abilitys in Musick of Rob*t* King one of Our Musitians and he having besought us to have Our Authority to sett up a Consort of Musick, And to have the Sole Government thereof And that none force their way in without paying such prices as shall be sett downe. Our will & pleasure therefore is, & We do hereby License and authorize y*e* s[ai]*d* Robert King to sett up a Consort of Musick to be performed by such as he shall appoint and as often as he shall think Fitt and We require & Command all persons to forbeare rudely or by force to enter in or abide there during the time of performing y*e* s[ai]*d* Musick without observing such Rules & paying such prices as shall be by him sett down. And all Our Officers Civill & Military are required to be aiding & assisting herein. Given at Our Court at Whitehall the 25th day of December 1689 in y*e* first yeare of Our Reigne.
        By his Maj*tys* Command
                        'SHREWSBURY.'[5]

We have no evidence that Purcell attended these concerts, but it is unlikely that he would have ignored them, if only to look at the possibility of having his own works performed. Apart from these activities and the theatre, there were the occasional concerts at Whitehall, despite the fact that King William was not renowned for his taste in music. One such event took place on New Year's Day, 1690. Luttrell tells us that the 'king and queen came to Whitehall, where many of the nobility and gentry came to wish them a happy new year;

and there was a great consort of musick, vocal and instrumental, and a song composed by the poet laureate. The mayor, aldermen and sheriffs waited on their majesties to compliment them from the citty.'[6] There is no record of the music performed, except for Shadwell's 'With Cheerful Hearts Let All Appear', set by Blow. Again we wonder if Purcell also contributed something, but so far there is no evidence to that effect.

However delighted the English were to know that their country was safe in Protestant hands, there were those who sometimes feared that on occasions William's Calvinist leanings made him too zealous. On 12 February 1690, we learn that

A proclamation has been published by their majesties for a general fast to be kept on Wensday the 12th of March next, and thenceforward to be observed on the third Wensday in every month successively during the present warr, for supplicating God for pardon of our sins, imploring his blessing and protection in the preservation of his majesties person and prosperity of his arms in Ireland, and navall forces.[7]

Inevitably these restrictions extended to musical performances and the theatre, also forbidden on fast days. But during the first few weeks of the New Year Purcell would have been busy putting the finishing touches to an ode, 'Of old when heroes thought it base', commissioned by the Society of Yorkshiremen in London. They had originally intended it for 14 February, but due to the forthcoming elections the performance was postponed. The result of these, by the way, brought into power not the Whigs who had put William on the throne, but the Tories, to whom William wisely switched his loyalties.

D'Urfey describes the piece as '*An* ODE *on the Assembly of the Nobility and Gentry of the City and County of* York, *at the Anniversary Feast*, March *the* 27th, 1690. *Set to musick by Mr* Henry Purcell. *One of the finest Compositions he ever made, and cost £100 the performing.*'[8] An advertisement also appeared in the *London Gazette* for 14 March 1690 confirming that the Feast will be 'held the 27th instant at the Merchant Taylor's Hall in Threadneedle Street, where will be a very splendid entertainment of all sorts of vocal and instrumental music'. The Whigs would not have been too happy about the Tory splendour, especially since they had been deserted. But the rousing lines in the final chorus might easily 'have served as a battle song for the Glorious Revolution':

Sound trumpets, sound, beat every drum
Till it be known through Christendom;
This is the knell of falling Rome . . .

Four weeks after the performance of the 'Yorkshire Feast Song' Purcell was commissioned to compose music for Queen Mary's birthday on 30 April. The text was a poem by D'Urfey, 'Arise my Muse', obviously too long for Purcell's taste so he omitted to set the two final verses. The unfortunate result was that the ode ended extolling William's brave deeds rather than Queen Mary's virtues, which was surely not what the poet intended. D'Urfey complained that Purcell had also disregarded his instructions for the choral section in the latter portion of the poem. The piece ends comically, with the chorus exhorting William to 'Go on, great prince, go on' just after Mary has been portrayed entreating him to stay at home. The Queen could not have been pleased at such tactlessness, and there is always the possibility that she took the opportunity to show her resentment, as in the delightful item of gossip provided by Hawkins:

This tune [Cold and Raw] was greatly admired by queen Mary . . . having a mind one afternoon to be entertained with music, [she] sent to Mr Gostling . . . to Henry Purcell and Mrs. Arabella Hunt, who had a very fine voice, and an admirable hand on the lute, with a request to attend her . . . Mr Gostling and Mrs Hunt sang several compositions of Purcell, who accompanied them on the harpsichord; at length, the queen beginning to grow tired, asked Mrs Hunt if she could not sing the old Scots ballad, 'Cold and Raw,' Mrs. Hunt answered yes, and sang it to her lute. Purcell was all the while sitting at the harpsichord unemployed, and not a little nettled at the queen's preference of a vulgar ballad to his music; but seeing her majesty delighted with this tune, he determined that she should hear it upon another occasion: and accordingly in the next birthday song, *viz.*, that for the year 1692, he composed an air to the words 'May her bright example chace Vice in troops out of the land,' the bass whereof is the tune 'Cold and Raw' . . . it is printed in the second part of the Orpheus Britannicus, and is note for note with the Scots tune.[9]

If indeed this anecdote is true, it confirms not only that Purcell possessed a sense of humour but how endearingly human he was. It is interesting also that he did not bow willingly to the royal will, and furthermore appeared not to have suffered because of it. He was soon asked to provide music for another of D'Urfey's verses in praise of the Queen, 'High on a Throne of Glitt'ring Ore'. When the text appeared in D'Urfey's *New Poems* of 1690, this was described as 'An Ode to the Queen especially set to music by Mr H. Purcell'.

We have several other instances of Queen Mary's love of music. In the summer when the weather was fine, she was known to go from Whitehall to 'Chelsey reach in her barge, and is diverted there with a consort of musick'.[10]

William has been censured for his apathy where music was concerned, and it is true his taste did not extend far beyond the sound of the trumpet and drum. But he deserves a certain amount of sympathy for the fact that his problems both in Holland and England could not be laid aside for a single moment. As a soldier, he led his men in the Battle of the Boyne, and was in fact wounded, although not seriously. Louis XIV was a constant threat to both countries, and whilst William was in the thick of the Irish battles, the English and Dutch fleets were defeated by the French at Beachy Head. This was followed by rumours that the French were preparing to invade Holland, whilst at the same time in London the Jacobites were said to be preparing to rise against Queen Mary.

The young Queen, only 28 years old and totally inexperienced in politics or administration, surprised everyone by taking over from her husband in one of the most critical periods in the history of her country. She was retiring and domesticated by nature, and frantic with worry during William's absence on the battlefield. We know from her letters and memoirs that on her part their marriage was founded on deep love and respect, so her concern was that of any wife left while her soldier-husband was fighting for his country. Despite her worries, she remained cool-headed and calm throughout her ordeal and was deserving of all the praise that was showered upon her for her courage in a situation that threatened both invasion and rebellion.

It was therefore very natural that when William returned from the wars, there was cause for celebration.

The 4th, being his Majesty's birth day, was observed here very strictly, by shutting up the shops, firing the great guns at the Tower, ringing of bells and bonefires at night; their majesties dined publickly at Whitehall where was a great resort of nobility and gentry, and at night was a consort of musick, and a play afterwards. And the next day, being the anniversary of the gunpowder plott, (being likewise the day of his majesties landing in England) was observed with great solemnity and general rejoicing.[11]

Unhappily these occasions were increasingly infrequent and the royal requirements for music diminished accordingly. As a result, the court musicians, Purcell among them, found their energies being directed elsewhere, the emphasis being towards the theatre. Unfortunately there are no records of Purcell's own thoughts upon the matter, but since he wrote such delightful music for the stage, clearly he had a special affinity with the medium, regardless of the sponsor.

Price describes 1690 as 'pivotal' for Purcell. In the last six months of that year, he saw no fewer than five dramatic productions for which he had written music, which included: *Sir Anthony Love, or the Rambling Lady,* a comedy by Thomas Southerne advertised in the *London Gazette* for December but probably produced at Drury Lane in late September: 'This Play was acted with extraordinary Applause, the Part of Sir Anthony Love being most Masterly play'd by Mr Montfort: and certainly who ever reads it, will find it fraught with true Wit and Humour';[12] and *The Gordian Knot Untied,* by an anonymous writer well versed in French. Motteux writes:

You have ask'd me, who was the Author . . . and wondred, with many more, why it was never printed. I hear that Gentleman who writ lately a most ingenious Dialogue concerning Women, now translated into *French,* is the Author of that witty Play, and it is almost a Sin in him to keep It and his Name from the World.[13]

Although *Dido* had been performed privately the previous year, it had certainly not gone unnoticed by the theatrical fraternity. Priest, already well known as a gifted choreographer, was a natural choice for taking care of the dances in *Dioclesian.* Betterton knew Purcell well enough through his various contributions to the theatre over the years, and therefore felt confident in asking him to write the music for the entire production.

The libretto was adapted by Betterton 'after the manner of an opera' from the play *The Prophetess: or the History of Dioclesian,* by Fletcher and Massinger, licensed for acting in 1622 and probably first published in 1647. Betterton took what he needed, making alterations for reasons concerning the operatic form, the changed political scene and the fact that women were now appearing on the English stage.[14]

The best description comes from Roger North:

It had bin strange if the gentlemen of the theaters had sate still all this while, seeing as they say a pudding creep, that is a violent inclination in the towne to follow musick, and they not serve themselves of it. Therefore Mr Betterton, who was the chief ingineer of the stage, contrived a sort of plays, which were called Operas, but had been more properly styled Semi-operas, for they consisted of half musick, and half drama.[15]

Certainly Betterton's *Dioclesian* was noticeably in advance of previous plays with music presented so far on the London stage. It contained a considerable amount of new music and 'business'. The final act was also embellished with a masque, for which a hundred lines of the text were deleted. It contained 16 musical items without intervening dialogue, lasting three-quarters of an hour, an innovation not found in the original at all.[16]

The story of *Dioclesian* is a straightforward tale of heroics, love, jealousy and disputes over territory. The prophetess is Delphia who foretells that Diocles, a private in the Roman army will become emperor 'providing he kills a mighty boar'. Diocles duly slays Aper, murderer of the late emperor, and is hailed as his successor. But there are complications when he abandons his sweetheart Drusilla, Delphia's niece, in favour of Aurelia, who had offered to marry the man who avenged the late emperor's death. Further complications arise when it appears that Maximinian, Diocles's nephew, also loves Aurelia. Meanwhile Diocles goes to war with the Persians and emerges victorious. Delphia, who had previously assisted the Persians, forgives him for his treatment of Drusilla. Diocles magnanimously restores the Persian King to his country and hands over the empire to Maximinian. An attempt on his life by Maximinian is thwarted by Delphia, and the happy scene is crowned with an entertainment by way of a country masque.

One addition that caused considerable controversy was the Prologue written by Dryden, spoken by Betterton and banned after the first performance. Only edited versions of the original script exist so it is difficult to know why it was banned, but various reasons were given: one is that Shadwell – who succeeded Dryden as Poet Laureate in 1688 – was there on the first night and complained of the double meanings regarding the Revolution. When asked why he would render one of his fellow authors such a disservice, he replied that while Dryden was Poet Laureate he would never allow one of his (Shadwell's) plays on the London stage. Another explanation, which would seem more likely, was that Londoners were railing against the taxes imposed to finance the war.

> But turn the Tube, and there we sadly view
> Our distant gains; and those uncertain too.
> A sweeping Tax, which on ourselves we raise;
> And all like you, in hope of better days . . .
> Money, the sweet Allurer of our hopes,
> Ebbs out in Oceans and comes in by Drops.

And the final couplet could be taken to imply that England would be
better off with Mary as Queen than William as King:

> That our Dead Stage, Reviv'd by your fair eyes,
> Under a female Regency may rise.

Many found the entire prologue politically distasteful, but it could
also be the case that, at such a time, anything coming from Dryden, a
devout Roman Catholic, would have been viewed with suspicion.

The Epilogue, probably written by Betterton, was spoken by a
woman, and the final lines also make the point about Mary:

> Let me propose a Project of my own,
> Depose our Men, our Male Administrators,
> And once trye us, us Female Regulators;
> I'll be content to live and dye a Nun,
> If ere we manage worse than they have done:
> Nay more; I will be bound to make it good,
> And that is very hard to flesh and Blood,
> If you our total ruine would prevent,
> Make ours, I say, a Female Government.

Have we here the seeds of Women's Liberation?

Another subject long associated with controversy is Purcell's
Dedication. It was almost certainly written by Dryden with the
collaboration of Purcell. The MS in the British Library[17] shows that
'the handwriting is Dryden's and looks nothing like Purcell's equally
distinctive fist. This is not a fair copy, but a draft, presumably for the
printer, as the paragraphs and words not deleted are those found in the
printed score, with very minor variations.'[18]

The work is dedicated to 'His Grace, Charles Duke of Somerset,
Earl of Hartford, Viscount Beauchamp of Hatch, Baron Seymour of
Trowbridge, Chancellor of the University of Cambridge, Lord High
Steward of Chichester and Knight of the Most Noble Order of the
Garter', with the usual grovelling deemed necessary when dedicating a
work with humility towards a person of rank. It continues:

Musick and Poetry have ever been acknowledg'd Sisters, which walking hand
in hand, support each other; As Poetry is the harmony of Words, so Musick is
that of Notes: and as Poetry is a Rise above Prose and Oratory, so is Musick
the exaltation of Poetry. Both of them may excel apart, but sure they are most
excellent when they are joyn'd, because nothing is then wanting to either of

their Perfections: for thus they appear like Wit and Beauty in the same person. Poetry and Painting have arriv'd to their perfection in our own Country: Musick is yet but in its Nonage, a forward Child, which gives hope of what it may be hereafter in England, when the Masters of it shall find more encouragement. 'Tis now learning Italian, which is its best Master, and studying a little of the French Air, to give it somewhat more of Gayety and Fashion. Thus being farther from the Sun, we are of later Growth than our neighbour Countries, and must be content to shake off our Barbarity by degrees. The present Age seems already dispos'd to be refin'd, and to distinguish betwixt wild Fancy, and a just, numerous Composition. So far the Genius of Your Grace has already prevail'd on Us: Many of the Nobility and Gentry have follow'd Your Illustrious Example in the Patronage of Musick. Nay, even our Poets begin to grow asham'd of their harsh and broken Numbers, and promise to file our uncouth Language into smoother Words.

The rest of the dedication is concerned with more obsequies, Purcell offering himself 'with all humility' and asking for his Ambition to be pardoned because 'there is no other means to obtain the Honour of being made known to you'. Above all, he craves acceptance as 'Your favour to this Trifle will be a good Omen not only to the Success of the Next, but also to all the future Performances', ending 'Your Grace's Most Obedient and most Obliged Servant, Henry Purcell'.

Many learned arguments exist as to the alterations in the wording of the dedication and several different meanings have been read into the need for Dryden or Purcell to make amendments. Certainly there are some rather brash statements which have been modified, such as the passage following the word 'Nonage', which was amended from 'a prattling foreign child which rather gives hope of what it may be hereafter in England, than what it has hitherto produc'd'. This is an insult to both foreign musicians and the older English ones, like John Blow. Purcell would certainly never have wished to offend his old teacher.[19] The passage 'Thus being farther from the Sun' refers, of course, to Louis XIV, the Sun King.

A private letter written by Amabel Grey to her brother, Lord Ruthyn, on 30 May, indicates that the date of the first performance of *Dioclesian* at Dorset Garden would have been well before the end of the month, not June, as some other accounts suggest. She writes: 'The new Opera call'd The Prophetess is come out I have not been able to see it & so can give little acompt of it but I hear there is very good musick to it.'[20]

We do not know who the performers were, except for Betterton. Colley Cibber mentions *Dioclesian* as being a play in which he excelled. It was generally held that he was best cast in tragedy, but he also took many other parts, not necessarily leading roles. One interesting observation on Betterton's stage presence comes from Anthony Aston who says he 'had fat, short Arms, which he rarely lifted higher than his Stomach. His Left Hand frequently lodg'd in his Breast, between his Coat and Waistcoat, while, with his Right, he prepar'd his Speech. His actions were few but just.'[21]

Of the production of that first performance of *Dioclesian*, we know very little, except that the main or 'Great' curtain would have been opened after the Prologue and remained so until after the Epilogue. The lighting in the auditorium was not dimmed during performances and therefore brought about a difference in the relationship between actors and audience. 'This relationship of illusion versus reality is important in the history of the stage. A practical problem related to it at that period, was keeping the audience off the stage during performances.'[22]

None the less, *Dioclesian* included some ingenious special effects which had to be organized in full view of the audience. A few excerpts from the stage directions give us some idea of the extent of their skill in this department:

While a Symphony is Playing, a Machine descends, so large it fills all the Space, from the Frontispiece of the Stage, to the farther end of the House; and fixes it self by two Ladders of Clouds to the Floor. In it are Four several Stages, representing the Pallaces of two Gods, and two Goddesses: The first is the Pallace of *Flora*; the Columns of red and white Marble, breaking through the Clouds; the Columns Fluted and Wreath'd about with all sorts of Flow'rage; the Pedestals and Flutings inrich'd with Gold . . . The last is the Pallace of the Sun; it is supported on either Side by Rows of *Termes*, the lower part white Marble, the upper part Gold. The whole Object is terminated with a glowing cloud, on which is a Chair of State, all of Gold, the Sun breaking through the Cloud, and making a Glory about it; As this descends, there rises from under the Stage a pleasant Prospect of a Noble Garden, consisting of Fountains, and Orange Trees set in large Vases: the middle Walk leads to a Pallace at great distance.

At this point the gods, goddesses, fauns, nymphs, shepherds and shepherdesses and the entire company enter whilst 'The Dancers place themselves on every Stage in the Machine: the Singers range themselves about the Stage.'[23]

In the Masque, the Palace of the Sun with its 'glowing cloud' called for special lighting effects for 'making a Glory'. This was a platform resembling a cloud, usually with a circlet of clouds with – in this case – children backed by a diminishing cloud-perspective.[24] Other special effects were thunder; distant rumbling was produced in a ' "thunder run"; a channel with steps, down which cannon-balls could be rolled'.[25] Nearby thunder came 'from a closed box, filled with rocks, which was tipped from side to side. It contained wooden pegs as dividers to make the movement irregular.' Wind was produced by a wind machine so ingenious that it has remained little changed from that time to this.[26]

Another novelty in Act III is the 'Chair Dance' when figures embroidered on the hangings step out and dance; 'when they have danced a while, they go to sit on the chairs, they slip from 'em and after join in the dance with 'em'. Exactly how this was performed remains unsure, but the dance was evidently a success, for in the Prologue of *The Fairy Queen* (1692), Dryden wrote:

> And, lest the Gallery should Diversion want,
> We had Cane Chairs to Dance 'em a Courant.

In *Dioclesian*, although music plays a large part, the principal actors do not sing, a characteristic of semi-opera at the time. Westrup suggests that one of the reasons for this may be the lack of experienced opera-singers in London at the time, and he quotes Grabu from his introduction to *Albion and Albanius* when presenting the play to James II, who also had problems in this respect:

the only Displeasure which remains with me, is, that I neither was nor could possibly be furnish'd with variety of excellent Voices, to present it to your Majesty in its full perfection.

Although this may sound ungrateful to his royal employer, there was probably some truth in the statement. Locke makes a similar protest in his preface to *Psyche*.[27] However, most of the music in *Dioclesian* is in the masque at the end of Act V. There are two instrumental pieces before the overture, known as the 'First' and 'Second' music, which is a legacy from the Elizabethan theatre when they would hold a concert before the play began. The rest is concerned mainly with ceremonial occasions and several dances, and of course the celebrated song 'What shall I do to show how much I love her?' in Act III, on which Curtis Price comments: 'Purcell seems to have badly misjudged the dramatic context; the music is far too good for its purpose, namely, to allow the puppet Maximinian to stand "gazing on the Princess all the time of the Song", while Aurelia is ready to run to his arms anyway.'[28] Clearly the division that caused this enforced immobility also elicited contemporary criticism; in 1702, an anonymous writer drew attention to the stage directions for the investment of Diocles in Act II when a martial song accompanied by trumpets and oboes is sung. He points out the absurdity of the action coming to a halt with the chief officers of the army standing still with their swords drawn while another fellow sings 'Let the soldiers rejoice'.

The scoring for *Dioclesian* is elaborate with strings, flutes (recorders), oboes, trumpets and for the first time ever in an English score, a French bassoon. In all probability a French musician would have been invited to take this part. Many of the songs are with continuo only, but some have obbligato accompaniment and all the choruses are scored for a full complement of instruments. A particularly fine example is in 'Sound, fame, thy brazen trumpet sound' where 'Purcell has introduced one of those florid obbligatos to which he was naturally tempted by the virtuosity of the Shore family' of trumpeters, of which John was the most famous. His sister, Catherine, married to the actor Colley Cibber, was also one of Purcell's pupils.

Westrup's summing up is apt:

It is not surprising that this music, so free from the insipid platitudes of the time, brought Purcell a reputation and forced the reluctant Dryden to conclude that there might possibly be an English composer worthy of his genius after all.[29]

None of Purcell's theatre music written prior to this date was included in the posthumous *Collection of Ayres for the Theatre* (1697), and very few songs from before this period are published in *Orpheus Britannicus*. 'He did not burst upon the London stage, Athena-like, after a ten-year apprenticeship frustrated by a revolution and Monsieur Grabu; but the young composer of *Dioclesian* was nonetheless a complete master of his art.'[30]

References

1. AA, Vol 2, pp 27–8.
2. Price, *Henry Purcell and the London Stage*, pp 60–4.
3. North, *Memoires*, p 112.

4. Ibid, pp 114–15.
5. Elkin, *The Old Concert Rooms of London*, pp 38–9.
6. Lutt, Vol 2, p 1.
7. Ibid, p 16.
8. D'Urfey, Thomas, *Songs Compleat, Pleasant and Divertive*, Vol 1, pp 114–16.
9. Hawkins, *A General History of the Science and Practice of Music*, Vol 2, p 564n.
10. Lutt, Vol 2, p 57.
11. Ibid, p 125 (7 November 1690).
12. LS, p 389.
13. Motteux, P.A. ed *The Gentleman's Journal; or The Monthly Miscellany, By Way of a letter to a Gentleman in the COUNTRY*, Baldwin, January 1691/2 – November 1694, January 1691/2, p 33.
14. Muller, Julia, *Words and Music in Henry Purcell's First Semi-opera, Dioclesian*, An Approach to Early Music through Early Theatre, Edwin Mellen, New York, 1990, p 93.
15. North, op cit, p 115.
16. Muller, op cit, p 30.
17. Stowe MSS 755, fols 34–5.
18. Muller, op cit, p 476.
19. Ibid, pp 475–8.
20. Ibid, p 33.
21. Aston, Anthony, A Brief Supplement to *Colley Cibber, Esq.* for the author, [?1747], pp 3–4.
22. Muller, op cit, pp 307–8.
23. Ibid, pp 262–3.
24. Powell, Jocelyn, *Restoration Theatre Production*, Routledge & Kegan Paul, 1984, p 45.
25. Langhans, Edward A., 'A Conjectural Reconstruction of the Dorset Garden Theatre', *Theatre Survey*, Vol 13, no 2, 1972, p 79.
26. Muller, op cit, pp 308–9.
27. Westrup, *Purcell*, pp 126–7.
28. Price, op cit, p 278.
29. Westrup, op cit, pp 128–30.
30. Price, op cit, p 21.

14

TWIN PEAKS OF GENIUS: PURCELL AND DRYDEN

The first collaboration between Dryden and Purcell was for the comedy, *Amphitryon*, which would have been a gratifying situation for Purcell for a number of reasons, not least the opportunity of working with the most distinguished dramatist of the day. But doubtless he also remembered the preface Dryden had written to his *Albion and Albanius* in 1687, extolling the virtues of the French Louis Grabu, who

has so exactly express'd my Sence, in all Places, where I intended to move the Passions, that he seems to have enter'd into my Thoughts, and to have been the Poet as well as the Composer. This I say, not to flatter him, but to do him Right; because amongst some *English* Musicians, and their Scholars (who are sure to judge after them,) the imputation of being a *French-man*, is enough to make a Party, who maliciously endeavour to decry him. But the knowledge of *Latin* and *Italian* Poets, both which he possesses, besides his Skill in Musick, and his being acquainted with all the Performances of the *French Opera's*, adding to these the good Sence to which he is born, having rais'd him to a degree above any man, who shall pretend to be his Rival on our Stage. When any of our Countrey-men excell him, I shall be glad for the sake of old *England*, to be shewn my Errour . . .

The music Grabu provided had turned out to be mediocre and Dryden – a proud man at the best of times – was now obliged to eat his words: in the Epistle Dedicatory to *Amphitryon* dated 24 October 1690, he wrote:

But what has been wanting on my Part has been abundantly supplied by the Excellent Composition of Mr *Purcell*; in whose Person we have at length found an *English - man* equal with the best abroad. At least my Opinion of him has been such, since his happy and judicious Performances in the late

Opera, and the Experience I have had of him, in the setting of my three Songs for this *Amphytryon*: To all which, and particularly to the Composition of the *Pastoral Dialogue*, the numerous Quire of Fair Ladies gave so just an Applause on the Third Day.

John Dryden was born in 1631 at Aldwinkle in Northamptonshire, the son of landed but impecunious gentry. His family had a powerful influence on the local community and were ardent supporters of the Puritan cause. Therefore, as a boy, he would have had contact with some of the political violence of the time. He was educated at Westminster School under the famous Dr Busby, where he showed poetic talent at an early age, and in 1650 was elected a Westminster Scholar at Trinity College, Cambridge where he took his degree four years later. After the death of his father that same year, Dryden went to London where his mother's cousin, the wealthy Sir Gilbert Pickering, Lord Chamberlain to Cromwell, organized a post for him in the Civil Service.

It was only after the death of the Lord Protector that Dryden began to write anything of consequence – his 'Heroic Stanzas' were dedicated to the 'glorious memory' of Cromwell, although remaining strangely silent on his politics.

Dryden had become disillusioned by all the wrangling and bloodshed during the Commonwealth era but when the monarchy was restored he was equally disgusted at the intrigues, treacheries and brutality of politics. None the less he was not above writing a poem on the happy return of 'His Sacred Majesty Charles II'. In an outburst of temper, he once declared:

No Government has ever been, or ever can be, wherein Time-servers and Blockheads will not be uppermost. The Persons are only chang'd, but the same juglings in State, the same Hypocrisie in Religion, the same Self-Interest and Mis-management will remain for ever.[1]

Inevitably Dryden's scepticism caused him to distrust both the Anglican and non-conformist churches, and this, combined with his love of order, led him to convert to Catholicism. As a result, religious arguments occur frequently in his plays, as in *The Indian Emperour or The Conquest of Mexico by the Spaniards* (1665):

> In seeking happiness you both agree;
> But in the search the paths so different be,
> That all Religions with each other Fight,

> While only one can lead us in the Right,
> But till that one hath some more certain mark,
> Poor humane kind must wander in the dark.

By 1663 Dryden had begun writing plays, a pursuit that was to take up most of his literary energies for almost 20 years. From the beginning:

we are increasingly made awake [*sic*] of where Dryden's passionate interest in literature lay, namely to improve, clarify and enrich the language . . . to bring order, grace, expressiveness, into verse writing . . . Finding as he progressed that he had no particular vision of life to import, except for his always constructive view of order, he was content to do what came to his hand to effect. He did not appear to mind what he wrote about, so long as in writing he could continue his great chosen mission.[2]

Bonamy Dobrée quotes Dr Johnson as saying that Dryden 'found the language brick and left it marble' and he explains the force of that remark:

In the middle of the century, it was something like a magnificent heap of rubble; he left it shapely and habitable; or if we prefer an organic metaphor, let us say that he found it a tangled forest shrubbery, and left it a grove of flowering trees. We have his beautifully modulated flow, the variation of phrase from the long supple sentence to the epigrammatic thrust, as also the vigour, the incisive stress where he wants it, the clarification of meaning.[3]

Dryden's love of order would surely have endeared him to Purcell, whose music might easily be described in similar terms; he, too, had this remarkable ability to keep within the order of things, but at the same time his writing abounds with the freedom that is only possible when genius partners that discipline.

Dryden was made Poet Laureate and Historiographer Royal in 1668, thus achieving added status and a small income – but one which was probably subject to the same fluctuations as those suffered by the musicians. After the 1688 Revolution, as a devout Catholic, he lost his official posts. He then turned to the theatre but earned his daily bread by making translations of the classics.

The collaboration with Dryden must have had social significance for Purcell, now being introduced to the fashionable members of London society, many of whom were keen theatre-goers. Whether this had any influence or not, the output of theatre music that flowed like a torrent from his genius over the next few years was phenomenal.

In *Amphitryon,* Dryden took many ideas from Molière's well-known story of Jupiter's adultery with Amphitryon's hitherto faithful wife, Alcmena. He provides added complications with gods taking human form and causing some compromising amorous triangles. The play progresses briskly with a plethora of transformations and machines, and was regarded as one of the best of the period. Price suggests that it is a prime candidate for a revival at the present time. The music for *Amphitryon* consists of three songs and an overture which Price believes were worked in after the play had already been written and cast. It was intended originally for presentation before royalty on 30 April (1690), but for some unknown reason the performance was cancelled. It was finally produced at the Inner Temple on 21 October by the United Company who received the customary fee of £20.

Although we know so little about Henry Purcell's personality or character, there are occasional revealing glimpses through his contacts with colleagues or friends. One such example shows us that he was no respecter of persons. Despite his recent association with Dryden, who was to become a close friend as well as collaborator, Purcell was not above writing music for one of the poet's deadliest rivals, Elkanah Settle. Settle had once written a series of bombastic dramas which endangered Dryden's popularity at Court: as a result the two authors were constantly attacking each other, either by publishing pamphlets or satirizing each other in their plays. The play for which Purcell wrote the Overture and seven Act tunes was *Distressed Innocence, or the Princess of Persia* produced at the Theatre Royal, Drury Lane by the United Company in October 1690.

Meanwhile it was a time for celebration in the royal family. William had finally returned to London where Mary was overjoyed at their reunion. Her memoirs reveal that the months of her husband's stay in Ireland had been some of the most difficult of her life so far. Luttrell tells us that

The 4th [November], being his majesties birth day, was observed here very strictly, by shutting up the shops, firing the great guns at the Tower, ringing of bells, and bonefires at night; their majesties dined publickly at Whitehall, where was a great resort of nobility and gentry, and at night was a consort of musick, and a play afterwards. And the next day, being the anniversary of the gunpowder plott, (being likewise the day of his majesties landing in England,) was observed with great solemnity and general rejoicing.[4]

William's personal popularity was now at its height and the festivities at Whitehall would seem to be reminiscent of an earlier reign. Whether Purcell composed any music for the 'consort of musick' we do not know, neither do we have any idea of the play given afterwards, but what we can be sure of was that in addition to his duties as organist and teacher, Purcell was working assiduously on music for the theatre. Amazingly, he also found time to write an elegy, 'Young Thirsis' fate, ye hills and groves deplore', on the death of a fellow musician, the young Thomas Farmer, one of the King's violinists and a composer of instrumental music and over 40 songs.

In January 1691, King William was 'earnestly entreated by the States of Holland, and the confederate Princes in Germany etc., to meet at a general Congress at The Hague, in order to concert military and economic forces for the next campaign'.[5] With the constant threat of invasion by Louis XIV, William welcomed the opportunity to participate in such an important conference. Besides which, he was homesick for his native land.

The Dutch were delighted: 'Great preparations are making at the Hague for the reception of the king of England . . . the states have caused to be made an extraordinary rich chair of state for his majestie to sitt in, and which they intend to present him with . . .'[6]

Although William's reputation for musical celebration at home was undistinguished, when it came to representing his adopted country abroad, he decided to make a memorable impression. And how better to do so than to take with him a large body of musicians? The arguments as to exactly how many musicians there were, and whether Henry Purcell was among that number, have been rife for many generations. There are, in fact four separate lists of musicians, the first being that published in *The King's Musick*. Andrew Ashbee has since found three further lists among the papers of Charles, 6th Earl of Dorset, Lord Chamberlain between 1689 and 1697. On one list we find Nicholas Staggins, Master of the King's Musick, a band of violins, 'Hooboys' and a 'Vocall Consort'; besides the Keeper of the Instruments and Chamberkeeper to the Musick, there is John Blow, Composer and 'Hene Pursell: Harpsicall'. The list is preceded by the following:

These are to certifie the Right Honble Ld Chamberlain of there Matis Household, that the Persons heereafter Nam'd Did Attend his Mati into Holland, who do Humbley crave yor Ldships faviourable Assistance towards the Attaining the Mony that is ordred them in the Treasury Chamber, which cannot Be received tell yor Ldship dus declare yor Pleasure therein.[7]

One of the reasons for dispute has been that part of the list is designated 'The Remaining Part that Attended the Queen', back in England, and this includes Robert King and John Banister among the violins. But since there follows the name of John Mosley, the Keeper of the Instruments and five 'Hooboys' that 'ware in Holland: onely for that viage [presumably extras]. These are to be payd for their Journey into Holland, & no longer,' followed immediately by the names of Blow and Purcell, it would seem fairly conclusive that they were included. On a second list, the conditions which precede it are identical except for one variation, that 'some of the Persons . . . did Attend . . .' But since the wording on the second list is the same as the first, – those left behind to attend the Queen – followed by the information about the oboes being only for that journey and the names of Blow and Purcell, this time as 'Composer', there can surely be little doubt that he did go to Holland.[8] For more detail, there is a full discussion in Zimmerman who also believes that Purcell was included,[9] if only because it is unlikely that the musicians would have travelled without a harpsichordist.

There are no details extant of the musicians' voyage to Holland or of the music performed there. We know from the riding charges that the musicians left England on 1 January and were in Holland for about three and a half months:

LC to TC. Warrant to pay 5s. a day to Dr Nicholas Staggins, master of his Majesty's musick, and 3s. a day to the following musicians, for the space of 103 days from 1 January 1690–1 to 13 April 1691, for their riding charges and other expenses in attending his Majesty to Holland, amounting to £24.15s. for Staggins and £15.9s. each for the others: (there follows a list of 12 musicians-in-ordinary and five others including 'one more hautboyes').[10]

Neither Purcell nor Blow are on this list but a number of other names are also omitted, so there must have been other warrants for payment that have since been lost.

It is just as well that the musicians and their precious instruments went in advance of their king, for the account of his crossing shows it to have been a series of disasters. The voyage was originally planned for 6 January, but strong winds made the sailing impossible. Ten days later, when conditions were better, William embarked on his yacht *Mary* at Gravesend and sailed the following day escorted by a convoy of twelve men-of-war. They finally reached Holland on 30 January, having battled daily with violent storms, but could not sail up the estuary because of dense fog and ice. Much to the concern of his companions, the King insisted on boarding his barge with four of his lords and seven rowers and set out for the coast. They then ran aground at the island of Goeree near Zeeland so had to wait until morning before they could refloat. They had reckoned on arriving in two hours, but the conditions were so appalling that the journey took 14. Fortunately they had taken with them seven bottles of beer and wine, two chickens and five loaves of bread.

When William and his entourage reached the Hague, their misadventures were, no doubt, quickly forgotten. Luttrell tells us that

to gratifye the magistrates and burghers of the Hague, his majestie was prevailed with to make his publick entry, which he did the 26th. His majestie went in his coach, attended with many others and 6 horses, out of the town, and so returned in again another way thro the triumphal arches erected for him. There were multitudes of spectators from the neighbouring parts; and the night concluded with the discharge of cannon and fine fire works.[11]

Unfortunately there are no accounts of the music played on any of these special occasions. We can only assume that the musicians would have participated in the triumphal entry and on William's formal reception by the States-General at the Hague, which would seem to have been another splendid affair:

The Hague had never seen times like this. The small peaceful seat of the Republic's government was filled up with the rulers of half Europe, their entourages, and their servants; the streets were jammed with their coaches. Fourteen English lords came with William, there were the two Electors of Brandenburg and Bavaria, there was the Prince Regent of Wurttemburg, the Landgrave of Hesse-Cassel, the Prince of Brunswick and the flamboyant Governor of the Spanish Netherlands, the Marquis de Castanaga. In Paris, the royal heads were counted with some alarm – it was said that there had been twenty-eight princes at the *levee* of the *Majestas Potentissime* – the title given William by the Emperor. As well as the princely guests, there were thirty ambassadors and numbers of princesses and ladies.[12]

The speech William made on this occasion was in Dutch, so the Englishmen would not have grasped the full meaning, which may be just as well, since it would not have been well received. He told them he was prepared to sacrifice everything for the good of the State and if he had accepted the English crown, it was not out of personal ambition or greed, but to support and maintain their religion and peace, 'and that he might be the better enabled more powerfully to assist his Allies, and more particularly this State, against the enterprise of France . . .'[13] Luttrell translates the meaning in deceptively mild terms, saying that William was 'supporting the protestant interest throughout Europe',[14] but in 1689 the more astute Halifax had remarked that William 'took England on the way to France'. It would seem he had not been far short of the mark.[15]

Shortly after the musicians returned from Holland, Purcell was concerned with publishing problems. The unqualified success of *Dioclesian* the previous year had encouraged him to publish the score, but his task had not been easy. In July 1690 he had placed an advertisement in the *London Gazette* stating that 'The Vocal and Instrumental Musick in the Opera, called The Prophetess, composed by Mr Henry Purcell, is designed to be printed by way of Subscriptions'. In the *London Gazette* of 26 February – 2 March 1691, there appeared notice that it was now finished and would be available from John Carr at his shop near the Middle Temple Gate, 'upon receipt of the remaining part of the subscription money'. When issued, it was a handsome folio volume of 180 pages at a price of ten shillings. Purcell appears to have had considerable difficulty in guiding the manuscript through to final production, and inserts a note in the printed edition:

In order to the speedier publication of this book, I employed two several printers; but one of them falling into some trouble, and the volume swelling to a bulk beyond my expectation, have been the occasions of this delay.

It has been objected that some of the songs are already common, but I presume that the subscribers, upon perusal of the work, will easily be convinced that they are not essential parts of it [some songs had been issued on single sheets by another publisher prior to the publication of the score].

I have, according to the promise in the proposals, been very careful in the examination of every sheet and hope the whole will appear as correct as any yet extant.

My desire to make it as cheap as possible [*sic*] I could to the subscribers, prevailed with me so far above the consideration of my own interest that I find, too late, the subscription money will scarcely amount to the expense of completing this edition.

Dioclesian was to enjoy frequent performances over the next few years, and seemed to be particularly suitable for entertaining foreign dignitaries. Peter the Great attended a performance in 1698 and two envoys from the Emperor of Morocco were present at a performance in 1700.

During the previous winter there had been rumours that the royal marriage was showing signs of a rift. The gossips had been at work, declaring that William was out of love with his wife and sleeping with Elizabeth Villiers, one of her ladies-in-waiting. Mary, it was said, had turned to Shrewsbury who was now so much in love that he had eyes for no other woman. Mary's total devotion to her husband manifests itself throughout all her letters and memoirs, so it is doubtful that she ever paid any attention to other men. Certainly she played cards with Shrewsbury, but their association was unlikely to have been more than friendship. On the other hand, William's affair with 'Betty' Villiers went on for some 15 years, and she was certainly much in evidence in London at this time. Of course, William always denied the liaison when challenged by Mary. Some historians consider that she believed him, but there is plenty of evidence in her memoirs and letters to show that in the first few months of 1691 the marriage was undergoing a period of extreme unhappiness and doubt.

Also that spring, Purcell produced the third of his birthday odes to Queen Mary, 'Welcome, welcome, glorious morn', to words by D'Urfey. It was performed on 30 April.

William's defeat at Mons coincided with the Queen's birthday so his return to England could have been for either reason; in any case, perhaps he was trying to make amends for the effects of the recent rumours. Certainly he stayed for the celebration itself, but left for the Netherlands at five o'clock the following morning with Mary travelling with him as far as Ingatestone. D'Urfey's words for the ode are to the point:

> He to the field by honour called shall go
> And dangers he shall know and wonders he shall do.
> The god of arms his godlike son shall bless
> And crown his fleet and armies with success,
> Whilst undisturbed his happy consort reigns
> And wisely rules the kingdom he maintains.

Westrup noted that Mary must have smiled at that 'undisturbed' understatement. In her *Memoirs*, she writes: 'I parted with him with all the trouble and concern which can be felt in my circumstances, which none can judge who have not felt the like.'[16]

Shortly after the return of the musicians from Holland, Purcell would have been working on an important new commission for the theatre, the second of his semi-operas, *King Arthur; or, The British Worthy* by John Dryden.

The plot of *King Arthur* is based on historical legend with a dressing of fantasy. Arthur, King of the Britons, and Oswald, the Saxon King of Kent, are both in love with Emmeline, the blind daughter of the Duke of Cornwall. After ten bloody battles the Saxons are driven back and are to face the decisive conflict taking place on St George's Day, which the British regard as an omen for their success. Oswald's collaborator is the magician, Osmond, who has two assistants, the spirits for earth and air, Grimbald and Philidel. Philidel is persuaded by Merlin to join the British side and foils attempts by Grimbald to mislead the British. In the meantime, Emmeline and her attendant Matilda are captured and Oswald forces his unwelcome attentions on her. In order to impress her with the power of his love, he restores her sight and then conjures up a display in which the countryside and all the inhabitants are frozen. Cupid breathes warmth on them and they are restored to life. There are the usual deceptions, masquerades, all of which are resolved by the triumph of right over evil, and in the final act the two armies fight it out 'with Spunges in their Hands, dipt in blood'. Arthur overcomes Oswald in a hand-to-hand fight, and gives him his freedom. Emmeline and Arthur are united and Merlin announces that he is the first of 'three Christian worthies' (hence the full title, *King Arthur, or the British Worthy*). Britain's island rises from the sea after which the company join in a rousing chorus in praise of St George, and a dance brings the celebrations to an end.[17]

In order to appreciate the background events surrounding *King Arthur*, we need to return to the year 1684 when Charles II sent Betterton to Paris to investigate the possibilities of putting on opera in England. We know that he returned with Grabu, former master of the French king's violins, who, it was hoped, would be able to advise on producing 'something at least like an Opera in England for his Majesty's diversion'. No opera was forthcoming, but we know that Grabu provided the music for Dryden's *Albion and Albanius*. In the preface, Dryden tells us that it is a play 'Written in blank Verse, adorn'd with Scenes, Machines, Songs and Dances', and it was to include an all-vocal Prologue representing the restoration of Charles II by a series of tableaux. In a letter to his publisher, Tonson, in August 1684 Dryden says he has already split the project into two parts. He thought 'the singing-opera', presumably *Albion and Albanius* was 'to be playd immediately after Michaelmasse'. He still had one act of the opera (*King Arthur?*) to write but was in no hurry to finish it. Because of 'some intervening accidents', the main body of the work was set aside and the Prologue extended to form a three-act opera, *Albion and*

Albanius. What brought about the change of plan is open to question. Price suggests that 'the king's Francophile tastes prevailed over Dryden's chauvinism', but still considers that the reasons for shelving it are more complex.[18]

The death of Charles II on 6 February 1685 had made Dryden's plans for a two-part production inoperable, so he hastily changed the symbolism in *Albion and Albanius* to compliment the new King James II, and the performance took place in June of that year. But to have held over the presentation of the second part for six years seems to infer something more than lethargy on Dryden's part. In his *Life of John Dryden*, Ward tells us that Dryden dedicated *King Arthur* to Halifax, an old acquaintance and a staunch Tory and Anglican: he had also been Lord Privy Seal, which would assure the play would be regarded with respect by its readers. 'But even before it was acted, Dryden seems to have employed his friends in high places' which included the Duchess of Monmouth – later Lady Cornwallis – who recommended it to Queen Mary who read it and gave it her 'royal approbation'. Dryden presumed 'That her Majesty was not displeased to find in this poem the praises of her native country, and the heroick actions of so famous a predecessor in the government of Great Britain'.[19]

Ward also tells us that in a recently discovered unique copy of the first edition of *King Arthur*, there is a leaf showing that there were in the Preface significant amendments to the original which, if retained, could have had disturbing consequences. The amended version reads:

But not to offend the present times, nor a government which has hitherto protected me, I have been obliged so much to alter the first design, and take away so many beauties from the writing, that it is now no more what it was formerly than the present ship of the Royal Sovereign, after so often taking down and altering, was the vessel it was at the first building.

The offending passage follows the words 'protected me' and would have read: 'and by a particular Favour wou'd have continued me what I was, if I could have comply'd with the Termes which were offered me'. We have no knowledge of what these terms were, but they would surely have required him to renounce his faith 'either by taking a modified oath of allegiance to the new joint sovereigns, or by renouncing the principle of transubstantiation, that prime battle-ground between the Anglican and Catholic Churches'. As Ward points out, whoever suppressed the passage did a favour to Dryden who would have been attacked on all sides. The government also would have suffered considerable embarrassment for the fact that this 'unrepentant Catholic laureate' had even been approached.[20] It also says a great deal for Dryden's integrity, that he held to his convictions in a difficult and dangerous situation.

For Dryden, it was a recurring dilemma. When he decided to collaborate with Purcell in 1691, he found that the play as it stood, still retained political implications which were unacceptable to William and Mary. But even when he had rewritten it to suit the present regime, there remained certain actions which could have caused further concern. Price puts it aptly:

it must surely have elicited knowing glances from both Whigs and Jacobites, despite Dryden's attempt to scramble the original allegory. Arthur was now clearly William III and Oswald the deposed James II. Their single combat in Act V, in which Arthur would emulate his 'Fam'd Ancestor' Aeneas when he 'Fought for a Crown, and bright *Lavinia's* Bed', not only reaffirms the royal blood line from the Trojan prince to Brutus of Alba, but also enacts the Battle of the Boyne, fought between William and James in late June 1690, almost exactly a year before the premiere of *King Arthur*.[21]

However, Price finds anomalies in this and other interpretations and for those desirous of pursuing the subject there is considerable discussion to be had in Price, Zimmerman, Buttrey, Dent and others.

No complete score of Purcell's music for *King Arthur* exists today, only 'a confused assortment of more than 60 manuscripts and miscellaneous publications'. One fragmentary score dating from before 1695, collected and evaluated by Margaret Laurie has at least brought all the available material together,[22] and Curtis Price gives a lively analysis of the music in relation to the words in *Henry Purcell and the London Stage*.[23] The music throughout shows how Purcell could conjure up atmosphere, colour and a dramatic element in his music that was much in advance of his time. It is the third act, 'The Prospect of Winter in Frozen Countries', with its famous 'frost' scene, which contains the most memorable music in the opera. This masque, considered by eighteenth-century critics to be one of Purcell's greatest works, was occasionally put on as a separate entertainment. Price's evocative description of some of the music in this act makes it easy to see why it was so popular:

The quavering strings begin with a conventional chain of harmonies, but in the fifth bar . . . the tonal centre is momentarily obscured by chromatically descending first-inversion chords, a progression that would have been regarded as daring even a hundred years later. The Genius's journey from beneath the stage is depicted by ascending semitones in the vocal part harmonized with an astonishing variety of sophisticated chords, all lying securely within the orbit of C minor. In the second section, 'See'st thou not how stiff, and wondrous old', Purcell spices the lush harmonies with more pungent dissonances – augmented triads, tone clusters, cross-relations – to bring the word 'bitter' into sharp focus. Until now the aria has been more dazzling, but the final phase sobs with passion; Purcell summons all his craft to capture the literal meaning of the stammering line 'Let me, let me, freeze again to death.'[24]

Another interesting observation comes from Dent:

The greatness of the scene lies not in the quaint notation or even in the particular device of instrumentation, but in the musical idea itself. The whole scene is nothing more than a masque, and has no real connection with the drama, though its ostensible function is to excite the passions of Emmeline by the presentation of Cupid's effects in a visible form. It is extremely difficult for the modern reader to enter into the seventeenth-century point of view in a case of this kind. The whole idea is essentially baroque, and belongs to an age which on every conceivable occasion was ready to represent abstractions in the form of allegorical sculpture in attitudes of frantic gesticulation. Yet we can at least admire the picturesqueness of Purcell's imagination, the bold contrasts of style, and the masterly piling up of the music to a climax at the end of the chorus ' 'tis Love that has warm'd us'.[25]

In passing, it is worth mentioning an article in the *Musical Times* in which J.A. Fuller Maitland draws our attention to a scene in Act IV of Lully's *Isis*, produced in 1677. A 'Choeur de Peuples des Climats glacés' would seem to anticipate Purcell's famous scene, especially as the words are set in a similar note pattern with slurs to indicate a tremolo effect. The refrain of the two stanzas sung by the chorus, 'La neige et les glaçons nous donnent de mortels frissons', seems to indicate clearly that a parallel effect is intended, and Purcell could have thought the idea worth imitating. But there the similarity ends. 'Purcell in all departments of his work was so thoroughly original a composer that he can well afford to yield this single effect to his French predecessor, and the actual music has little in common, Purcell being, I need hardly say, far the grander of the two.'[26]

When it came to fitting the words to the music, Purcell had no hesitation in changing them to suit his purpose, and was doubtless aware that Dryden had little ear for music. If anyone knew how to set

English words to music it was Purcell: he knew how to place the vowels and avoid spluttering consonants, a fact that receives acknowledgement from Arundell, who adds:

but as this sensitiveness to a musical balance of consonants and vowels has not, I think, been pointed out before, here are a few examples from *King Arthur* of how he always altered words that read well to words that sound better and fit the movements of the singer's mouth easier.

In the evil spirit Grimbald's song against the good spirit Philidel, Dryden's line

> Too far, alas, he has betrayed ye

became:

> To fear, alas, he has betrayed ye

so avoiding the ugly-sounding repetition of the open-mouthed 'ah' in 'far' and 'alas'. In the famous Frost Scene Dryden made Cupid sing:

> What! dost thou dream of freezing here?

which Purcell made easier to sing and understand as

> What dost thou mean by freezing here?

In the praise of Britain in the final masque the sibilants are weeded out of the line

> Foreign lands thy fishes tasting

by making it

> Foreign lands thy fish are tasting:

Finally the first lines of Venus's lovely song, which, as Burney said 'time has not the power to injure. It is of all ages and countries', were simply changed for the better from Dryden's version

> Fairest isle, all isles excelling,
>   Seat of pleasures and of loves,
> Venus here will choose her dwelling
>   And forsake her Cyprian groves.

which reads perfectly well, to

> Fairest isle, all isles excelling,
>   Seat of pleasure and of love,
> Venus here will choose her dwelling
>   And forsake her Cyprian grove.[27]

Dryden obviously agreed with the alterations made by Purcell but Dent suggests that there may have been more, since in his preface he refers to the changes made for political purposes and then writes:

There is nothing better, than what I intended, but the Musick; which has since arriv'd to a greater Perfection in *England* than ever formerly, especially passing through the Artful Hands of Mr Purcel, who has Compos'd it with so great a Genius, that he has nothing to fear but an ignorant, ill-judging Audience.

However, Dryden is not prepared to let Purcell have things all his own way and with two such strong characters one can visualize arguments. Dryden has to explain to his readers the difference between reading and hearing:

But the Numbers of Poetry and Vocal Musick, are sometimes so contrary, that in many places I have been oblig'd to cramp my Verses, and make them rugged to the Reader, that they may be harmonious to the Hearer; Of which I have no Reason to repent me, because these sorts of Entertainment are principally design'd for the Ear and Eye, and therefore in Reason my Art on this occasion ought to be subservient to his.

He then spoils it all by implying that his own poetic skill remains more important regardless.

And besides I flatter myself with an Imagination, that a Judicious Audience will easily distinguish betwixt the Songs wherein I have comply'd with him, and those in which I have followed the Rules of Poetry in the Sound and Cadence of the Words. Notwithstanding all these Disadvantages, there is somewhat still remaining of the first Spirit with which I wrote it.

This was a bold statement considering the number of spirits in which it had already been written.

King Arthur received its first performance by the United Company sometime in May 1691 at Dorset Garden. King Arthur was played by

Betterton, who also spoke the Prologue, and the celebrated Mrs Bracegirdle played Emmeline and spoke the Epilogue. Downes describes it in glowing terms: 'King Arthur, an Opera, wrote by Mr Dryden; it was Excellently Adorn'd with Scenes and Machines: The Musical Part set by Famous Mr Henry Purcel; and Dances made by Mr Jo. Priest; The Play and Musick pleas'd the Court and City, and being well perform'd, twas very Gainful to the Company.'[28]

Roger North was also impressed and makes an interesting observation of a practice that must have been unusual for the time:

I remember in Purcell's excellent opera of King Arthur, when Mrs Butler, in the person of Cupid, was to call up Genius, she had the liberty to turne her face to the scean, and her back to the theater. She was in no concerne for her face, but sang a recitativo of calling towards the place where Genius was to rise, and perform'd it admirably, even beyond any thing I have ever heard upon the English stage. And I could ascribe it to nothing so much as the liberty she had of concealing her face, which she could not endure should be so contorted as it is necessary to sound well, before her gallants, or at least her envious sex. There was so much of admirable musick in that opera, that it's no wonder it's lost; for the English have no care of what's good, and therefore deserve it not.[29]

Mrs Butler had been Purcell's leading female singer since 1689 when he started working regularly for the theatre. He wrote three songs especially for her: 'For Iris I sigh', 'Hang this whining way of wooing' and 'No, no, poor suff'ring heart'. These songs relied on the singer's ability to communicate with her audience and here she was in her element. Mrs Charlotte Butler was of noble birth and a favourite of King Charles II, who recommended her for the theatre. She possessed an all-round talent for acting, singing and dancing, and was extremely attractive with a trim figure, hence her frequent appearances dressed as a boy. She was seldom cast in virtuous roles but her personality gave the impression of being witty rather than coarse. All these attributes were admirably suited to the parts written for her by Dryden and Purcell in King Arthur.[30]

Dryden had expressed the hope that King Arthur would be 'the chiefest entertainment of our ladies and gentlemen this summer'.[31] Certainly it was a great deal more successful than some of his later plays. No doubt on account of Purcell's music, it was destined to retain its popularity throughout the eighteenth century and would become Dryden's most revived play.

References

1. Dryden, John, 'Dedication', *Examen Poeticum*, Tonson, 1693.
2. Dobrée, Bonamy, *John Dryden*, Writers and their Work, No 70, Longmans, 1961, pp 14–15 (for the British Council).
3. Ibid, p 17.
4. Lutt, Vol 2, p 125.
5. Quoted in Zimmerman, *Henry Purcell, 1659–1695, His Life and Times*, p 183.
6. Lutt, Vol 2, p 136.
7. AA, Vol 2, p 38.
8. Ibid, pp 38–40.
9. Zimmerman, op cit, pp 184–90.
10. AA, Vol 2, pp 40–1.
11. Lutt, Vol 2, pp 168–9.
12. van der Zee, *William and Mary*, pp 342–3.
13. Ibid, p 342.
14. Lutt, Vol 2, p 172.
15. van der Zee, op cit, p 342.
16. Quoted in Westrup *Purcell*, p 71.
17. Ibid, p 132.
18. Price, *Henry Purcell and the London Stage*, p 289.
19. Ward, *Life of John Dryden*, p 251.
20. Ibid, pp 250–1.
21. Price, op cit, pp 293–4.
22. The Purcell Society Edition, Vol XXVI.
23. Price, op cit, pp 317–19.
24. Ibid, pp 304–5.
25. Dent, *Foundations of English Opera*, p 213.
26. Fuller Maitland, J.A., 'Foreign Influence on Henry Purcell', *Musical Times*, Vol 37 (January 1896), pp 10–11.
27. Arundell, *The Critic at the Opera*, pp 150–1.
28. Downes, *Roscius Anglicanus*, p 88 [42].
29. North, Roger, *Roger North on Music*, ed John Wilson, Novello, 1959, pp 217–18.
30. Baldwin, O. and Wilson, T., 'Purcell's Sopranos', *Musical Times*, Vol 123 (September 1982), pp 602–3.
31. Ward, op cit, p 251.

15

THE FAERIE QUEENE

One of the criticisms levelled at William by the British was that he was more often absent from the English throne than sitting upon it. Certainly there was some excuse for his wars with the French, but it was noted that whenever a lull in battle provided the opportunity, he would take himself off to one of his country-houses in Holland for a few weeks' hunting. His British subjects did not take kindly to his neglect of the Queen, who was enormously popular with her people. Mary had no word of reproach for her husband and her memoirs tell of the great love she had for him. But it affected her in other ways. Her health suffered and, when William's absences spanned the entire summer, as in that year of 1691, she began to lose her zest for life. In a meditation she shared with her journals, she wrote: 'I do not know what will happen to me, but, life being so uncertain, I prepare myself for death. I bless God that the only thing which makes death uneasy to me is that some might suffer for it.' In a note for the King, she added: 'I beg him to burn this and my other papers, and to preserve a tenderness for my memory, as for someone who has always been entirely his.'[1]

Perhaps it was her poor state of health, allied to the religious fervour that prevailed at these periods, that prompted Mary to enforce stricter moral standards upon her people. Luttrell tells us that, on 10 July, 'the queen sent a letter to the justices of peace of Middlesex, at Hicks hall, requiring them to use the most effectual means for putting the lawes in execution against prophane swearing and cursing, prophaning the Lords day, drunkennesse, and such immoralities'.[2] As delighted as the English were with their Protestant monarchy, for many this would seem like a return to the puritanical dictates of the Commonwealth. It certainly would not have pleased the musicians who often held concerts in the taverns and naturally enjoyed a glass or two in the process.

However, there would seem to be few restrictions in evidence at William's homecoming. It worked miracles for the Queen and she was a dazzling hostess for her husband's 41st birthday on 4 November – also their 14th wedding anniversary: 'The court was all in their splendour, the queen very rich in jewells. Their majesties dined publickly; the night concluded with a great ball and dancing at court, bonefires and illuminations throughout the citty, with ringing of bells, etc.'[3] It was noted that William was seen to pay more attention than usual to his wife, and Mary wrote in her memoirs: 'I must not forget to observe how kind the King is, how much more of his company I have had since he came home this time, than I used to have.'[4] And well he might, for so far that year William had spent only three weeks at home.

That autumn William was mainly concerned with asking a somewhat hostile parliament to provide him with an army of 65,000 men to fight the French, a request that was for the most part granted.

Perhaps it was his satisfaction in obtaining his army that prompted the King to show an interest in the Feast of St Cecilia in November; or maybe it was Mary, who was known to be a lover of music. In any case, the musicians would have welcomed any response after the neglect by James II of this very important celebration. That year (1691) it was Blow who set the music to D'Urfey's words. From the *Gentleman's Journal* we learn that on the 23 November (the 22nd was a Sunday)

most of the Lovers of Music, whereof many are persons of the first Rank, meet at *Stationers-Hall* in *London*, not thro' a Principle of Superstition, but to propagate the advancement of that divine Science. A splendid Entertainment is provided, and before it is always a performance of Music by the best Voices and Hands in Town; the Words, which are always in the Patronesses praise, are set by some of the greatest Masters in Town. This year, Dr *John Blow*, that famous Musician, composed the Music, and Mr *Durfey*, whose skill in things of that nature is well enough known, made the Words ... Whilst the Company is at Table, the Hautboys and Trumpets play successively. Mr *Showers* [Shore] hath taught the latter of late years to sound with all the softness imaginable, they plaid us some flat Tunes, made by Mr *Finger*, with a general applause, it being a thing formerly thought impossible upon an Instrument design'd for a sharp Key.[5]

Meanwhile Purcell was increasingly busy writing for the theatre and soon it would have been difficult to attend a play in London where some of the music was *not* written by him. John Dryden's play, *The*

Indian Emperor, first performed at Bridges Street in 1665, had seen many revivals. In December of that year (1691) it was revived by the United Company at either Drury Lane or Dorset Garden with an additional song by Purcell, 'I look'd, I look'd, and saw within the Book of Fate', which was published in *The Banquet of Music* no 5 in 1692. Also in December was a performance at Drury Lane of *The Wives' Excuse; or, Cuckolds Make Themselves* by Thomas Southerne with music by Purcell. One song, words by Thomas Cheek, 'Corinna I excuse thy face', was published in *The Banquet of Music*, the sixth and last book in the series, in 1692. 'Say, cruel Amoret' was sung by Mountfort and 'Hang this whining Way' by Mrs Butler.

A few days after the New Year of 1692, the court celebrations continued with a great 'Twelfth Night' ball at Kensington. All the nobility were there and dancing continued until one in the morning. The King slipped away to indulge in his traditional visit to the Groom Porter's gambling session. He lost 200 guineas before his luck changed when he recovered £100. On the following evening the Queen and the Queen Dowager went to see Dryden's opera, presumably *King Arthur*, but for the King there was a counter-attraction. He took himself, *incognito*, to the House of Lords where the Duke of Norfolk was suing for £50,000 damages a man by the name of Germain, whom he claimed had enticed the Duchess away. It was one of the liveliest scandals of the day and Society consumed every morsel with relish. There were 28 sworn witnesses and, on the day the King was there, two of them swore 'that they saw Germain between a pair of sheets with the dutchesse'.[6] The case continued throughout the year and in the end the Duke received only token damages of 100 marks for his pains.

Apart from William's long absences, Mary had recently suffered another domestic problem, which brought further loneliness into her life: in the previous autumn the rift between her and Princess Anne had become final, never to be reconciled. Ever since Mary's return to England, relations between the two sisters had been cool, although in public they seemed friendly for the sake of appearances. Even as girls the two sisters had never had much in common and were temperamentally incompatible. Over the years they had grown further apart, a situation that was not helped by the dominant influence of the notorious Sarah Marlborough who did everything within her power to come between them. She once wrote: 'It was indeed impossible they should be very agreeable companions to each other, because Queen Mary grew weary of anybody who would not talk a great deal, and the

Princess was so silent that she rarely spoke more than was necessary to answer a question.'[7]

Egged on by Sarah, Anne had complained first about her apartments in Whitehall and then that her allowance was insufficient. The Duchess persuaded Anne to request that this matter should be settled in Parliament rather than be left to William's generosity. The matter was raised in the House of Commons by friends of Marlborough without either William or Mary being notified. When Mary pleaded with Anne to terminate her friendship with Sarah, she refused. There then followed a sequence of events that brought about the removal of Anne's guards, and the withdrawal of all public honours. The breach was complete and the sisters never spoke to each other again.

In January 1692 Purcell wrote a duet, 'As soon as the chaos was made into form', for a new comedy by D'Urfey, *The Marriage-Hater Match'd*. Motteux writes: 'It hath met with very good success, having been plaid six days together, and is a diverting play.'[8]

The next play in which Purcell was concerned contained only one of his songs, 'No, no, poor suff'ring heart' for Dryden's *Cleomenes*, but the première, originally planned for 9 April 1692, was delayed on account of an unexpected controversy. Luttrell tells us: 'By order of the queen, the lord chamberlain has sent an order to the playhouse prohibiting the acting of Mr Dryden's play called the tragedy Cleomenes, reflecting much on the government.' A week later, 16 April, he notes that 'Mr Dryden's play has been acted with applause, the reflecting passages upon this government being left out'.[9]

The story is about Cleomenes, the King of Sparta, who, after being beaten in battle by the Macedonians, flees to Alexandra with his family to gain Egyptian support. Cleomenes is frustrated at being kept waiting for an audience by the decadent King Ptolomy, who, in turn is preoccupied with paying attention to the beautiful Cassandra. William and Mary were normally not too strict in censoring plays, but this sympathetic treatment of an exiled king must have touched on a particularly sensitive nerve.

Although William had defeated James in the Battle of the Boyne in 1690, it must be remembered that the English had also been defeated at Beachy Head one day before. James, who had returned from Ireland to France, was, by the spring of 1692, known to be planning an invasion with the help of his French allies. As it happened, these plans were thwarted but 'At such a time could a London audience have failed to be reminded of James and the Battle of the Boyne when Cleomenes alludes to a defeat which had forced him into exile?'

I fought the battle bravely, which I lost;
. . .
I fled; and yet I languish not in exile;
But here in Egypt whet my blunted horns,
And meditate new fights, and chew my loss

John Loftus argues that Dryden's assertion in his preface 'that there is no Parallel to be found' lacks credibility, and suggests that the play was finally produced owing to the influence of the Earl of Rochester, a Jacobite sympathizer, to whom Dryden addressed his Dedicatory Epistle.[10]

The political significance would not have affected Purcell's one song, besides which he had other more important matters to hand. In the *Gentleman's Journal* Motteux prints the words of two songs written by himself and tells us:

The first is set by Mr Purcell, to whom I must own my self doubly obliged; for he hath not only made the notes extremely fine but nicely adapted them to my words. I am not without hopes of having the honour to have it sung before Her Majesty.[11]

The song was 'Stript of their green our Groves appear', but there is no record of it having been sung before the Queen.

On 30 April 1692 the Queen's birthday was celebrated at Court with a new ode, Sir Charles Sedley's 'Love's goddess sure was blind', set to music by Henry Purcell. Apparently it was a grand affair: 'the nobility and gentry, with the lord mayor and aldermen of this citty, attended to compliment thereon.'[12]

At the end of April, Luttrell noted: 'On Monday will be acted a new opera, called the Fairy Queen: [it] exceeds former playes: the clothes, scenes, and musick cost £3,000.'[13] On 2 May the 'opera', with music by Purcell, received its first performance by the United Company at Dorset Garden. It is the most controversial of the semi-operas mainly because it was an adaptation of Shakespeare's *A Midsummer Night's Dream*. These adaptations, which were common practice during the Restoration, have been frowned upon by several generations of scholars, but more recent writers have 'treated them more as theatre pieces than as butchered literary masterworks'.[14]

Price restates two important considerations that he feels are often overlooked by both sides. He suggests that Sir William Davenant, most strongly condemned of the early Restoration adaptors, may well have been legally bound by the terms of his patent (1660) to modernize the plays before producing them. There has been recent debate on whether this required more than divesting them of 'all prophanenesse and scurrility'. He suggests that since the trend was set it was then a matter of whether the adaptation was good or not which ensured its success in the theatre. In fact some were revived regularly well into the eighteenth century.*

The name of the adaptor is unknown. There have been many suggestions, which include both Dryden and Settle, but there is no evidence to make a strong case for either. Price's suggestion that Betterton is a reasonable guess, seems the most likely, especially as he had been involved with all the previous productions of opera at Dorset Garden. In addition, we know that Josias Priest, who had worked with Betterton on many occasions, arranged all the dances, of which there were ten.

Whoever made the adaptation, it would seem that Purcell had some hand in planning the text for the masques – a view held by Moore. He maintains that not only are they different in tone from the spoken dialogue 'but it is through them that he [Purcell] is able to impose a kind of unity out of disparateness, creating a notable example of baroque art'. He goes on to point out that the creative spirit involved was one of integrity. 'If Purcell had demanded less than the highest that the genre could give, the opera would have failed to attain anything beyond pleasant irrelevancies, but, aware of the masque's noble tradition, he was able to formulate from a most unpromising libretto, a unified whole of rare beauty.'[15]

Downes, prompter for the United Company, gives us some detail as to the production:

This in Ornaments was Superior to the other Two [*King Arthur* and *The Prophetess*]; especially in Cloaths, for all the Singers and Dancers, Scenes, Machines and Decorations, all most profusely set off; and excellently perform'd, chiefly the Instrumental and Vocal part Compos'd by the said Mr *Purcel*, and Dances by Mr *Priest*. The Court and Town were wonderfully satisfy'd with it; but the Expences in setting it out being so great, the Company got very little by it.[16]

---

* The same thing happened to the libretti of Metastasio 100 years later when the fashions of 'opera sina' changed at the end of the eighteenth century and his 'classic' texts were 'modernized'; the most famous illustration being Mozart's *Clemenza di Tito* – brought 'up to date' by Mazzola – in fact he was 'required' to do so by the Bohemian Estates. Admittedly, Metastasio is not Shakespeare, but the principle is the same. It remains a sad reflection on the scholars who persist in judging one thing in terms of another.

No wonder that a plea for financial support is included in the preface, although the aspersions cast on English singers would not have been well received:

That a few private Persons should venture on so expensive a Work as an Opera, when none but Princes, or States exhibit 'em abroad, I hope is no Dishonour to our Nation: And I dare affirm, if we had half the encouragement in *England* as they have in other Countries, you might in a short time have as good Dancers in *England* as they have in *France*, though I despair of ever having as good Voices among us, as they have in Italy. These are the two great things which Travellers say we are most deficient in. If this happens to please, we cannot reasonably propose to our selves any great advantage, considering the mighty Charge in setting it out, and the extraordinary expence that attends it every day 'tis represented. If it deserves their Favour? if they are satisfied we venture boldly, doing all we can to please 'em? We hope the *English* are too generous not to encourage so great an undertaking.

It is not difficult to see why it was such a costly production. The number of performers must have been around 100, consisting of about 20 actors and actresses (who did not sing) a similar number of singers, at least 24 dancers and a band of about 24 instrumentalists.

This is the longest of Purcell's dramatic operas and contains some of his most splendid music in a series of striking masques. Moore discusses the stage directions in some detail and from these we can visualize the scope of the scenes and machines employed in the production and why it was so costly to mount. The scenic splendours begin in the masque at the end of Act II where the earth has just opened to receive Titania's Indian Boy in order to hide him from Oberon.

The scene changes to a prospect of grottos, arbours, and delightful walks: The arbours are adorned with all variety of flowers, the grottos supported by terms, these lead to two arbours on either side of the scene, of a great length, whose prospect runs toward the two angles of the house. Between these two arbours is the great grotto, which is continued by several arches, to the farther end of the house.

This is the simplest of the four sets. The fairies dance their moonlight revels before it whilst the singers in the Masque of Night move across the stage in procession.

At the close of the next act, Titania commands the stage-hands to 'change this place to my Enchanted Lake'. At the time, changes of scenery took place in full view of the audience who enjoyed this part of the proceedings almost as much as the play itself. This would have been particularly interesting because it involves what was literally a transformation.

The scene changes to a great wood; a long row of large trees on each side; a river in the middle; two rows of lesser trees of a different kind just on the side of the river, which meet in the middle, and make so many arches; two great dragons make a bridge over the river; their bodies form two arches, through which two swans are seen in the river at a great distance ... While a symphony's playing, the two swans come swimming on through the arches to the bank of the river, as if they would land; these turn themselves into fairies, and dance; at the same time the bridge vanishes, and the trees that were arched, raise themselves upright.

The cardboard swans would glide off imperceptibly as two suitably white-feathered ballerinas suddenly appeared out of nowhere, 'as in the second act of *Swan Lake*'.

The masque concerning the celebrations of King Oberon's birthday calls for special lighting effects, with only wax candles and lamps at their disposal. This, then, is the scene ordered by Titania:

The scene changes to a garden of fountains. A sonata plays while the sun rises, it appears red through the mist, as it ascends it dissipates the vapours, and is seen in its full lustre; then the scene is perfectly discovered, the fountains enriched with gilding, and adorned with statues: The view is terminated by a walk of cypress trees which lead to a delightful bower. Before the trees stand rows of marble columns, which support many walks which rise by stairs to the top of the house; the stairs are adorned with figures on pedestals, and rails; and balusters on each side of 'em. Near the top, vast quantities of water break out of the hills, and fall in mighty cascades to the bottom of the scene, to feed the fountains which are on each side. In the middle of the stage is a very large fountain, where the water rises about twelve foot.

The lighting effects would probably have been achieved through the glass bowls filled with coloured liquid (see p 65), and the cypress trees and columns painted in diminishing perspective on the side flats, with the stairs and fountains on the backdrop. After the chorus 'Let the fifes and the clarions and shrill trumpets sound', a cloud machine descends centre-stage:

A machine appears, the clouds break before it, and Phoebus appears in a chariot drawn by four horses.

The final masque is the most spectacular of all, with more machines and the famous Chinese scene. When the lovers' quarrels have been set to rights, the goddess Juno 'appears in a machine drawn by peacocks. While a symphony plays, the machine moves forward, and the peacocks spread their tails, and fill the middle of the theatre'. Moore thinks this implies that, after the clouds have drawn apart, the machine is lowered to the stage and Juno steps forward to sing while the peacocks spread their tails to provide the colourful background.

Oberon, this time stealing a march on Titania, gives orders that 'a new transparent world be seen':

While the scene is darkened, a single entry is danced; then a symphony is played: after that the scene is suddenly illuminated, and discovers a transparent prospect of a Chinese garden, the architecture, the trees, the plants, the fruit, the birds, the beasts quite different to what we have in this part of the world. It is terminated by an arch, through which is seen other arches with close arbours, and a row of trees to the end of the view. Over it is a hanging garden, which rises by several ascents to the top of the house; it is bounded on either side with pleasant bowers, various trees, and numbers of strange birds flying in the air, on the top of a platform is a fountain, throwing up water, which falls into a large basin.

The stage would have been darkened by closing a pair of shutters, leaving room for the dancers to perform whilst the Chinese garden was being set up. When the shutters were drawn back it would reveal the 'transparent prospect'. Lamps with reflectors would provide the light for the 'new transparent world' and probably there would be lights placed on movable machines which were worked by pulleys at the sides or the top of the stage. The hanging gardens, birds, beasts and fountains would have been painted on the back scene.

No record of the designer's name for this exotic scenery has survived. But Moore gives us some interesting information on a set of decorative panels acquired in the early 1960s by the Victoria and Albert Museum, painted by Robert Robinson, an English decorator who specialized in the painting of rococo *chinoiserie*, long before that style came into being. Robinson certainly worked for the theatre and there are contracts in existence between him and Elkanah Settle for 'severall sets of scenes and Machines for a new Opera' for 18 March 1700.[17]

Of all the semi-operas so far, *The Fairy Queen* contains some of Purcell's most imaginative music. It also shows clearly that impish sense of fun which he exploits whenever possible. A typical example is the delightful duet between Corydon and Mopsa, 'Now the Maids and the Men', when Corydon does his best to convince Mopsa that she should accept his kisses and that he is to be trusted. Mopsa clearly thinks otherwise:

> I'le not trust you so far, I know you too well;
> Should I give you an Inch, you'd take a whole Ell.
>   Then Lordlike you Rule,
>   And laugh at the Fool.
> No, no, etc.

And again we have the scene where the blindfolded Drunken Poet sings 'fi-fi-fi-fill up the bowl' to the amusement of Titania's fairies who tease and pinch him from top to toe. Dent writes: 'In songs and dialogues such as these Purcell exhibits not merely an inexhaustible vein of vigorous popular melody, but a great sense of humour in the setting of words which sometimes startles us by its life-like and even modern effect.'[18] This view is confirmed by Moore: 'In making the stage directions explicit through the music, Purcell reaches the eye through the ear.'[19]

The Fairy Queen was also the last opera of Purcell's in which his favourite Mrs Butler appeared, before taking herself off to Dublin, attracted by a higher salary. As the 'ever grateful spring', she sang 'When I have often heard young maids complaining'. Although the words are 'cynical and flippant', Purcell's delightful tune makes them charming. 'One is reminded of Colley Cibber's description of Mrs Butler acting in comedy . . . she had a manner of lending her assuasive Softness, even with the Gay, the Lively, and Alluring.'[20]

The score of *The Fairy Queen* has had a chequered existence. It is fortunate that a theatre score written by three unidentified copyists – supervised by Purcell with a number of autographed sections – survives in the library of the Royal Academy of Music (MS 3). From 9–11 October 1701 the managers of the Theatre Royal advertised in two London newspapers, one of which was *The Flying Post*:

The Score of Musick for the Fairy Queen, set by the late Mr Henry Purcel, and belonging to the Patentees of the Theatre-Royal in Covent Garden, London, being lost upon his Death; Whoever shall bring the said Score, or a true Copy thereof, fii st to Mr Zachary Baggs, Treasurer of the said Theatre, shall have twenty guinea's for the same.

Since there was apparently no response, the advertisement was placed in the *London Gazette*, 16–20 October, with a postscript: 'twenty Guinea's reward, or proportional for any act or acts thereof'. The score then remained in oblivion for 200 years, when it was discovered by J.S. Shedlock in the library at the Royal Academy of Music around 1900,* apparently in mint condition.[21]

Despite all this activity in the theatre, Purcell had somehow found time to move house. The parish accounts of St Margaret's for Bowling Alley East at Lady Day (25 March 1692) show a note had been written in the margin against the name, Purcell, saying, 'Gone'. Then follows 'Ann Peters–2 houses'; presumably the new resident was a member of his wife's family. It seems that Purcell did not relinquish ownership of the house in Bowling Alley East, but merely sublet it. The records refer to it as belonging to him. Some confusion then arises when we learn that on 28 April 1692 'At Mr Purcell's in Bowling Alley' four other females were also living there, (not including Ann Peters): 'Mrs Ann Davis, Mrs Lucy Davis, Rebecca Davis, Letitia Davis [who were] to be summoned to appear to show cause why they should not be assessed £1 per quarter'. Further down on the same page a fifth name appears: 'Madame Carhile at Mr Purcell's to be summoned'.

The full title of the book from which these entries are taken, is: 'A true Duplicate of Schedule of the Assessment of the Several Wards and Divisions within the Parish of St Margaret's Westminster, in the County of Middlesex. Made by virtue of an Act of Parliament for raising money by a Poll payable quarterly for one year for carrying on Vigorous War against France . . . After all appeals determined'; a sum total of £919 15s was collected from the parish of St Margaret's and delivered on May Day 1692. Appeals had been lodged by those who had been advised that they might be excused payment if they were worth less than £300, or were 'married women'. Since the title of 'Mrs' was such a loose one in Restoration times, and there was no real proof that they *were* married women, it is difficult to know on what basis their appeal was lodged.[22]

Presumably this would have been when Purcell moved to a house in nearby Marsham Street, as his name is in the 'Overseers' Accounts' two years later in a house where someone named Ann Law had resided until 1692. It would seem that there are two years where he paid rates at neither Bowling Alley East nor Marsham Street. Since we know that

---

* In the interim it was owned first by the composer and collector Dr Pepusch, subsequently by R.J.S. Stevens, organist and composer who bequeathed it to the Royal Academy of Music in 1837.

Purcell was given apartments in the Gate House at St James's Palace, it is safe to presume that these quarters were occupied by him from 1690 until his death. It was also in these rooms that he would have sheltered his friend Dryden from his creditors for months at a time, after he had been deprived of his laureateship. Purcell also had another house in Dean's Yard – on the site of the Precentor's House at Westminster.

One thing is certain. Wherever Purcell was domiciled it does not seem to have interrupted the flow of his output. The next play in which he was involved was the revival of *The Libertine, or the Libertine Destroyed* by Thomas Shadwell, first produced in 1675. Unfortunately there is no date for the revival. The story is based on the Don Juan legend but 'Except for the stone-guest episode and the immolation, Shadwell's Don John is largely home-grown, a complete perversion of Molière's libertine and even of its immediate source, Dorimon's *Le Festin de pierre* (1659).'[23]

This English 'John' rapes, commits patricide and murders his way through five acts – including the massacre of a band of shepherds – before he is brought to justice. What Price calls an 'exuberant bloodbath' was evidently too much, even for the mid-eighteenth-century taste, when David Erskine Baker wrote:

that the Incidents are so cramm'd together in it, without any Consideration of Time or Place as to make it highly unnatural, that the villainy of Don *John's* Character is worked up to such an Height, as to exceed even the Limits of Possibility, and that the Catastrophe is so very horrid, as to render it little less than Impiety to represent it on the Stage.[24]

Price considers that modern critics view Don John as a tragic rake and the play in general as an attack on seventeenth-century morals. Hume, on the other hand, asks if it might have been a burlesque of 'both horror tragedy and the ethic of libertine comedy'.[25]

But Shadwell's preface is so defensive in his pleas for readers to excuse the irregularities demanded by the subject, and the need for them to 'see a dreadful punishment inflicted' upon the Don, that the question remains open to doubt.

Purcell contributed music to only the fourth and fifth acts, but they contain two songs that remain unforgettable. 'Nymphs and Shepherds' in the pastoral masque in Act IV has been sung by so many children's choirs, especially in our own time, that it has become 'a hackneyed emblem of schoolboy innocence, a particularly sweet irony considering its dramatic origins'. Price considers that Purcell's 'flouncing jollity is on purpose, a faithful representation of the all-too-precious revels of Shadwell's stilted Arcadians, whose celebration is about to be squashed by the rakehells'.[26] In this chorus there is a fine example of Purcell's evocative treatment of words, so that he achieves the effect of laughing to the word 'laugh'.

The other song in the same act, for four-part chorus, is 'In these delightful pleasant groves'.

Another song, 'To Arms, heroic prince', published in the second volume of *Deliciae Musicae* in 1695, was sung with trumpet obbligato by 'the Boy'. This would almost certainly have been Jemmy Bowen whose professional career began when Drury Lane theatre was reopened in 1695. Bowen would have been only ten at the time of *The Libertine* revival but he was said to have not only a remarkable voice, but also a natural feeling for the music. There is the famous story about someone trying to offer the boy advice on how to ornament a certain song, when Purcell retorted: 'O let him alone, he will grace it more naturally than you or I can teach him.'[27] This is one of those rare occasions when Purcell's character comes into focus for one brief moment, yet tells us so much about the man himself.

References

1. van der Zee, *William and Mary*, p 349.
2. Lutt, Vol 2, p 263.
3. Ibid, p 302.
4. van der Zee, op cit, p 349.
5. Motteux, *Gentleman's Journal*, January 1692, pp 4–5.
6. Lutt, Vol 2, p 344.
7. van der Zee, op cit, p 353.
8. Motteux, op cit, February 1692, p 26.
9. Lutt, Vol 2, pp 413, 422.

10. Loftus, John, 'Political and Social Thought in the Drama', *London Theatre World*, 1660–1800, Southern Illinois University Press, 1980, pp 266–7.
11. Motteux, op cit, January 1692, p 36.
12. Lutt, Vol 2, p 437.
13. Ibid, p 435.
14. Price, *Henry Purcell and the London Stage*, p 320.
15. Moore, *Henry Purcell and the Restoration Theatre*, pp 103–4.
16. Downes, *Roscius Anglicanus*, p 89 [42–3].
17. Moore, op cit, pp 125–9.
18. Dent, *Foundations of English Opera*, p 220.
19. Moore, op cit, p 108.
20. Baldwin, O. and Wilson, T., 'Purcell's Sopranos', *Musical Times*, Vol 123 (September 1982), p 603.
21. Mandinian, Edward, ed *The Fairy Queen, as presented at the Royal Opera House, Covent Garden*, Lehmann, 1948, pp 12–18.
22. Zimmerman, *Henry Purcell, 1659–1695, His Life and Times*, p 202.
23. Price, op cit, p 111.
24. Baker, David Erskine, *The Companion to the Playhouse*, Vol 1 (s v 'The Libertine'), T. Becket, 1764.
25. Hume, Robert D., *The Development of English Drama in the Late Seventeenth Century*, Clarendon, 1976, p 312.
26. Price, op cit, pp 114–15.
27. Cibber, *An Apology for the life of Mr Colley Cibber comedian. With an historical view of the stage during his own time. Written by himself*, printed for the author, 1740, Vol 2, p 312.

16

TIME CLOSES IN

At the end of May 1692, the combined English and Dutch fleets
defeated the French on the open sea. They then chased them right into
their own harbours of Cherbourg and La Hogue, and burnt their ships
as they lay in port. This significantly dashed James II's dwindling
hopes of returning to England, a cause for much rejoicing in that
country. Purcell must also have been delighted that the tune 'Let the
Soldiers Rejoice' from *Dioclesian* was chosen to celebrate the occasion
and used for a broadside which speedily appeared with the words:

The Royal Triumph Or, The Unspeakable Joy of the three Kingdoms, for the
glorious Victory of the FRENCH, by the English and Dutch Fleets; to the Joy
and Comfort of all True Subjects. Tune is, Let the Soldiers Rejoice . . .
Valiant protestant boys
Here's millions of Joys
And triumph now bro . . . ught from the ocean; etc.,[1]

At this time, Purcell's activities as church musician and composer
would seem to have been lighter than usual, as no anthems or services
appeared during this period. However, he did receive a rise in salary
and also gained a new appointment. He had previously received only
£70, as did his fellow musicians, but he was now listed along with the
other two organists, William Child and John Blow, as receiving £100.
He is also termed, 'Master of the Twelve Children', which is included
in his £100. It is generally assumed that this title was a slip, as Blow is
known to have held the post on a regular basis. However, even if the
records are silent on this matter, it is fairly certain that Purcell did hold
the appointment for a time and is described as such by both Thomas
Ford and Dr Busby.

If, indeed, Purcell was Master of the Children, he would have been busier than ever. The theatre seems to have occupied most of his energies and play after play appeared with at least one or two songs from his pen. In June 1692, Purcell set one song for John Crowne's *Regulus*, produced by the United Company at Drury Lane, 'Ah me! to many deaths decreed'. When it was published in the *Gentleman's Journal* in August of that year, Motteux wrote: 'The first of these songs which I send you is set by *Mr Purcell* the *Italian way*; had you heard it sung by Mrs Ayliff, you would have owned that there is no pleasure like that which good Notes, when so divinely sung, can create!'[2] Mrs Ayliff was a more highly trained singer than her predecessor, Mrs Butler, and since Purcell was now exploring the Italian style and the deeper emotional possibilities it offered, she would have arrived at an opportune moment. For the next two years Purcell was to write a number of songs for Mrs Ayliff. She was

The finest singer with whom Purcell worked in the theatre and it is impossible not to speculate whether some of the other big solo pieces he composed at this time were not written with her voice in mind. It is tempting to think that she may have performed *The Blessed Virgin's Expostulation* to Purcell's accompaniment at concerts or in private houses.[3]

In the autumn of 1692, Purcell also wrote two songs, 'I see she flies me' and 'Were she but kind', for the revival of Dryden's *Aureng-Zebe, or the Great Mogul*, previously presented at Drury Lane in 1675. And again, with Dryden and Lee in the revival of *Oedipus*, in October 1692, first produced at Dorset Garden in 1678/9, Purcell provided the music for the parts written by Dryden in Acts I and III: 'The most memorable necromantic scene in a Restoration tragedy'[4] is in the third act of this play when the ghost of Laius is raised to Purcell's beautiful air for counter-tenor, 'Music for a while'. As if the play were not gruesome enough, it seems the audience also witnessed an unexpected and accidental death on stage: 'Sandford and Powell acting their parts together, the former by mistake of a sharp dagger for one that runs the blade into the handle, stab'd the other 3 inches deep.'[5]

Throughout this period Purcell would certainly have been completing what was to be a major work, and as it happened, of immortal dimension. 'Hail, Bright Cecilia', an ode for the celebrations on 22 November, included a short solo, 'Thou tun'st this world', for Mrs Ayliff. This music throughout shows Purcell in his maturity with the employment of new techniques and a blossoming of his 'Italianate' style. It has all the colour and rhythmic drive which is the hallmark of

his writing, and above all, imagination and variety in an unprecedented degree. And of course, his skill at setting words in the English
language is never more evident than in this work. Motteux tells us
something else about Purcell's skill as a performer. The ode

was admirably set to Music by Mr *Henry Purcell* and perform'd twice with
universal applause, particularly the second Stanza ['Tis Nature's Voice]
which was sung with incredible Graces by Mr *Purcell* himself. Though I was
enjoyned not to name the Authour of the Ode, I find a great deal of
relunctancy to forbear letting you know whom you must thank for so
beautifull a Poem.[6]

In a following issue the poet is identified as Nicholas Brady.

The year 1692 closed on a sad note for the theatre. William
Mountfort, favourite actor of Queen Mary, and whose pleasant tenor
voice had graced so many productions for which Purcell had written
the music, was murdered by the 20-year-old Captain Richard Hill,
newly returned from campaigns in Flanders and Ireland. It seems he
was an admirer of the singularly virtuous actress-singer Mrs
Bracegirdle, who had rejected his advances. He even made an attempt
to kidnap her, which was foiled by her host whose house she was
leaving when the attack took place. The disgruntled Hill mistakenly
thought that Mountfort was her lover. Later that night, when walking
with his friend, the young Lord Mohun, also just returned from service
abroad, he encountered Mountfort. Mohun, who was acquainted
with the actor, embraced him as a friend, whereupon Hill stabbed him
through the heart and bolted. Mountfort died within a few hours, and
with his passing the theatre had lost one of its most accomplished and
well-loved actors.*

Through their mutual connection with the theatre, Purcell and
Mountfort knew each other well and were almost certainly friends.
Mountfort was not only a fine actor and singer but also a playwright of
considerable gifts. He had collaborated in the writing of several plays
for which Purcell had contributed music, and acted in at least a dozen
more. There is a touching account of his funeral:

On the night of Tuesday, the thirteenth [December], the unfortunate actor
was laid to rest in the vault of St Clement Dane's. The funeral ceremonies

---

* Hill was caught, imprisoned and released. He was finally killed in a duel. Mohun was also put
on trial but was released to become an influential figure in the House of Lords: a typical example
of one law for the rich and one for the poor.

were said to have been attended by a thousand persons among whom were a great many gentlemen, 'who thus showed their respect for one whom they loved and esteemed.' Royalty was not indifferent at the passing of a player, for the funeral anthem was sung by a group of choristers from Whitehall accompanied by Henry Purcell. The great bell of the church, as it was ringing Mountfort's knell, cracked, a circumstance which was 'taken much notice of by the criticks.'[7]

Unfortunately we do not know which anthem was chosen for this service, but it would certainly have been written by Purcell himself.

Mountfort was not the only casualty in the theatre. Anthony Leigh, a famous comedian, who had achieved a great success in the role of Dominic in Dryden's *The Spanish Fryar*, also died tragically from illness around the same time. Consequently several productions were affected. Both Leigh and Mountfort had bought shares in Thomas Betterton's United Company which was steadily becoming more profitable. In the season 1692/3 more new plays had been produced than in the early years following 1682, some with moderate success.

Purcell had been commissioned to write music for a number of forthcoming plays, so it was not only the loss of a friend, but a possible reduction of income that he faced that season. Motteux bemoans the fact that: 'We are like to be without new Plays this month and the next; the Death of Mr *Mountfort*, and that of Mr *Leigh* soon after him, being partly the cause of this delay. The first that is promised us is a comedy by Mr *Southerne*, whose Plays are written with too much Politeness and Wit, not to be read by you with un-common pleasure.'[8]

It would seem that this was *The Maid's Last Prayer; or, Any rather than Fail*, produced at Drury Lane sometime in February (1693). Purcell set three of the songs, 'Tho you make no return to my passion', 'No, no, no, no, resistance is but vain' and 'Tell me no more I am deceiv'd'. A month later another important production by the United Company took place at Drury Lane. It was *The Old Batchelor*, the first play by the 21-year-old William Congreve, for which Purcell wrote the music consisting of an overture in three parts, eight act-tunes and two somewhat risqué songs, 'Thus to a ripe consenting maid' and 'As Amoret and Thyrsis lay'. The play was very successful and established Congreve's reputation as a brilliant playwright of the then fashionable comedy of manners. When the play was published the same year, it was reprinted three times. It is interesting that Dryden evidently recognized Congreve's talent, and had a hand in the editing prior to production. In the *Memoirs Relating to Mr Congreve Written by Mr*

Thomas Southerne (in Macdonald, *Bibliography of Dryden*, p 541), we learn:

When he began his Play the Old Batchelor haveing little Acquaintance with the traders in that way, his Cozens recommended him to a friend of theirs, who was very usefull to him in the whole course of his play, he engag'd Mr Dryden in its favour, who upon reading it sayd he never saw such a first play in his life, but the Author not being acquainted with the stage or the town, it would be a pity to have it miscarry for want of a little Assistance: the stuff was rich indeed, it wanted only the fashionable cutt of the town. To help that . . . Mr Dryden putt it in the order it was play'd, Mr Southerne obtained of Mr Thos. Davenant who then govern'd the Playhouse, that Mr Congreve should have the privilege of the Playhouse half a year before his play was play'd, wh. I never knew allowed anyone before.

Another comedy, *The Richmond Heiress, or A Woman Once in the Right* by Thomas D'Urfey, was produced at Drury Lane – probably in April – and contained at least two songs by Purcell: a dialogue between a madman and a madwoman, 'Behold the man that with gigantic might', and a catch, 'Bring the Bowl and Cool Nantz'. It is also possible that a third, 'How vile are the sordid intrigues of the town' from *The Marriage-Hater Match'd*, first produced in 1691, was also written by Purcell. Dryden, in a letter to Walsh on 9 May 1693, manages to praise one or two performances, but is mainly in derisive mood:

Durfey had brought another farce upon the Stage: but his luck has left him: it was suffered but foure dayes; and then kick'd off for ever: Yet his Second Act, was wonderfully diverting; where the scene was in Bedlam: & Mrs Bracegirdle and Solon [Doggett] were both mad: the Singing was wonderfully good, And the two whom I nam'd, sung better than Redding and Mrs Ayliff, whose trade it was: at least our partiality carryed it for them. The rest was woefull stuff, and concluded with Catcalls; of which the two noble Dukes of Richmond and St Albans were chief managers.[9]

In fairness one should not take Dryden's comments on the singing too seriously as his ear for music was not known to be particularly sensitive. That spring, Purcell would have been busy composing the music for the Queen's birthday celebrations at the end of April (1693). The ode, *Celebrate This Festival*, with words by Nahum Tate, was performed at Whitehall on 1 May, 30 April being a Sunday. This is one of Purcell's most elaborate and exciting works 'in his best Italian manner'. He was fortunate in having the services of two highly gifted sopranos, Mrs Ayliff and Jemmy Bowen, 'for whose talents there was ample scope in the trills and flourishes of the soprano solos'.[10]

Matthew Shore would almost certainly have played and excelled in the trumpet solos on this occasion, where the obbligatos range from G below the treble stave to the C above it. Although the text refers to the wars in the Netherlands, the main message is for peace, with mention of that ever-recurring subject, the English weather. It had so far been very wet and he voices the familiar cry:

> Expected spring at last is come,
> Attir'd in all her youthfull bloom;
> She's come and pleads for her delay,
> She waited for Maria's day
> Nor would before that morn be gay.

The Female Virtuosos, adapted from Molière's *Les femmes savantes* by Thomas Wright, produced at Dorset Garden in May, contained one duet by Purcell, 'Love, thou art best of human joys', the words by Anne, Countess of Winchelsea. Since it was sung by two characters not in the cast, presumably it would have been in between acts.

The question of payment to musicians was still a problem at Court. The debts inherited from Charles II and James II did not alleviate the situation. William was absent so much that Queen Mary was obliged to battle with the complaints herself. In the reigns of the two previous monarchs the vocal and instrumental music had been amalgamated and each musician received £40 per annum. In May 1693 the singers submitted a protest to the Lords of the Treasury maintaining that whereas the instrumentalists had been paid to date, they had not received any money since Lady Day 1690. The Queen sidestepped the issue, approving the minute but ordering that the complaint be 'respited till the establishment is altered'.[11]

None the less, the outstanding debt did not prevent the Queen from commanding them to play for her. On one such occasion 'The queen went lately on board Mr Shores pleasure boat against Whitehall, and heard a consort of musick, vocall and instrumentall; it was built for entertainment, having 24 sash windows, and four banquetting houses on top.'[12] Indeed, a very grand kind of boat.

In fact, no action had been taken the entire summer, and on 17 August Nicholas Staggins was petitioning for settlement of his allowance of £200 per annum 'which he had received in the time of Charles the second, as Master of Music'.[13]

In the *Gentleman's Journal* of June 1693, there is an announcement:

A Music Book, intituled *Harmonia sacra* [part II], will shortly be printed, for Mr Playford. I need not say any thing more to recommend it to you, that you will find in it many of Mr *Henry Purcell's* admirable Composures. As they charm all men, they are universally extoll'd and ev'n those who know him no otherwise than by his Notes, are fond of expressing their Sense of his Merit. Mr *Tho. Brown* is one of those, as you will find by these Lines.

To his unknown Freind Mr H. Purcel, *upon his excellent Compositions in the* Harmonia Sacra.

> *Long did dark Ignorance our Isle o'respread,*
> *Our Music and our Poetry lay dead:*
> *But the dull Malice of a barbarous Age,*
> *Fell most severe on* David's *sacred Page* . . .
>
> *For what escap'd in* Wisdoms *ancient Rimes*
> *Was murder'd o're and o're by the Composer's Chimes.*
> *What Praises* Purcell *to thy Skill are due,*
> *Who hast to* Judah's *Monarch been so true?*
> *By thee he moves our Hearts, by thee he reigns,*
> *By thee shakes off his old inglorious Chains,*
> *And sees new Honor's done to his immortal strains* . . .
>
> *Thus I unknown my Gratituide express,*
> *And conscious Gratitude could do no less,*
> *This Tribute from each* British *Muse is due,*
> *Our whole Poetic Tribe's oblig'd to you:*
> *For where the Author's scanty Words have fail'd,*
> *Your happier Graces,* Purcell, *have prevail'd,*
> *And surely none but you with equal ease*
> *Cou'd add to* David, *and made* D— *please.*[14]

Purcell was no doubt flattered to have such praise from an unknown admirer but he does not give the impression of being a man who would have dwelt too long on such matters. His main occupation at this time was to provide music for forthcoming productions in the theatre. He wrote individual songs for two more plays, 'There's not a swain upon the plain', reusing an instrumental tune from *The Fairy Queen* for *Rule a Wife and Have a Wife* by John Fletcher, and 'Leave these useless arts in loving' for a revival of Shadwell's comedy *Epsom Wells*, but the dates of the productions are not known.

However busy he was, Purcell always seemed to have had time for others, especially young musicians needing a helping hand. A letter from Roger Herbert to the Earl of Rutland, on 14 October 1693, tells of one such young man, although Purcell's role is not specified:

I am now with Dr Blow and Mr Purcell and some other great masters of musick. The doctor presents his humble service to your Lordship and offers a gentleman to be your Lordship's organist, who is a German . . . a Roman Catholick. His name is Alberrix, his father was Master of the Chapel at Whitehall to King Charles the Second, and he has had very great salaries but will – if your Lordship be pleased to grant it to him – serve you for twenty pounds a year.[15]

A new comedy by William Congreve, *The Double Dealer* was produced at Drury Lane, probably in late October, and Purcell was again commissioned to write the music, which entailed one song 'Cynthia frowns whene'er I woo her', an overture and several theatre airs. Dryden's interest in the young Congreve was shown once more in his expression of good wishes and congratulations in the preface to the printed play. In a letter to Walsh on 12 December 1693, he writes:

His Double Dealer is much censur'd by the greater part of the Town: and is defended onely by the best Judges, who, you know, are commonly the fewest. Yet it gains ground daily, and has already been acted Eight times. The women thinke he has exposed their Bitchery too much; & the Gentlemen, are offended with him; for the discovery of their follyes: & the way of their Intrigues, under the notion of Friendship to their Ladyes Husbands. My verses, which you will find before it, were written before the play was acted.[16]

In December of that year, the Purcell family celebrated the birth of another daughter, baptized Mary Peters: it was probably to mark this event that Purcell wrote an anthem, 'O Give Thanks unto the Lord'. Unfortunately there is no evidence that the child survived.

John Dryden's last play, produced at Drury Lane that December, was not a success, but Motteux would seem to question the reasons:

Whatever Mr *Dryden* writes spreads so soon every where, that I can tell you no news of his *Love Triumphant, or Nature will prevail*, since that Play has been printed long enough to have reach'd your hands before this; and I do not doubt, but that when you did read it, particularly the serious Scenes, you wisht that it might not be, as he intends, his last.[17]

The one song that Purcell wrote for it, 'How happy's the husband', was to words by Congreve, not Dryden. It was sung by Mrs Ayliff, but 'Young I am, and yet Untried', with Dryden's text set to music by John Eccles, was sung by 'The Girl', who was making her debut in this play. In all probability she was 'the young Gentlewoman of 12 years of age' mentioned in the *London Gazette* for 26 November 1693 in connection with the concerts in Charles Street. Purcell evidently liked her voice, for during the last two years of his life he wrote several songs for her in a number of stage productions. As Mrs Letitia Cross, 'a pert and lively personality',[18] she was to become a leading actress and singer. In 1698 she went off to France with a baronet but returned in 1704 when she resumed her acting and singing roles and also established herself as a dancer.

Besides his almost constant employment in writing for the theatre, Purcell's songs were frequently appearing in print. Quite a number were published in the *Gentleman's Journal* and others in *Comes Amoris*, Book IV, and Part II of *Harmonia Sacra*, which, as its title implies, comprised only sacred songs.

Clearly, Purcell was now being recognized as the great composer that he was, and his music could be heard everywhere. But, like Mozart a century later, time was closing in on this young genius. He had so much more music to give to the world, but less than two more years to secure it for posterity.

References

1. Zimmerman, *Henry Purcell, 1659–1695, His Life and Times*, p 203.
2. Motteux, *The Gentleman's Journal*, August 1692, p 26.
3. Baldwin, O. and Wilson, T., 'Purcell Sopranos', *Musical Times*, Vol 123 (September 1982), pp 603–4.
4. Price, *Henry Purcell and the London Stage*, p 105.
5. Lutt, Vol 2, p 593.
6. Motteux, op cit, November 1692, p 18.
7. Borgman, Albert S., *The Life and Death of William Mountfort*, Harvard Studies in English, Vol 15, Cambridge, Mass., 1935, p 145.
8. Motteux, op cit, December 1692, p 15.
9. Ward, Charles E., *The Letters of John Dryden*: with letters addressed to him, Duke University Press, Durham, North Carolina, 1942, pp 52–3.
10. Westrup, *Purcell*, pp 77–8.
11. Cal Treas Papers, 24 May 1693.
12. Lutt, Vol 3, p 88 (2 May 1693).

13. Cal Treas Books, 17 August 1693.
14. Motteux, op cit, June 1693, p 196.
15. Quoted in Zimmerman, op cit, p 221.
16. Ward, *Letters*, p 63.
17. Motteux, op cit, January 1694, pp 26–7.
18. NG, Vol 5, p 61.

THE BELLS TOLL FOR MARY

In the New Year of 1694, Purcell provided the music to an ode, 'Great Parent Hail', for the centenary celebrations of Trinity College, Dublin, performed at Christ Church Cathedral on 9 January. The words were by Nahum Tate, a graduate of the college. In the *London Gazette* the event was described in detail:

Dublin, Jan. 9. This day was celebrated in the University of this city, the secular day of their Foundation by Queen Elizabeth, being one hundred years since their first establishment; the solemnity began in the morning about 10, with prayers in the College Chapel . . . The afternoon was taken up with speeches, verses and music, both vocal and instrumental, in praise of their foundress and benefactors, of their majesties King William and Queen Mary under whose auspicious reign they were restored . . .

It seems there was a great deal of Latin in the ceremony with laudations of King James I, Charles I, Charles II, and William and Mary, but for obvious reasons there was no mention of James II.

On the following day there was a revival by the United Company at Dorset Garden of *Dioclesian*, in the operatic version which had been produced in 1690. It had four new songs by Purcell: 'When first I saw the bright Aurelia's eyes', 'Since from my dear', 'Let monarchs fight' and 'Let the soldiers rejoice', the latter two to words by Betterton.

The popularity that Purcell's music had gained in the theatre was now spreading to the concert-room. In the *London Gazette*, 22–5 January, there was an announcement that: 'At the consort-room in York-buildings, on this present Thursday, at the usual hour will be perform'd Mr Purcell's Song composed for St Cecilia's Day in the year 1692, together with some other compositions of his, both vocal and instrumental, for the entertainment of his Highness Prince Lewis of Baden.' According to Motteux: 'A song set by Mr *Henry Purcell.* The words by the Authour of this *Journal*, [were] Sung at an entertainment for Prince Lewis of Baden, "Sawney is a bonny, bonny lad." "[1] The prince had also attended a performance of *Dioclesian* put on in his honour some two weeks prior to this concert.

In February, yet another play with music by Purcell was produced at Drury Lane, Southerne's *The Fatal Marriage: or, the Innocent Adultery*. The basic idea stemmed from the novel by Aphra Behn, *The Nun*, and concerns a former nun married to a man who has been missing for years, presumably killed in battle. Her father-in-law knows he is still alive but organizes a second marriage in order to cut her off from the family fortunes. The husband returns, the 'innocent' adulteress becomes mad and commits suicide. Elizabeth Barry, who played the part at the first performance, was so convincing that she 'forc'd Tears from the Eyes of her Auditory'.[2]

Purcell's four songs, 'The danger is over', 'I sigh'd and own'd my love', 'But, oh! her change' and 'But while she strives' lie at the heart of the drama but 'avoid the excessive pathos of the final scene'.[3] The play was highly successful and Motteux tells us that 'it has been so kindly receiv'd, that you are by this time no stranger to its merit. As the world has done it justice, and it is above my praise, I need not expatiate on that subject.'[4]

Sometime in late April, the successful comedy *The Married Beau*, by John Crowne, was put on at Drury Lane with one song and all the incidental music supplied by Purcell. The song 'See! where repenting Celia lyes', sung by Mrs Ayliff, who did not have a speaking part, is a prime example of Purcell's genius in setting words to convey the dramatic elements of the situation. The plot is that of the husband testing the wife's ability to resist seduction by his friend, Polidor. The wife, Mrs Lovely, 'fails with flying colours' and is consumed with remorse. In the final act, afraid that her husband has learned of her infidelity, she asks her maid for a song to reassure her. She has a final meeting with her erstwhile lover and, sensing that he will betray her, she praises her husband vociferously and storms off the stage. Price makes an interesting observation on Purcell's handling of the text:

How did Purcell interpret this important scene? Is his song a clear signal of repentance, or a parody of tragic remorse, as the *double entendre* in the first line strongly implies?

See! where repenting Celia lyes,
With Blushing Cheeks, and down-cast eyes,

Bemoaning, in a mournful shade,
  The ruins in her heart and fame,
  Which sinful love has made.
Oh! let thy Tears, fair Celia flow,
  For that Celestial, wondrous dew,
  More Graces on thee will bestow,
Than all thy Dresses, and thy Arts cou'd do.

Because Mrs Lovely neither weeps at her sins nor confesses them to her husband, Purcell's pathetic, even tragic setting comes as a great surprise. The opening . . . is stark, the singer alone, like Mrs Lovely, exposed to the world. Seizing prematurely on the image of cleansing tears, Purcell altered 'downcast eyes' in the second line to the more liquid 'melting eyes' over which he draped a long melisma [a group of more than five or six notes sung to a single syllable]. 'Oh! let thy Tears, fair Celia, flow' is a passionate lament that draws the singer to the depths of despair . . . [via a change of key to G minor] from which she arises renewed, her tears having granted absolution. Importantly, the exaltation of the final phrase . . . is achieved by the music alone, since the satirical meaning of the text is delayed and thus obscured by repeating the insignificant words 'than all'. The song may not erase all about this complex character, but it suggests that her declaration of marital obedience be taken seriously. However one may view Mrs Lovely's progress in Act V, the singer has died of shame and been reborn through repentance.[5]

Coinciding with the revival of *The Married Beau* on Monday 30 April, Purcell's ode to celebrate the Queen's birthday, 'Come Ye Sons of Art away' was performed, presumably at Whitehall. Luttrell is not very forthcoming on the subject and merely states that 'she was 33 years old, and it was observed'.[6] The ode is one of Purcell's best-known compositions; the only manuscript copy of the complete work is in the Royal College of Music, London.

In mid-May, the United Company produced d'Urfey's *The Comical History of Don Quixote*, Part I, at Dorset Garden, the musical honours being shared almost equally between Purcell and John Eccles. There is no reason to suppose that Purcell minded the division of labour. He would have recognized Eccles as a composer of considerable ability and probably enjoyed working with him. The songs, 'Sing, sing, all ye muses', 'When the world first knew creation', 'Let the dreadful engines' and 'With this, this sacred charming wand' were all set by Henry Purcell, and, as Price reminds us, contain some of his most passionate music. 'Let the dreadful engines' is probably the best-known from this play and is one of the longest lyrics Purcell ever set. It is sung by Cardenio who goes mad because he believes that his beloved has deserted him for his best friend. He does not appear until the fourth act so Purcell is given the difficult task of establishing his personality immediately through this song. Like King Lear, Cardenio is tormented by the realization of his own insanity. Purcell's setting covers the entire compass of human emotions and shifts of mood, giving no quarter to the singer, who had to scale the heights of the stave as well as the depths. Price maintains that the 'lofty tessitura confirms that the actor-singer [Bowman] was not a bass but a true baritone, with complete control of high G'.[7]

John Eccles was born in London about 1668, the son of Henry Eccles, a member of the King's Private Musick, who went to Holland with William III instead of Robert King. Eccles published his first songs in 1691 and in 1693 became very active as a composer for the United Company at Drury Lane. The dialogue he wrote for the singing debut of the celebrated Mrs Bracegirdle in *The Richmond Heiress* was so successful that he shortly became one of the leading theatre composers. She quickly recognized his ability to write for her voice and from this time would only sing his music. It was Mrs Bracegirdle for whom Eccles created the famous mad song 'I burn, I burn' in *Don Quixote*.

The plot of *Don Quixote* is clothed in fantasy but 'While Durfey may have tongue in cheek, the music is pure of heart' and 'The most striking aspect of both Purcell's and Eccles's music is that it takes itself absolutely seriously'.[8]

There is also an interesting example in this production of how some incident in the private lives of the actors could have a parallel in the action on stage. In *Don Quixote*, there is a scene for the funeral of Chrysostome, a young Englishman who, because of his unrequited love for Marcella, has died of a broken heart. The main purpose of the scene is to portray the unrepentant 'cruel Tygriss' Marcella so unfavourably that Don Quixote's later defence of her will appear ridiculous. Marcella proceeds to go mad, expressing her torment in 'I burn, I burn'. The role of Marcella was played by Mrs Bracegirdle and, although two years had passed since the scandalous circumstances surrounding the death of the actor Mountfort, the event would still be remembered by the public. When Marcella is asked if she feels pity for the man she rejected, she replies that 'Pity's the Child of Love; and I ne'er yet Lov'd any of your Sex, I might have some Compassion for his Death; but still the Occasion of it moves my Mirth'. She insists she has no responsibility for his death, that he was a good actor, singer, composer and an Englishman, but was not her lover. His death was a misadventure not caused by her rejection. It is clear that D'Urfey was providing Anne Bracegirdle with a platform to defend herself against the rumours that had persisted since the disastrous event. Price suggests that the tragic tone of Eccles's dirge may well have been inspired by Mountfort, and that 'Perhaps Purcell felt no urge to write the music for this scene because he had already honoured the actor by supplying the anthem sung at his interment in St Clement Danes on 13 December 1692'.[9]

Purcell was so taken with Mrs Bracegirdle's singing of 'I burn, I burn' that he wrote 'Whilst I with grief did on you look' as a tribute to her artistry and it was introduced into a revival of John Dryden's *The Spanish Fryar* that same year.

In late May the second part of *Don Quixote* was produced at Dorset Garden with the same cast. Motteux reports: 'The first part of Mr *Durfy's* Don *Quixote* was so well received, that we have had a second Part of that Comical History acted lately, which doubtless must be thought as entertaining as the first; since in this hot season it could bring such a numerous Audience.'[10]

Again the songs were contributed by both Eccles and Purcell; the former's, 'I burn, I burn' from Part I; and five songs, 'Genius of England', 'Since times are so bad', 'Lads and Lasses, blithe and gay', 'Ambition's a trade', 'Then follow brave boys' and a Prelude were by Purcell.

Throughout the time he was so busy writing for the theatre, Purcell still had to carry out his duties as organist of Westminster Abbey. In July 1694 when a decision was made to rebuild the organ, Bernard Smith was commissioned for the work and Purcell, as organist of the Abbey, was obliged to supervise each stage as it was carried out. The original agreement, in the Abbey archives, gives us an insight into the conditions of such a contract:

An Agreemt made betweene the Deane & Chapter of Westmr & Bernard Smyth Organist the 20th of July 1694. That in consideration of the summe of £200 to be paid by the said Deane & Chapter to the said Bernard Smyth in manner followinge vizt. £50 in hand £50 more upon the 28th day of November next £50 more upon the 28th day of May then next ensewinge & £50 more residue thereof upon the 28th of Nov. 1695.
The said Bernard Smyth hath undertaken & doth hereby undertake, That by or before the 1st day of November next ensewinge the date hereof he and the said Bernard Smyth shall and will new make the present organ belonging to the Deane & Chapter of Westmr (excepting the pipes and case), & add thereto a double sett of Keys & 4 new stops, vizt. one principall of mettle, one

stop Diapason of wood, one Nason of wood, & one fifteenth of mettle, wch are to be added to the present Organ by enlarging the case backwards, And that such pipes as are defective in the present organ shall be made good the said Bernard Smyth & he is to complete and finish the same by or before the 1st day of November next. And that when the said organ is compleated and finished by the said Bernard Smyth; It is hereby agreed by & betweene the partyes aforesaid That the same shall be viewed & approved of by Stephen Crespian Clerke Chaunter of The Collegiate of St. Peter in Westmr and Henry Purcell gent. organist of the said Church; And what defaults shall be found by them or either of them in the composinge and makeing of the said Organ; shall be altered amended & made good by the said Bernard Smyth.

BER. SMITH

Subscribed by the said
Bernard Smyth in the
presence of STEPH. CRESPION
  HENRY PURCELL
JOHN NEDHAM[11]

Of the four stops mentioned in this agreement, two — the stopped diapason and the nason — were still in the organ up to the time of it being dismantled in 1936, and were subsequently incorporated into the new instrument.

In September there was a revival of D'Urfey's comedy, *The Virtuous Wife, or, Good Luck at Last*, which had first been produced at Dorset Garden in 1679. Purcell's music for the revival consisted of ten instrumental ayres but no songs.

There were five songs by Purcell in *Thesaurus musicus* (The Third Book), when it was published in early 1695, one of which was 'The Knotting Song' to words by Sir Charles Sedley. It tells of a frustrated lover trying to woo his beautiful Phillis, who is so preoccupied with her handiwork that she ignores him, and each verse ends with the refrain: 'Phillis without a Frown, or Smile, sat and Knotted, and Knotted, and Knotted, and Knotted all the while.'

The craft of knotting was introduced to England by Queen Mary who had learnt the skill in Holland where they imported Chinese embroidery which used knotted threads. We know that Mary abhorred idleness but also that she, like her sister Anne, suffered from sore eyes. When her eyes became tired from too much reading, she took up knotting. 'Her Example soon wrought on, not only those that belonged to Her, but the whole Town to follow it: So that it was become as much the Fashion to Work, as it had been formerly to be Idle.'[12]

Knotting was carried out by 'using a shuttle to produce a closely knotted thread which would then be couched down to form elaborate patterns on furnishing fabric or looped to form fringes. The great advantage of knotting over other forms of needlework was that the movement of shuttle and fingers soon became automatic and could be carried out in poor light. It was even possible to work in a coach, as we learn from Sir Charles Sedley's poem *The Royal Knotter*, where Mary is contrasted with James II's Catholic queen:

> Bless'd we! who from such Queens are freed,
> Who by vain Superstition led,
> Are always telling Beads;
> But here's a Queen now, thanks to God,
> Who, when she rides in Coach abroad,
> Is always knotting Threads.[13]

The poem of 'The Knotting Song' was published in the *Gentleman's Journal* for August/September 1694, and Motteux comments that the craze for knotting 'possesses the best part of the finer half of human kind, and leaves them as unconcern'd for Sighs and Vows as the fair Subject of this Song'.

William III had been campaigning in the Low Countries for several months and, much to Mary's delight returned to London on 11 November. His main achievement had been to hold the French at bay and recapture Huy, but there were no events which called for loud musical rejoicing. Purcell dutifully composed an anthem to celebrate his return, 'The Way of God is an Undefiled Way', on verses from Psalm 18. Also at this time, Purcell was working on the revision of John Playford's *Introduction to the Skill of Musick* for its twelfth edition. 'The changes that he made and the new material that he incorporated are an interesting indication of the importance he attached to technique and of his own skill as a teacher.'[14]

In late September, Purcell provided one song, 'Good neighbour, why do you look awry?' for the United Company's production of Edward Ravenscroft's farce, *The Canterbury Guests, or a Bargain Broken*, at Drury Lane. The plot is 'a laboured variation of the old story in which a clever heiress, mismatched with a fool, tricks her guardian/parent into letting her marry a gay blade'. It has a number of sensational scenes including 'a frantic episode of bedroom farce as

obscene as any devised during the period'. Purcell's song is a dialogue
between two feuding housewives for the entertainment of two men
and their accompanying whores.

> For this piece Purcell removed his peruke and painted the crudity of the verses
> with an abandon that rivals Eccles's coarser essays in the genre. The two
> women merrily exchange insults in 6/4 time until one accuses the other of
> trying to seduce her husband. A change to duple metre [2/4] and furious
> dotted rhythms underscore the rude reply. The argument becomes even more
> heated until the wives sing different words at the same time . . . When the
> second wife threatens violence, the husbands intervene in a homophonic duet
> to stress their peace-making role. This rebarbative piece has none of the
> graceful humour of the composer's better-known dialogues, such as 'Now the
> maids and the men' from The Fairy Queen, but it perfectly compliments the
> debauchery.[15]

On 23 November, the celebrations at the annual church service
sponsored by the 'sons of the Clergy' saw the performance of Purcell's
festive setting of the Te Deum and Jubilate in D major, the first of its
kind by an English composer. The theatrical element in Purcell's
writing for the church is well exemplified in this piece, where he was
following a tradition established by Giovanni Gabrieli and other
Venetian composers for ceremonial music with a martial flavour. This
particularly rousing music, with Purcell exploiting his trumpets and
drums to the full, would have pleased King William when 'Sunday last
[9 Dec.] was performed before their majesties in the chappel royal the
same vocal and instrumental musick as was performed at St Bride's
Church on St Cecilia's Day last'.[16] But here there seems to be some
confusion; The London Stage tells us that it was performed at
Stationers' Hall, following the traditional St Cecilia's Day celebrations. Tudway, however, maintains that Purcell composed the Te
Deum and Jubilate 'principally against the opening of St Paul's, but
did not live till that time',[17] a statement that suggests it was
commissioned for that occasion. However, when Purcell's widow
published the work in 1697, she states clearly that it was 'Made for St
Cecilia's Day 1694'. Regardless of its origins, this magnificent work
was destined to undergo some adulteration by Boyce in the eighteenth
century, fortunately to be restored in the nineteenth.

That autumn, Queen Mary was much in need of a rest. William's
continued absence, her responsibilities in matters of state, with
politicians harassing her on every side, were beginning to lower her
resistance. In the previous spring she had fallen an easy victim to a

feverish chill, and had written to a friend: 'I believe that I am becoming old and infirmities come with age, or with the chagrin or the inquietude which one has so regularly all summer.'[18] She was 32.

In May, acting on the advice of her doctors, and following the current fashion, she had undertaken a course of asses' milk which cost her £21 12s. Her personal accounts revealing enormous dress bills tell us that she resorted to a very feminine cure for reviving low spirits. She suffered from periodic depression, it is true, but she also loved 'the glitter of a silver ribbon, the gleam of a pretty little satin slipper, the flash of a golden girdle'.[19] She had a standing order for two dozen pairs of white gloves and seven pairs of shoes a month. Her lingerie followed the same luxurious style with black embroidered stays stitched with silver. And her bill for accessories alone for the last three-quarters of 1694 came to £1321.

In the autumn of that year, smallpox was rampant. The disease had claimed 1325 lives in contrast to 257 in the same period of the previous year. In the beginning of December when Mary fell ill, it caused great consternation. At first her physicians thought she was suffering from measles, but the Queen herself had more serious doubts. An interesting glimpse into the character of this remarkable woman was that, at the first sign she had of a fever and a slight rash on her arms, she confided in no one. Instead, she locked herself up in her study, and made an inventory of her jewels and listed her debts in great detail. Most remarkable of all, she wrote detailed instructions for her own funeral. In a letter to a friend, the last she is known to have written, she ended: 'I pray God to make us all ready [for death] as we ought to be.'[20]

When, in the middle of December, William announced that he would soon be off again to Flanders, it was more than Mary could bear. William's own health had also been poor all summer and his wife was concerned that, because she was unwell herself, she could not look after him properly. From this point onwards, her condition worsened and smallpox was finally diagnosed. The more superstitious Londoners were prepared for the worst when they learned that the eldest of the lions in the Tower, who had been there for 20 years, had died suddenly: exactly the same thing had happened at the death of Charles II.

Mary's calm thoughtfulness never left her, even in those last days. Immediately she knew the diagnosis, she ordered every member of her household who had not had the disease, to be sent away for fear of becoming infected. William, who had himself survived the disease that had killed both his parents, ordered a bed to be put in her room and he insisted upon administering all her needs himself. It is interesting that this cold and undemonstrative man suddenly gave way to tears and said, from being the happiest man he would now be the most miserable. Of his queen, he said that 'during the whole course of their marriage, he had never known one single fault in her'.[21]

The poor Queen, in addition to smallpox, developed St Anthony's Fire, which causes blue spots. She was attended by nine doctors who gave her potions, bled her, and 'sacrifyed' with hot irons on her forehead to prevent the effects of St Anthony's Fire. But all to no avail. Just before one o'clock on the morning of Friday 28 December, Mary died. As a mark of respect, all the coffee-houses and theatres had been closed and shivering Londoners awaited news in a snowbound city. The bells tolled for the passing of their beloved queen and the reign of William and Mary slipped quietly into history. But William was to reign as a lonely monarch for another seven years.

References

1. Motteux, *Gentleman's Journal*, January–February 1694, p 33.
2. Price, *Henry Purcell and the London Stage*, p 72.
3. Ibid, p 73.
4. Motteux, op cit, March 1694, p 63.
5. Price, op cit, pp 194–5.
6. Lutt, Vol 3, p 303 (1 May 1694).
7. Price, op cit, p 212.
8. Ibid, p 207.
9. Ibid, p 211.
10. Motteux, op cit, p 170 (June 1694).
11. WAM 9834 (signatures are autograph).
12. Burnet, Gilbert, *An Essay on the Memory of the Late Queen*, London, 1695.
13. Baldwin, O. and Wilson, T., 'Purcell's Knotting Song', *Musical Times*, Vol 128 (July 1987), pp 379–81.
14. Westrup, *Purcell*, p 82.
15. Price, op cit, p 198.
16. Lutt, Vol 3, p 410 (11 December 1694).
17. Harlean MSS, 7342, BM.
18. van der Zee, *William and Mary*, p 379.
19. Ibid, pp 379–80.
20. Ibid, p 383.
21. Ibid, p 384.

REBELLION IN THE THEATRE

William's grief at the Queen's death was a surprise to everyone. He was quite inconsolable and refused to see anyone but a few close friends. He talked long with Archbishop Tenison about religion and promised to mend his ways. This had encouraged the Archbishop to tackle him on the subject of Betty Villiers and the harm he had done to Mary through his adulterous relationship with her. William freely admitted his guilt and swore he would have no more to do with her. He kept his word, made the final break and never saw her again. From this time he also attended prayers twice daily instead of once as previously.

Another gesture for which William receives little appreciation from the historians is that he promised 'the late queens servants shall have their salaries paid them during his life as if she were living'.[1]

Within a few hours of her death Queen Mary's body was embalmed and her heart placed in a small violet velvet-covered box and put in an urn next to that of Charles II in the Henry VII Chapel at the Abbey. An order was published by the Earl Marshal for everyone to wear deep mourning and 'from 13 January, the Lords, the Councillors and all members of the Royal Household were ordered to have their coaches, carriages and chaises completely draped in black, any shiny ornaments on them painted black, and their servants put into black liveries'.[2]

The Privy Council had originally intended to give the Queen a private burial on similar lines to that of Charles II in 1685. But public opinion was so strongly in favour of a public funeral, with all the ceremony and respect that could be given to their beloved queen, that the Privy Council had no option but to concede. The date was fixed for 5 March and the lying-in-state was to begin on Sunday 6 January, although Luttrell gives the date as 21 February.[3] He also informs us that the total cost to the State was expected to be around £100,000. The irony of the situation is that Mary's wishes were diametrically opposed to such ceremonies. Far too late, a paper was discovered among her effects 'wherein she had desired that her body might not be opened, or any extraordinary expense at her funeral, whenever she should die'.[4]

On the death of a monarch, Parliament is normally dissolved, but as William and Mary had reigned jointly, all that was needed was to break the existing Great Seal and issue one for William alone. The scene in both houses must have been electrifying. The members offered the King their condolences and begged him not to indulge his personal grief to the prejudice of his own health, since the welfare of his subjects and 'of all Christendom is so nearly concerned'.[5] It was all too much for William: when he made his reply thanking them he broke down uncontrollably.

In England, the public grief over the Queen's death was indescribable, although on hearing the news several Jacobites in Bristol 'made publick rejoycings, by ringing of bells'.[6] But they were soon rounded up and prosecuted, and, in order to prevent any further outbreak, soldiers were sent to make their quarters among them. In the Protestant United Provinces, where Mary had arrived as a young bride, the news came as a severe shock. The English ambassador wrote from the Hague: 'These people, who had never any passion before, are now touched, and marble weeps . . .'[7]

One good result of William's reaction to Mary's death was that it brought about a reconciliation between him and his sister-in-law, the Princess Anne. She had written him a simple heartfelt letter of sympathy to which he responded by sending the Archbishop of Canterbury to see her on New Year's Day; and as a gesture of reconciliation reinstated her guards and received her again at Kensington Palace. He also restored her income of £5000 a year which had not been paid since the two sisters had their final and irrevocable disagreement. Shortly afterwards, Marlborough, whose wife Sarah had always held a strong influence over the Princess, had an audience with William thereby making it clear that he considered Anne's future looked brighter than that of the ill-fated James.

Meanwhile, despite the extremely cold weather – the Thames had been frozen solid since the New Year – there were crowds queuing from six in the morning to pay their respects to Mary, now lying in state in Whitehall Palace. Thousands of yards of black cloth and purple velvet covered the walls, and the Queen was lying on a bed of purple hung with a canopy fringed in gold with the arms of England painted and gilt, 'the head piece embroyder'd richly with a crown and cyphers of her name, a cusheon of purple velvet at the head on which was the Imperiall Crown and Scepter and Globe, and at the feete another such a cusheon with the Sword and Gauntlets, on the corps . . .'[8]

One of the most popular anecdotes of this period was that a robin returned each day to sing over her as she lay in state. In fact, Grinling Gibbons's monument in Westminster Abbey has a robin perched on the top with the words: 'The Robin Redbreast Famous for singing every day on the Top of Queen Mary's Mausoleum Erected in Westminster Abbey, 1695.'[9]

The theatres remained closed, but all the poets, writers and composers, including Purcell, were busily turning their hand to writing for the Queen's funeral, or to praising her memory. On 5 March, 'all the shops throughout the citty were shutt'[10] and the long procession, with the Princess Anne as chief mourner, set out from Whitehall to Westminster Abbey in a severe snowstorm 'so that the Ladies had but draggled trains by the time they got thither'.[11]

There are numerous accounts of the ceremony itself. John Evelyn writes: 'I went to see the ceremony. Never was so universal a mourning; all the Parliament-men had [black] cloaks given them, and [also] four hundred poor women; all the streets hung, and the middle of the street boarded and covered with black cloth. There were all the Nobility, Mayor, Aldermen, Judges, &c.'[12] Luttrell says there were 300 old women, each of whom had a long gown, and a boy to hold up their trains as they walked before the Queen's corpse. Prior to the funeral they had been paid weekly maintenance of £5 each 'till things can be gott ready'.[13]

The procession moved to the solemn 'March for the Queen's Funeral' by Henry Purcell, played on trombones and slide trumpets (*Flatt* trumpets) accompanied by muffled drumbeats. The Lord Chamberlain's account for January 1694/5 gives some idea of the preparations involved:

Account for 20 yards of black baize to cover five drum cases, at 3.6d per yard
£3.10s

And for 8 yards ditto to cover one pair of kettle-drums at 3s.6d per yard
£1.8s

10 January, 1694/5. Warrants for the providing of mourning for the late Queen:
To the first regiment of foot-guards, 25 covers for drumms and 6 banners for the hautboys.

To the 16 gentlemen of the Chappell Royall.
To the Sergeant Trumpett, 16 trumpeters and a kettle-drummer.
To Dr Staggins, master of the musick.[14]

And on 3 January:

His Majesties upholster has orders to buy 6000 yards of black cloth for the
hanging of Whitehall, Kensington, Hampton Court and the presence
chamber at Windsor; he is also to provide 400 yards of purple velvet for the
king's bedding apartment.[15]

The music for the solemn march had originally been composed for
the ghost sequence in the 1692 revival of Shadwell's *The Libertine* –
based on the Don Juan legend, and evoked an uncanny supernatural
atmosphere in keeping with a funeral.

Inside the Abbey, the Queen's body was laid under a silver-fringed
black velvet canopy, from which hung 'a bason supported by cupids or
cherubims shoulders, in which was one entire great lamp burning the
whole tyme',[16] while hundreds of wax candles blazed in every corner.
Then came Purcell's beautiful anthem, 'Thou knowest, Lord, the
secrets of our hearts'. Westrup tells us:

He had set these sentences before as a young man, but the occasion called for
more than the revival of an early work. Inspired by the solemnity of death he
disciplined himself to a noble simplicity and set the words to pure note-
against-note counterpoint, with the four trombones strengthening and
deepening the vocal harmony.

Many years later, Thomas Tudway recalled the occasion:

I appeal to all that were present, as well such as understood Music, as those
that did not, whither they ever heard any thing so rapturously fine and solemn
& so Heavenly in the Operation, which drew tears from all; & yet a plain,
Naturall Composition; which shows the pow'r of Music, when 'tis rightly
fitted & Adapted to devotional purposes.[17]

After the anthem came a Canzona for four trombones, also by
Purcell. Outside, the shivering crowds stood in silence as the great
guns from the Tower fired every minute throughout the service.

Purcell's involvement with the royal bereavement did not end with
the funeral service; afterwards he wrote two elegies: 'O Dive custos
Auriacae Domus' for two sopranos, and 'Incassum, Lesbia' for solo

voice, both of which were published that May together with a setting of an English elegy by John Blow.

With the Court in mourning, there had been no New Year's ode for 1695, and even the Coronation Day celebrations on 11 April were cancelled owing to the funerals of both Lord Halifax and Dr Richard Busby, Purcell's old headmaster from Westminster School, falling on that day. Purcell, to whom Busby left a mourning ring, would certainly have attended the funeral service.

The spring of 1695 was not only a sad period for the nation's loss of the Queen they had so loved; it was also an anxious time for all those who earned their living from the theatre. The suspension of all public performances until 30 March was bad enough, but the Actors' Rebellion, which had festered throughout the winter of the previous year, now developed into open warfare. The main cause of the disruption was mismanagement and shady financial dealings over a number of years. Back in 1687, Alexander Davenant had bought his brother Charles's shares in the United Company with money borrowed from a well-known 'backer', Sir Thomas Skipworth; he secretly 'farmed' the shares to Alexander, who paid him a weekly rent in exchange for the profits due. Alexander then deposed the Betterton–Smith management and installed his younger brother Thomas as manager. In order to make the deal appear more attractive, Alexander gave Betterton a quarter and one-half a quarter share. In January 1689, Henry Killigrew attempted to set up a new company; it will be remembered (see p 63) that the temporary closure of Drury Lane in 1678 was entirely owing to the wrangling between the Killigrew brothers and the pressure of their accumulated debts.

In March 1690, Alexander Davenant had sold his one share to Christopher Rich, a lawyer by profession and one of the most devious and disreputable characters in the entire history of the theatre. He lied, stole, and oppressed his actors, his sole aim being to line his own pockets. Rich secured the Davenants' share and the Patent for £80, thus becoming Patentee and Manager of the Theatre Royal. One of his ploys was to enlist stage-struck young men in order to train them as actors for 10s per week. They were always paid short and never received any lessons.

However, Rich was not to have it all his own way. Killigrew brought a suit against him for a three-twentieth share of the profits and Sir Robert Legrand was briefed to investigate the company's finances. They were found to be £800 in debt and operating unprofitably. Killigrew tried, unsuccessfully, to prevent Alexander Davenant from receiving any of the 'aftermoney', and the court ordered that profits be held in a separate account to defray company debts.

Meanwhile Betterton, who had recently lost his life savings in a private investment, returned to working for a salary after having been employed on a one-share basis since 1691. In September 1692, he had conferred with his colleagues, Mountfort, Leigh and others, to produce a statement of the rights of sharing actors. Unfortunately there is no trace of this document today.

In July 1693, the Legrand report was made public and, in October, Alexander Davenant fled to the Canary Islands. Skipworth and Killigrew then successfully pleaded with Betterton to resume management and it was through his personal intervention that defecting actors like Doggett and Bowen were persuaded to return to the company. It was then that Rich took over the financial responsibilities, but his slippery dealings with fraudulent salary lists and balance sheets, as perpetrated by his treasurer, Zaccary Bagges, was too much for honest men like Betterton. It was now civil war.

In November 1694, Betterton and his fellow actors presented their Petition of the Players to the Lord Chamberlain, but on 12 December the Patentees were awarded a government decree that no one might receive a licence to act or build a playhouse without notice being given to Skipworth, Rich and Charles Killigrew. The infuriated Betterton had resigned from the Patent company just a few days before the death of the Queen brought about the closure of the theatres.

By February 1695, the Patentees and the Lord Chamberlain were making attempts at reconciliation, but the rebels refused to negotiate. Betterton even obtained an audience with the King, who responded by granting a licence for them to perform elsewhere than the Theatre Royal. It was issued to Thomas Betterton and most of the leading actors in the profession, Elizabeth Barry, Anne Bracegirdle, John Bowman, Joseph Williams, Cave Underhill, Thomas Doggett, William Bowen, Susan Verbruggen, Elizabeth Leigh and George Bright.

So far, so good. Unfortunately, Betterton had neither money, nor a theatre, but he did have a number of friends among the nobility. They supported him wholeheartedly and raised sufficient money for him to reconvert the old Tennis Court in Lincoln's Inn Fields in Portugal Street, where the Royal College of Surgeons now stands.

Betterton also had one tremendous advantage over Rich. William Congreve, who, two years earlier, had achieved overnight success with his first play, The Old Bachelor, was clever enough to recognize that if he threw in his lot with Betterton, he would ensure that he had the best cast for his plays. So Congreve signed a contract undertaking to write a new play every year for Betterton. Even when Mrs Verbruggen and Joseph Williams left to join Rich at Drury Lane, Betterton knew that Congreve's support weighed more heavily in his favour. He was looking forward to the reopening of his theatre on 30 April with the first play he had received from Congreve under their contract: it was called *Love for Love*, and destined to become one of the most popular plays for the next hundred years.

Meanwhile, Rich could not wait to celebrate the reopening of the theatres, and on Easter Monday at Drury Lane, he presented a revival of Aphra Behn's *Abdelazer, or the Moor's Revenge*, which had originally appeared at Dorset Garden in 1676. The house was full and Rich was overjoyed. But his delight was short-lived. Colley Cibber, who had thrown in his lot with Rich for a further 10s a week (his total salary was now 30s) tells us: 'The house was very full, but whether it was the Play or the Actors that were not approved, the next Day's Audience sunk to nothing.'[18] Presumably the new management had hoped to arouse interest by commissioning Purcell to write the music for the new production, but even that was not sufficient attraction.

Abdelazer is probably the bloodiest of all Restoration plays, with the villain committing adultery with Queen Isabella of Spain and poisoning her husband; and as if this were not enough, he solicits lovers for his own wife. As Price says: 'To call it a tragedy is to dignify the protagonist's crimes.' Today, it would be called 'black comedy'.[19]

Purcell contributed a complete set of incidental music which includes the D-minor rondeau made famous by Benjamin Britten in the twentieth century when he used it as his theme for *The Young Person's Guide to the Orchestra*. There is only one song, the charming 'Lucinda is bewitching fair', written for the young Jemmy Bowen.

Later that month an operatic version of *The Indian Queen*, the last major work for which Purcell composed the music, was produced at Dorset Garden. As a play it had first appeared at Drury Lane in 1664 and was published the following year. The conversion into an opera was made expressly for the 1695 production. The plot is the usual tragic mixture of love, honour, wars, a usurping monarch, a hero who insults the King, consultation with a soothsayer and a suicide. The play was a collaboration between Dryden and his brother-in-law Sir Robert Howard, and many arguments have raged as to how the labours were divided. An interesting and detailed account can be found in Curtis Price's *Henry Purcell and the London Stage*. There are also differing opinions as to when the revival took place: Price considers that an early spring première does not seem likely as 'Betterton's dispute with the patent-company managers was so bitter that he could never have agreed to "gett up the Indian Queen" after reading "The Reply of the Patentees" in December 1694'. However, since the promoters were still intent on producing the play in the spring, once state mourning was over on 30 March, they probably looked to someone loyal to the company, possibly Dryden himself, to take over the job Betterton had refused. Price is of the opinion that Purcell had finished most of the vocal music before the Lord Chamberlain announced the establishment of Betterton's new company on 25 March. The songs appear to have been written for singers employed by the Theatre Royal: Bowman, Ayliff, Hodgson, Freeman, and probably even Mrs Bracegirdle. When most of these experienced artists joined Betterton's company, *The Indian Queen* was put aside whilst Drury Lane recruited and trained new singers.[20]

The reorganization of the company must have been a great disappointment for Purcell, who was clearly a perfectionist in everything he undertook. When *The Indian Queen* was finally produced, the casting was makeshift to the point of absurdity. The Prologue was intended to be sung by a boy and a girl, counter-tenor and soprano, respectively. John Freeman, one of the few singers who had stayed with the patent company after the split, took the boy's part whilst the difficult song for Quevira, the Indian girl, had to be sung by Jemmy Bowen – 'the boy' thus becoming 'the girl'. The lengthy aria in the third act for the God of Dreams, 'Seek not to know', was also sung by Bowen although one early eighteenth-century score states that it is 'for the tenor'. The two very well-known songs, 'I attempt from Love's Sickness to fly' and 'They tell us that you mighty powers above', were sung by Letitia Cross. There were 16 songs and 22 instrumental pieces in all, and at some time after this performance an additional masque by Purcell's brother, Daniel, was added. It is not certain exactly when this was incorporated, but as *The Indian Queen* was probably still being performed around the time that Purcell died, it could have been in the autumn of that year.

In May or June, Shadwell's adaptation of Shakespeare's *Timon of Athens* was given one of its many revivals at Drury Lane. In the original production, Grabu had written the music for the masque in the second act, and in 1693 Peter Motteux wrote some verses that were later included in the version for which Purcell wrote the music. There were 19 items of incidental music and 12 songs. However, considerable controversy exists as to whether all these tunes were written by Purcell, and some are of the opinion that only the Overture and 'Curtain' tune are by Purcell; unfortunately, only the D major trumpet overture survives.* The rest of the incidental music was supplied by James Paisible, a French composer and wind-player resident in London since 1674. He had been appointed an instrumentalist in James II's private chapel in 1685 – although he received payment for many years prior to this date. His name disappears from the records after 1688, not surprisingly since being both French and Catholic he suffered dual disadvantages under Protestant rule. He was associated with the Duchess of Mazarin and her circle in Chelsea, and went on to become a much respected musician under the reigns of Anne and George I, and his reputation as a player and composer was said to be high.

Fortunately no doubts exist as to the identity of the composer of the masque of Cupid and Bacchus in *Timon*. Here is Purcell at his best. The opening duet, 'Hark how the songsters', has Purcell extolling the pleasures of the grove with 'sweet Italianate figuration shared between voices and recorders', always a source of delight in Purcell's writing. This and the treble solo which follows, 'Love in their little veins', show an interesting development in that they 'are almost completely devoid of dissonance, a purity rare in either Purcell's vocal or instrumental music. For a moment one might assume he had finally "shaken off his barbarities" and had embraced the supposed regularity of the Italian style. But he is simply painting a picture of the harmony enjoyed by the plants and animals of the grove.'[21] The chorus 'Who can resist such mighty charms' is the highlight of the *Timon* score. For those who wish to go further, Price's analysis of the music is well worth exploring.

Throughout that summer the rivalry between the two companies continued unabated. In June, the playhouse at Dorset Garden 'was broke open, and their rich garments, to the value of £300, [were] taken away'.[22] And in what can only be described as open warfare, Drury Lane, on the discovery that Lincoln's Inn Fields were to act *Hamlet* on a Tuesday, posted the same play for Monday. Betterton's company, having announced *The Old Bachelor* for Monday, cancelled it in favour of *Hamlet*. Drury Lane then quickly altered their programme to *The Old Bachelor* on Monday. They then were dismayed to find that they had no one to play the part of Fondlewife, originally played

---

* This is also a transposition of the C major symphony for the young Duke of Gloucester's birthday song, 'Who can from joy refrain'.

by Doggett. Undeterred, they gave Colley Cibber the part to learn at very short notice and he acted it to great applause. It was said that his make-up was so accurate a replica of Doggett's, that many in the audience doubted it was Cibber. It was later discovered that Doggett had been sitting in the pit, watching the performance intently – a fact carefully noted by Cibber in his memoirs.

It would be interesting to know why Purcell stayed with Rich's company. Undoubtedly pressures would have been exerted upon him to join Betterton, with whom he had worked for some years. Clearly Rich must have given the composer a free hand and, as such, he would not have to share the honours with Eccles, who was proving to be a composer of considerable gifts. Perhaps it was a personal choice as far as Purcell was concerned. Unfortunately, there is no evidence to support any of these theories. Price considers that the surviving calendar of stage performances strongly suggests that Drury Lane owed what success it enjoyed in the difficult season of 1695–6 to Purcell's music, which may well have been the case.[23]

Unfortunately, what no one knew was that time was running out for Purcell, and, sadly, he would not live to see a reconciliation between the rival companies. Meanwhile, he was busy writing song after song for autumn productions that would sink into obscurity whilst his music for them was destined for immortality.

References

1. Lutt, Vol 3, p 422 (5 January 1695).
2. van der Zee, *William and Mary*, p 388.
3. Lutt, Vol 3, p 421 (5 January 1695).
4. ED, Vol 2, p 336 (8 March 1695).
5. van der Zee, op cit, p 389.
6. Lutt, Vol 3, p 423 (19 January 1695).
7. van der Zee, op cit, p 389.
8. Ibid, p 392.
9. Drawn from life by F. Barlow, engraved by P. Tempest (Bodleian, Gough Maps 45, fo 50).
10. Lutt, Vol 3, p 447 (7 March 1695).
11. van der Zee, op cit, p 393.
12. ED, Vol 2, pp 335–6 (5 March 1695).
13. Lutt, Vol 3, p 423.
14. Lafontaine, *The King's Musick*, p 418.
15. Lutt, Vol 3, p 420.

16. van der Zee, op cit, p 394.
17. Harl. MSS 7340, fo 3, BM (Westrup, pp 82–3).
18. Cibber, *An Apology for the Life of Mr Colley Cibber*, pp 158–9.
19. Price, *Henry Purcell and the London Stage*, p 85.
20. Ibid, pp 127–8.
21. Ibid, p 91.
22. Lutt, Vol 3, p 488.
23. Price, op cit, p 199.

DEATH OF THE 'VERY GREAT MASTER'

Although by the spring of 1695 King William had recovered from the initial shock of the Queen's death, he still looked sad and frail, and continued the habit of having prayers said twice daily. Kensington was still his home, but every weekend he took himself to Richmond or Windsor for hunting and shooting. He had also resumed control of state affairs and begun preparing for his next campaign against the French. If the Jacobites had imagined that without Mary, he would not dare to leave England, they were wrong. William had appointed a Council of seven men: Shrewsbury, Devonshire, Dorset, Pembroke, Godolphin, Somers and the Archbishop of Canterbury to act as a Regency in his absence, and on 12 May, he set out for Flanders to spend a summer of bitter fighting against the French under Marshal Boufflers.

Purcell spent that summer in what must have been feverish activity. His first commitment was to the Abbey and the Chapel Royal, and although few of his pupils are named, he certainly would have been involved in teaching some of the Children of the Chapel Royal. We also know that he gave lessons to the young Katherine Howard, and no doubt had other adult pupils. In addition to all these activities he was writing for at least four more stage productions to be performed in the autumn. And if this were not enough, he had the task of setting another ode, 'Who can from joy refrain', for a royal occasion: this time to celebrate the sixth birthday of Princess Anne's son, the young William, Duke of Gloucester, who was now second in line for the throne. Although virtually unknown today, it is one of the most beautiful of all the court odes. Despite Purcell's phenomenal work-load, there is no trace of a diminution of his powers. The only concession he made was to borrow the overture he had written for *Timon of Athens*.

By late summer 1695, the theatre was coming back to life, although the rivalry between the two companies was still a disruptive influence. *The Mock-Marriage*, a comedy by an inexperienced playwright, Thomas Scott, was produced by Rich at Drury Lane, probably in September. The plot concerned several women trying to extricate themselves from arranged marriages with all the predictable complications. It seems that the absence of actresses like Mrs Bracegirdle and Mrs Barry in leading parts was a considerable disadvantage, but all in all, the play met with 'pretty good Success, for the Season of the Year, considering it the first Essay by a Young Writer, unacquainted with the Town'.[1]

The play contained three songs, 'Oh! how you protest and solemnly lie', 'Twas within a furlong of Edinboro' town' and 'Man is for the woman made'. There are doubts as to whether the first two songs are by Purcell, but the third is certainly vintage Purcell. The foppish Sir Arthur – a part that cried out for Bowman – played by Michael Lee, boasts that he is a composer and asks 'a pretty *Miss*', presumably Letitia Cross, to sing the song. The lyric by Motteux 'is a catalogue of tasteless metaphors. Purcell exposes the fool with great style.' His great gift for creating atmosphere by musical means is seen here by a thrice-repeated triad imitating Sir Arthur's *faux pas* and,

When one can no longer stand the broken record, the refrain returns abruptly. The stroke of genius allowing one to tolerate all three verses in the reharmonizing of the first bar of the chorus to break the inane alternation of tonic and dominant chords. 'Man is for the woman made' is one of Purcell's funniest songs, hinting at an appealing facet of his musical personality. In the midst of composing the highly sophisticated and deeply moving scores for *Bonduca* and *The Indian Queen*, the great tragedian found time to write a deceptively simple song for an entirely forgettable comedy.[2]

Sometime in 1695 there was a revival of Shadwell's version of Shakespeare's *The Tempest*, which had first appeared in 1674, with two revivals in the intervening years. The music had been contributed by Banister, Humfrey, Reggio, Draghi and Locke, but the question as to who composed the music for the 1695 revival has occupied scholars for several decades, and we are probably no nearer a firm decision today. Westrup firmly believes that Purcell 'took it over', and comments:

It is *The Indian Queen* and *The Tempest* that show the full flowering of

Purcell's gifts as a composer for the stage. Both these works were written in the last year of his life and show him at the very height of his powers.[3]

Moore supports Westrup and offers the following deductions:

This is owing to his complete mastery of the latest developments of the Italian style, both vocal and instrumental, which he uses throughout with unfaltering technical facility. To the critics of the score this is just what is wrong. *Da capo* arias follow one upon another, nearly always with a motto beginning, a short instrumental symphony after the first vocal phrase which is then repeated and developed along fairly predictable lines, and with a faultless unity of style.[4]

He continues:

No one can seriously doubt that *The Tempest* is predominantly Purcell's. The Italianate manner of so much of the score may already have become conventional on the Continent, but for Purcell the departure from the style of his other theatre music was in the nature of an experimental adventure, and his excitement leaps forth in the exuberant virtuosity with which the familiar formulas are treated in the many bravura arias. Not one of his contemporaries could possibly have produced the great concluding masque of Neptune. It is as simple as that.[5]

Dennis Arundell disagrees:

It is said that towards the end of his life he began to write more in the Italian style that became typical of the early eighteenth century, but, if this is so, and if 'The Tempest' with its false accentuation of words is really by Purcell, then it is as well he did not live long enough to outgrow the music of his that we know – the strength of which lies in its truth rather than in its formalities, in its union with words and thoughts rather than in its unity of style, in its instinct rather than in its technique, and in its spontaneous vitality rather than in its considered academicism.[6]

And finally, Curtis Price draws our attention to the fact that in the early 1960s Margaret Laurie assembled bibliographic data supporting the suspicions shared by Arundell, Thurston Dart and others that Purcell did not compose the version of *The Tempest*, in Vol XIX of the Purcell Society Edition. In a paper delivered to the Royal Musical Association in 1963 she argues that he composed only 'Dear pretty youth' and the rest of the score, which came as a shock to those whose familiarity with the famous songs, such as 'Come unto these yellow sands' and 'Full fathom five', was unquestionable. To those who claimed that the music is too good to have been written by anyone but Purcell, Dr Laurie argued that 'John Weldon was *capable* of having written the bulk of the music'.[7]

Price maintains that Purcell did not set *The Tempest*, except for the song 'Dear pretty youth', added to the fourth act in 1695. It is sung by Letitia Cross as Dorinda, sister to Miranda, an additional character in the Shadwell version, and described by Price as 'innocently cheerful'. Price continues:

The singer, having recently discovered the power of her sexuality, asks how Hippolito [her lover] can sleep in her irresistible presence. But when she touches him (Alas! my dear, you're cold as stone), Purcell interjects a moment of panicky, chromatic recitative, after which Dorinda continues the revivication. Though the song would appear to pander to the then current vogue for maudlin effects, especially involving children, the composer found in her naîveté a pure vein of pathos.[8]

As we know that Letitia Cross joined the reorganized Drury Lane company in the spring of 1695 as Purcell's main soprano, we can assume that the revival took place sometime between the spring and Purcell's death in November.

*   *   *   *   *

By the end of August, William had defeated the French at Namur and so earned himself more universal respect than at any other time. Even the French were speaking of him as 'a great man'. It was 'not only one of the rare victories in William's military career: it marked a turning-point in the Allied fortunes'.[9] He returned to a tremendous welcome from the English people and decided to make a tour of many parts of the country he had never visited previously. It so happened that the Council had also voted for a general election whilst the people were in a good mood. William's personal electioneering could not have been better timed.

But before leaving on these travels William had ordered an official thanksgiving to be held on 8 September and another on the 22nd of the same month:

This day was published a proclamation for a publick thanksgiving by the lords justices for the successe in taking the town and castle of Namur, to be observed on Sunday the 8th of September here in London . . . and on Sunday the 22nd of September in all other places.[10]

Unfortunately we know nothing of the music played on any of these occasions.

Rich's envy of Betterton's continued successes at Lincoln's Inn Fields would no doubt have precipitated the production of *Bonduca* with music by Purcell, at Drury Lane, probably in early October. It would also have been timely to bring out a play which contained the martial music William so favoured. Several of the songs praised the gallantry of the British soldier, with flutes, oboes and trumpets much in evidence in the band. This royal preference may well have exacerbated the haste with which it was presented.

The original tragedy by Beaumont and Fletcher had first appeared in the early seventeenth century, and the 1695 production was an adaptation by George Powell. In the preface to the play when it was published in 1696, Powell writes that he 'prompted a Friend of mine, a much abler Hand than my own' to make the adaptation, but we do not know whose hand it was. There were many misprints and inaccuracies, but as Price points out, 'the choice of *Bonduca* for transformation into a musical was sound, since the original requires more songs than most Jacobean plays'.[11] There were 13 airs and nine songs; 'Hear us great Rugwith', 'Hear, ye gods of Britain', 'Sing ye Druids all', 'Sing divine Andate's praise', 'Divine Andate', 'To arms, your ensigns straight', 'Britons, strike home', 'O lead me to some peaceful gloom' and 'There let me soothe'; there is also a catch for three voices 'Jack, thou'rt a toper', for which Cummings claims that Purcell wrote the words himself. It seems that Dr Arne gave a concert at Drury Lane on 21 June 1768, for which he published a book of the words, one of the pieces being Purcell's catch. To this Arne appended a note:

The words of this catch are said to be written by Mr Purcell, wherein, it is obvious, that he meant no elegance with regard to the poetry; but made it intirely subservient to his extream pretty design in the music.[12]

The original *Bonduca* is a story of Romans versus Britons, with villains and men of honour, the Romans emerging as the successful invaders, with Bonduca (or Boadicea), as the British heroine. Powell's attempt to switch the sympathy from Romans to Britons fails. She is depicted as a crude character unable to rise to the defence of her country, and kept very much in the background until the fourth and

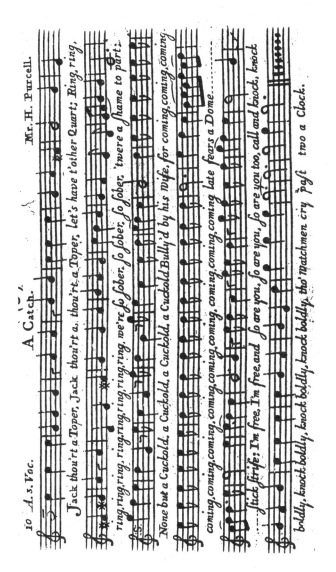

10 A. 3. Voc.

A Catch.

Mr. H. Purcell.

Jack thou'rt a Toper, Jack thou'rt a. thou'rt a. thou'rt a Toper, let's have t'other Quart; Ring, ring,

ring, ring, ring, ring, ring, ring, ring, ring, we're so sober, so sober, so sober, so sober, 'twere a shame to part.

None but a Cuckold, a Cuckold, a Cuckold, a Cuckold Bully'd by his Wife, for coming, coming, coming,

coming, coming, coming, coming, coming, coming, coming, coming late fears a Dome——————

stick strife; I'm free, and so are you, so are you, so are you, so are you too, call and knock, knock

boldly, knock boldly, knock boldly, knock boldly, tho' Watchmen cry past two a Clock.

final act where she should be singing her heart out in the song, 'O lead me to some peaceful gloom', before committing suicide. But Mrs Knight, the actress who played Bonduca, was given the spoken part only; the singing was entrusted to the young Letitia Cross.

Despite these shortcomings, Price considers *Bonduca* to be one of Purcell's finest works and regrets that it tends to be overshadowed by *The Indian Queen*, a full explanation of which is given in *Purcell and the London Stage*. The main points he stresses are that here Purcell was moving in a new direction, his contrapuntal technique is heightened and he finds new ways of expressing emotions and colour. The most striking feature of the score is its unity, in which respect it compares with *Dido and Aeneas*. Almost all the music is linked by characteristic figures and even the act tunes are related to the music as a whole. His summing-up is apt:

Bonduca is a cheap and careless revision of Fletcher's tragedy. Onto the original theme of honour among enemies is grafted brassy patriotism and mindless bloodshed. One of Purcell's greatest theatrical achievements is the reconciliation of these disparate themes through music: the patriotism is treated cynically, and from the bloodshed emerges tragedy.[13]

Bloodshed was again the theme in *The Rival Sisters; or The Violence of Love*, produced by Rich at Drury Lane, also in October, for which Purcell composed some of the music.

The play is set in Portugal and concerns two sisters who become hopelessly entangled in problems caused by being in love with the wrong person. Sibling rivalry and spurned lovers provide the mood of the music, the lyrics of which are 'designed to reveal the unspoken thoughts of the principal characters' but are sung by attendants. The part of the little boy who attends Alonzo, the spurned lover, was obviously written in for Jemmy Bowen, who sings 'Celia has a thousand charms'. Two other lyrics were set by Purcell, 'Take not a woman's anger ill', sung by Richard Leveridge and 'How happy is she' sung by Letitia Cross. Price describes this as 'a mild bit of child pornography', which at the time was much in vogue. However, the most important song in the play, 'To me y'ave made a thousand vows', was not set by Purcell, but by Blow, who rarely wrote for the theatre at that time. We know that Purcell was under great pressure at Drury Lane during the last months of his life and probably turned to Blow as an emergency measure. He certainly borrowed the curtain tune from the overture to 'Love's goddess sure was blind', the 1692 Ode for

Queen Mary's Birthday, but this borrowing was common practice throughout the Restoration period. Price reminds us that of this incidental music, only the treble and bass parts survive. He writes: 'They certainly have a few awkward passages. But without the inner voices, which more than anything else, distinguish Purcell's four-part orchestral writing from that of his contemporaries, the question of authorship must remain open.'[14]

For his next production at the Theatre Royal in November, Rich chose the tragedy *Oroonoko* by Thomas Southerne, based on a plot from a novel by Aphra Behn. It contained only one song by Purcell, 'Celemene, pray tell me'.

The play is set in the West Indies and concerns two sisters who have arrived there in the hope of finding themselves husbands. There is also an evil lieutenant-governor, who desires Celemene, a beautiful white slave-girl. Complications arise when we learn that she is in fact Imoinda, the bride of Oroonoko, an African prince, now a slave himself. Imoinda had been sold into slavery by her father-in-law when she refused to join his harem. She fares no better with the wicked lieutenant-governor, who tricks her into a reunion with Oroonoko, only to separate them so that he can have her for himself. It is a tale of unrelieved gloom throughout as both hero and heroine die in the final act.

Purcell's one song, which is directly related to the drama, is yet another example of how children were exploited in plays of the period. Sung by Jemmy Bowen and Letitia Cross, the lyric is all about the first awakenings of sexual desire. The verses by D'Urfey avoid overt eroticism, but it was obviously too suggestive for Alan Gray, the editor of Vol XXI of the Purcell Society Edition, for he asked R.A. Streatfeild 'to supply some polite Edwardian phrases in a few sensitive places'. Price comments further that 'The censorship tells more about the censor than the objectionable work itself, and Gray obviously ordered the alterations because of the delicate age of the singers'.[15] After they have kissed for the first time, the boy sings:

> Though I could do that all day,
> And desire no better play:
> Sure, sure in love there's something more,
> Which makes Mamma so big, so big before.

Purcell here shows himself as a master of writing harmonies that are as evocative as the words.

Time was running out for the great composer, but he was still
writing. Sometime in early November he set the allegorical poem
'Lovely Albina's Come Ashore', which was described in *Orpheus
Britannicus* as 'the last song the author set before his sickness'. From
this period on we know only that he became ill and was eventually
confined to his bed. But again, there are no records that give us any
idea of the nature of the illness. Westrup has suggested that he may
have suffered from tuberculosis, a very common disease at the time.

Whilst Purcell was on his sickbed, Rich's company presented the
third part of D'Urfey's *Don Quixote*, at Dorset Garden. The two
previous instalments had met with some success, but the third was a
pronounced failure. Rich was obliged to keep a wary eye on the rival
company's activities, and maintain his flow of plays irrespective of
their quality. Consequently, the comedy was rushed into production
and presented by Rich's inexperienced players with disastrous results.
D'Urfey, in the preface to the 1696 edition of the play, writes:

I must inform the Reader, that this Third Part before it came upon the Stage
was acknowledg'd and believ'd by all that saw it, and were concern'd (as well
those that heard it read, as those that were Actors, who certainly, everyone
must own, are in their Affairs skilful enough to know the value of things of
this Nature) to be much the best of all the Three Parts; of which Opinion I
must also confess my self to be, and do not doubt, that when it is impartially
read and judg'd, find many more to join me in that belief . . . tho prepar'd by
indefatigable Diligence, Care, Pains, nay, the variety which I thought could
not possibly miss the expected Success, yet by some Accidents happening in
the Presentment; was disliked and exploded; The Songish part which I used to
succeed so well in, by the indifferent performance the first day, and the
hurrying it on so soon, being streightned in time through ill management –
(tho extreamly well to Musick, and I'm sure the just Critick will say not ill
Writ) yet being imperfectly performed, was consequently not pleasing; and
the Dances too, for want of some good Performers, also disliked; all which,
tho impossible for me to avoid, and not reasonably to be attributed any way
to a fault in me, yet the noisy Party endeavoured to use me as ill as if it were,
till the generous Opposition of my Friends gave me as much reason to thank
them for their Justice, as to despise the others Malice . . . as to the Poppet
Shew in the Fourth Act, the Accident of it being plac'd so far from the
Audience, which hindred them from hearing what either they or the
Prolocuter said, was the main and only reason of its diverting no better.

Furthermore, although D'Urfey is concerned that certain ladies found
some actions and sayings in the parts played by Mary the Buxome and

Sancho, in poor taste, he excuses himself on the grounds that in order to 'do the characters right, a Romp speaks like a Romp, and a Clownish Boor blunders on things proper to such a Fellow', and explains that these 'little distant obscenities and double Entenders' are in deference to the 'Genious of the Pit'. He goes on to say that in 19 of the 20 plays he has written, he has shunned these innuendos, not only for his own satisfaction but also to oblige the 'Nicer Part of the Audience'. But he cannot leave it there and quotes 'a famous wit':

> Let but some few, whom I omit to name,
> Approve my Work, I count their Censure Fame

So here we have a case of the blame being cast upon everybody but the unrepentant D'Urfey.

Purcell wrote only one song for this production, 'From rosy bowers', sung by Letitia Cross in the character of Altisidora, a highly spirited young girl who enacts a charade in an effort to tempt the ageing Don Quixote. In *Orpheus Britannicus* I (1698) it is described as 'The last SONG the Author Sett, it being in his Sickness'. Price considers it his greatest theatre piece.

It is far less sophisticated than 'Let the dreadful engines' and lacks the tragic grandeur of Dido's Lament; it cannot ravish the body and soul as does 'Two daughters of this aged stream' in *King Arthur*, nor does it raise the hackles as effectively as the Frost Scene. But Purcell's swan song strikes closer to the heart of the human condition than any of these, with the pure and unguarded expression of an artist who had no time left for artifice. This piece transcends the drama, as if the composer, perhaps working from his deathbed, had no idea of the role in the play.

Price's analysis of the music is most revealing, and well worth studying: 'Like several of his [Purcell's] best songs, "From rosy bowers" concerns the power of music to move the gods.' He believes that Purcell was writing *in extremis*. 'This is a cry of real despair. The setting of [the word] "Death" is bone-chilling'.[16]

Death was now very close for Purcell, and apart from the conjecture that the cause was tuberculosis, we have no medical evidence to prove that it was otherwise. It is well to remember that Purcell spent his early childhood in a time of great hardship for the British people and would almost certainly have suffered from malnutrition as a consequence. His own father died when still a young man, so that the possibility of these two influences having some effect should not be ignored even if they cannot be proved.

There is also the well-known version by Hawkins, which is, of course, the most popular, although he gives no source for his information. He tells of how Purcell's wife, not approving of his frequent late-night drinking with friends in the local tavern, 'The Hole in the Wall' in Baldwin's Gardens, gave orders for the servants not to let him in after midnight. He is supposed to have returned home 'heated with wine' an hour after the appointed curfew, and 'through the inclemency of the air contracted a disorder of which he died'. Evelyn, who was obsessed with the weather, comments it had been mild throughout October and early November, so it is unlikely that Purcell would have suffered unduly, even if this story is true. Hawkins then confounds the issue by saying that Purcell's illness was probably lingering rather than acute, which again suggests tuberculosis.

Fortunately we have firmer evidence concerning Purcell's will, which he made on 21 November:

In the name of God, Amen. I, Henry Purcell, of the Citty of Westminster, gent., being dangerously ill as to the constitution of my body, but in good and perfect mind and memory (thanks be to God), doe by these presents publish and declare this to be my last Will and Testament. And I doe hereby give and bequeath unto my loveing Wife, Frances Purcell, all my Estate both reall and personall of what nature and kind soever, to her and to her assigns for ever. And I doe hereby constitute and appoint my said loveing Wife my sole Executrix of this my last Will and Testament, revokeing all former Will or Wills. Witnesse my hand and seale this twentieth first day of November, Annoq. Dni., One thousand six hundred ninety-five, and in the seventh year of the Raigne of King William the Third, &c.

H. PURCELL

'Signed, sealed, published and declared by the said Henry Purcell in the presence of Wm. Ecles, John Capelin.

'B. Peters'[17]

The haste in which this will was made would point to a sudden worsening of his condition. Zimmerman observes that the document is very rough and the clerk had not even time to sharpen the quill before handing it to Purcell for his signature. The writing, by this time, is the most conclusive evidence. The hesitant, uncontrolled scrawl is nothing like the beautiful rounded hand which we know so well from previous documents. This was probably his last conscious act, for he died just before midnight, appropriately on the eve of the feast for the patron saint of musicians.

The following day the St Cecilia Society met for its annual celebrations, commencing with sacred music, prayers and services at St Bride's Church, Fleet Street, and in the afternoon at Stationers' Hall where the secular part of the proceedings was held. John Blow had composed the main items of music, a *Te Deum* for the morning and an ode, 'Great Quires of Heaven', for the afternoon. It is not difficult to imagine the emotions engendered that day, with everyone present remembering the glorious music that their great colleague had provided for so many earlier and happier occasions.

Arrangements were made to have the funeral on 26 November at Westminster Abbey, and the *Flying Post* gives us advance details:

Mr Henry Pursel one of the most Celebrated Masters of the Science of Musick in the Kingdom, and scarce Inferior to any in Europe, dying on Thursday last (21 November); the Dean of Westminster summoned the Chapter, and unanimously Resolved that he shall be interred in the Abbey, with all the Funeral Solemnity thay are capable to perform for him, granting his widow the choice of the ground to Reposite his Corps free from any charge, who has appointed it at the foot of the Organs, and this Evening he will be Interred, the whole Chapter assisting with their vestments, together with all the Lovers of that Noble Science, with the united Choyres of that and the Chappel Royal, when the Dirges composed by the Deceased for her late Majesty of Ever Blessed Memory, will be played by Trumpeters and other Musick; And his place of Organist is disposed of to that great Master, Dr Blow.[18]

So, on that misty but mild day in November,[19] the burial took place. It needs little imagination to visualize the scene and feelings of those who mourned this brilliant young man, who, at the age of 36, at the height of his powers, was suddenly taken from them. His mother was still alive, having to bear the sorrow of losing a child, let alone such a gifted one. His wife had been deprived of a husband and breadwinner with the prospect of rearing their three infant children single-handed.

Since we know that Purcell had complied with the Test Act of 1603, the funeral service would have been according to the rites of the Anglican Church. As the procession of clergy and choir, led by his old friend Stephen Crespion, entered the Abbey, Purcell's *March and Canzona* from the funeral music for Queen Mary was played. Moving slowly forward, they intoned the first three funeral sentences: 'I am the resurrection,' 'I know that my redeemer liveth,' and 'We brought nothing into this world.' The mourners and officials then assembled in the north aisle and stood beside the open grave whilst verses from Psalms 39 and 40 were read. This was followed by the lesson for burial from the first chapter of Corinthians, verse 15, after which the soloists and choir sang four of the funeral sentences composed by Purcell himself: 'Man that is born of a woman'; 'In the midst of life we are in death'; 'Yet, O Lord'; and that beautifully moving version of 'Thou knowest, Lord, the secrets of our hearts' which he had composed for the funeral of Queen Mary just a few months prior to his own. The coffin was then lowered into the grave, and, after the earth had been thrown upon it, the last of the funeral sentences, 'I heard a voice from heaven', was sung. The service closed with the final collect. Ironically, Purcell had not only composed his own funeral music but had also rehearsed the singers participating on this sad occasion; for whom it would have had a very special significance.

The *Post Boy* of 28 November tells us that 'Dr Purcel [there is no evidence that he ever received a doctorate] was Interred at Westminster on Tuesday night in a magnificent manner. He is much lamented, being a very great Master of Musick'; and Luttrell: 'Mr Purcell, the great master of musick, was this evening buried in the Abby of Westminster'.[20]

References

1. Gildon, Charles, *The Lives and Characters of the English Drammatick Poets*, Tho. Leigh, 1698, p 121.
2. Price, *Henry Purcell and the London Stage*, pp 201–2.
3. Westrup, *Purcell*, pp 112, 140.
4. Moore, *Henry Purcell and the Restoration Theatre*, p 188.
5. Ibid, pp 191–2.
6. Arundell, Dennis, 'The Dramatic Element in Purcell', *Eight Concerts of Purcell's Music*, Arts Council of Great Britain, 1951, p 23.
7. Laurie, Margaret, 'Did Purcell Set *The Tempest*?', *Proceedings of the Royal Musical Association*, 90 (1963–4), pp 43–57.
8. Price, op cit, p 205.
9. van der Zee, *William and Mary*, p 397.
10. Lutt, Vol 3, p 519 (31 August 1695).
11. Price, op cit, p 118.
12. Cummings, *Purcell*, p 84.
13. Price, op cit, p 125.

14. Ibid, pp 75, 77–8.
15. Ibid, p 80.
16. Ibid, pp 219, 221.
17. Testamentum Henrici Purcell PCC: 243 Irby (Somerset House), December 1695.
18. Newssheet no 83, 23 September – 26 November 1695.
19. ED, Vol 2, pp 340–1.
20. Lutt, Vol 3, p 555 (30 November 1695).

AFTERMATH

There is no doubt that, quite apart from the love of his family and friends, Purcell was greatly respected by his fellow musicians. Cummings tells us that in his own copy of *Dioclesian* he found some lines in Latin written by Jacob Talbot; translated, they read:

The gift of the most beloved and most esteemed author, Henry Purcell, Priest of the Muses, who perished in the year of Our Lord, 1695, the Day before the Feast of St Cecilia, bewept by many, but no one more than his Friend and Admirer, Jacob Talbot.

Jacob Talbot was a Fellow of Trinity College, Cambridge, and author of an 'Ode for the Consert at York Buildings, upon the death of Mr Purcell'. The words of the ode concluded:

> Purcell's large Mind informs some active Sphere,
> And circles in melodious raptures there,
> Mixt with his Fellow Choristers above
> In the bright Orbs of Harmony and Love.[1]

The tributes to Henry Purcell were many, and most, including the above, are to be found in *Orpheus Britannicus*, published by his widow in 1698.

Shortly after his burial a memorial stone was carved with a Latin inscription, which in translation reads:

> Immortals, welcome an illustrious guest,
> Your gain, our loss, yet would not earth reclaim
> The many-sided master of his Art,
> The brief delight and glory of his age:
> Great Purcell lives, his spirit haunts these aisles

While yet the neighbouring organ breathes its strains,
And answering choirs
Worship God in song.[2]

By 1722, the inscription had become practically illegible through so
many people walking over it, and it remained in this condition until
1876 when Henry F. Turle, son of the well-known organist at the
Abbey, raised a private subscription to provide funds for restoring the
inscription. At the same time, Purcell's wife's name was added so that
it now reads:

FRANCISCA
HENRICI PURCELL Uxor,
Cum conjuge sepulta est.
XIV. Feb. MDCCVI

On a pillar adjacent to the grave a tablet has been placed with an
inscription which reads:

Here lies Henry Purcell, Esq., who left this life, and is gone to that blessed
place where only his harmony can be exceeded. Obiit 21 mo die Novembris,
aetatis suae 37 mo. Annoq. Domini 1695.

It was almost certainly placed there by Annabella, Lady Howard, the
fourth wife of Sir Robert Howard, the dramatist, who had a long
association with Purcell in the theatre. Lady Annabella was also the
dedicatee of *Orpheus Britannicus*. Zimmerman maintains that the
donor was Lady Elizabeth Howard, Dryden's wife, and that Dryden
wrote the inscription. Since Sir Robert was Dryden's brother-in-law it
is probable that this was so, but the claim that the donor was Dryden's
wife is incorrect. Lady Elizabeth married Dryden in 1664, and would
certainly not have been known by her maiden name in 1695.

There was also another, somewhat unusual tribute from the Revd
Arthur Bedford, known for his condemnation of the theatre and its
deleterious effects upon public morality, as expressed in *On the Evil
and Danger of Stage Plays*. In a companion volume on music, he
wrote:

It must be confess'd, that whilst *Musick* was chiefly imploy'd in this Nation for the *Glory of God*, *God* was pleas'd to shew his Approbation thereof, by wonderfully improving the Skill of the *Composers*, insomuch that I believe, no Art was advanced from so mean a Beginning to so vast a Height, in so short a Time as this *Science* in the last *Century*. Our *Musick* began to equal that of the *Italians*, and exceed all other. Our Purcel was the Delight of the Nation, and the Wonder of the World, and the Character of Dr *Blow* was but little inferior to him. But when we made not that use thereof which we ought, it pleas'd *God* to shew his Resentment, and put a stop to our Progress, by taking away our Purcel in the Prime of his Age, and Dr *Blow* soon after. We all lamented our Misfortunes, but never consider'd them as Judgements for the Abuse of this Science; so that instead of growing better we grew worse and worse. Now therefore, *Musick* declines as fast as it did improve before.[3]

It tells us nothing about Purcell that we do not already know, but it gives an evocative picture of the time. In both volumes, Bedford vigorously exposes the vice and immorality so prevalent in his day and castigates poets and musicians alike for their part in the lowering of moral values.

Another important contribution is from Thomas Tudway, who was some five or six years older than Purcell. He was a Chapel Royal chorister whose voice broke in 1668, so it is possible that they sang together in the choir; but in any case, their musical paths would have crossed many times. Tudway became organist at King's College, Cambridge in 1670, and in 1700 was appointed Professor of Music at Pembroke College, following the death of Nicholas Staggins. Tudway writes:

I knew him [Purcell] perfectly well. He had a most commendable ambition of exceeding every one of his time, and he succeeded in it without contradiction, there being none in England, nor anywhere else that I know of, that could come in competition with him for compositions of all kinds. Towards the latter end of his life he was prevailed on to compose for the English stage. There was nothing that ever had appeared in England like the representations he made of all kinds, whether for pomp or solemnity, in his grand chorus, &c., or that exquisite piece called the freezing piece of musick; in representing a mad couple, or country swains making love, or indeed any other kind of musick whatever. But these are trifles in comparison of the solemn pieces he made for the Church, in which I will name but one, and that is his *Te Deum*, *&c.*, with instruments, a composition for skill and invention beyond what was ever attempted in England before his time.[4]

Henry Hall, organist of Hereford Cathedral, a fellow chorister at the Abbey and life long friend, published an ode 'To the Memory of my Dear Friend Mr Henry Purcell', which concludes with the following verse:

> Hail! and for ever hail, Harmonious shade,
> I lov'd thee living, and admire thee Dead.
> Apollo's harp at once our souls did strike;
> We learnt together, but not learnt alike:
> Though equal care our Master might bestow,
> Yet only Purcell e'er shall equal Blow:
> For thou, by Heaven for wondrous things design'd
> Left'st thy companion lagging far behind.
> Sometimes a Hero in an age appears,
> But once a Purcell in a Thousand Years.[5]

Perhaps the most important tribute to the great composer was the 'Ode on the Death of Mr Henry Purcell' for two counter-tenors, two treble recorders and figured bass, set by Blow to verses by Dryden. Both men had close professional associations with Purcell, and also had enjoyed his friendship.

> Mark how the Lark and Linnet Sing,
> With rival Notes
> They strain their warbling Throats,
> To welcome in the Spring.
> But in the close of Night,
> When *Philomel* begins her Heav'nly lay,
> They cease their mutual spite,
> Drink in her Musick with delight,
> And list'ning and silent, and silent and list'ning, and list'ning
>   and silent obey.
>
> So ceas'd the rival Crew when *Purcell* came,
> They sung no more, or only Sung his Fame.
> Struck dumb they all admir'd the God-like Man,
> The God like Man,
> Alas, too soon retir'd,
> As He too late began.
> We beg not Hell, our *Orpheus* to restore,
> Had He been there,
> Their Sovereigns fear
> Had sent Him back before.
> The pow'r of Harmony too well they knew,
> He long e'er this had Tun'd their jarring Sphere,
> And left no Hell below.

The Heav'nly Quire, who heard his Notes from high,
Let down the Scale of Musick from the Sky:
They handed him along,
And all the way He taught, and all the way they Sung,
Ye brethren of the *Lyre*, and tunefull Voice,
Lament his lott: but at your own rejoyce.
Now live secure and linger out your days,
The Gods are pleas'd alone with *Purcell's Layes*,
Nor know to mend their Choice.

With the exception of the possibility of the trip to Holland with
King William, Purcell never set foot outside his own country. But if we
are to believe Roger North, his fame was beginning to be acknowledged abroad. Writing soon after Purcell's death, North asserted that
he had 'raised up operas and musick in the theatres to a credit, even of
fame as farr as Italy, where Sigr Purcell was courted no less than at
home'.[6] But more recently, Richard Luckett writes: 'Nevertheless,
despite Purcell's national celebrity, and this at a period when Britain's
intellectual and artistic achievements were beginning to attract
continental attention, his reputation remained insular.'[7]

So it would seem that in the period immediately after his death, and
for some 20 years afterwards, Purcell's music was still popular both in
concert-rooms and at the playhouses. Playford had published the first
and second books of *Deliciae Musicae* during 1695, and *The New
Treasury of Musick* that same year; this latter publication was a
reissue of ten-year-old books – Volumes I, II and IV of *The Theater of
Music* (1685–7), and Books IV and V of 'Choice Ayres and Songs'
(1683–4), which contained much Purcell as well as the works of other
composers described as the 'greatest masters in that science'. There
were also separate publications of songs from *The Indian Queen* and
Bonduca and a *New Song* by Mr Congreve, set to music by Mr Henry
Purcell, 'Pious Celinda goes to pray'r'.

The following year saw the publication by Playford for Purcell's
widow, Frances, of *A Choice Collection of Lessons for the Harpsichord or Spinnet*, and in 1698 came the first volume of *Orpheus
Britannicus* which contained a collection of 'SONGS FOR one, two
and three voices ... With ... A THROUGH-BASS to each Song;
Figur'd for the Organ, Harpsichord, or Theorbo-Lute'. There were
also catches by Purcell and new editions of works already published.
Although this publication of successive editions continued throughout
the eighteenth century, they were less frequent and the volumes
became slimmer as time progressed.

What was probably the first professional performance of *Dido and Aeneas* – as a masque, not an opera – took place in 1700, when Betterton's company put on a production of Shakespeare's *Measure for Measure* at Lincoln's Inn Fields. It was revived in 1704 for at least two performances which were independent of *Measure for Measure*, but was then entitled *The Loves of Dido and Aeneas*.*

In 1712 a concert performance of *Dioclesian* at Stationers' Hall was advertised as: 'Composed by the Immortal Henry Purcell, which for Beauty of Expression, Excellence of Harmony, and Grandeur of Contrivance, gives a first place to no Musical Opera in Europe'. But *King Arthur*, renamed *Merlin or the British Enchanter* had to wait until December 1735 for a revival by Henry Giffard at Goodman's Fields where it was given 35 highly successful performances. 'Giffard himself played Oswald, and published the libretto as his own revision of the original, but in fact it is very hard to find any alterations, and the text of the sung sections seems unchanged.'[8]

In the summer of 1770, David Garrick decided to mount a 'lavish armour and banners' production of Purcell's *King Arthur*, and turned to Thomas Arne to revise the score. After a cursory glance at the original, Arne, known for being arrogant and high-handed at the best of times, wrote to tell Garrick which numbers should be retained and which recomposed. He described 'Come, if you dare' as 'tolerable', but not as good as what he had written in its place, but

All the other Solo Songs of Purcell are infamously bad; so very bad, that they are privately the objects of sneer and ridicule to the musicians . . . I wish you would only give me leave to *Doctor* this performance . . .

As Fiske remarks, 'he wanted to doctor it to the point of castration, but either Garrick or the singers saw to it that nearly all the best Purcell items were preserved'. When the music was published, Purcell's items were in full score, a number of which had been reset by Arne; Arne's own contributions were in vocal score. In a later more restrained letter to Garrick, Arne wrote:

Several other things that employed my utmost efforts, were laid aside, in favour of Purcell's music, which (though excellent in its kind) was Cathedral, and not to the taste of a modern theatrical audience.[9]

* For more details, see Ellen T. Harris, *Henry Purcell's Dido and Aeneas*

As we know already, the score of *The Fairy Queen* was mislaid, so, apart from one act, no performance was given in the eighteenth century, but the charming masque Purcell composed for *Timon of Athens* remained popular for many years. Purcell's music was often chosen for the interval of a play, and 'Britons, strike home' from *Bonduca* was a great favourite. In fact, during what were known as the 'half-price' riots of 1763 at Drury Lane, the *London Chronicle* reported that 'when the third music began . . . the audience insisted on Britons, Strike Home and the Roast Beef of Old England (by Richard Leveridge), which were played accordingly.'[10]

Another popular form of entertainment in the eighteenth century, in which Purcell's music was used, was the ballad opera. This took the form of a play, usually with a satirical comic plot in which spoken prose dialogue alternated with songs, set mostly to traditional or popular melodies. The composers, even if known, were seldom identified. The first of these ballad operas, *The Beggar's Opera* by John Gay, with an overture and basses by Pepusch, was first performed at Lincoln's Inn Fields on 29 January 1728. The plot concerns the exploits of receivers of stolen property, highwaymen and pickpockets. Gay rails at those who are so infatuated with Italian opera, and presents them with 'a nosegay of old ballads in the desire to bring home to them the fragrance of their national folk-lore'.[11] As such it became the greatest theatrical success of the century. Purcell's 'What can I do to show how much I love her?' was sung to 'Virgins are like the fair Flow'r in its lustre' telling the sorry tale of how the flower, once plucked, dies and ends up being 'trod under feet'. Purcell's beautiful music manages to bestow a special enchantment on verses that are, at best, commonplace.

The changing public taste was beginning to affect many aspects of life, particularly music, and in this respect, Henry Carey, writing in 1729, bemoans the diminishing interest in native talent:

> Ev'n heaven-born Purcell now is held in scorn;
> Purcell, who did a brighter age adorn,
> That nobleness of soul, that martial fire
> Which did our British Orpheus once inspire
> To rouse us all to arms is all forgot;
> We aim at something . . . but we know not what.
> Effeminate in dress, in manners grown,
> We now despise whatever is our own.[12]

As for Purcell's church music, it was still played for a few years following his death, but when Handel settled in London in 1711, he gradually overtook Purcell in the public imagination. Nevertheless it is interesting that Handel's earlier settings of English texts show that he had studied Purcell's music very closely. Until he arrived in England, his choral music, apart from his *St John Passion* had consisted of Latin psalms and Catholic liturgical music in the choral cantata forms of Alessandro Scarlatti and other Italian composers. When Handel was resident at Cannons, the seat of the Duke of Chandos, he wrote the 12 *Chandos Anthems*, which represent 'a synthesis of the form and style of the late baroque Italian motet and the more massive choral writing of the English tradition', which he had learnt from Purcell, and, in these he 'laid the foundations of his "English" style and learnt, as far as he ever did learn, how to set English words correctly; he returned to them over and over again as a source from whence he drew material for his oratorios.'[13] We must not, however, overlook the tremendous overall impact Handel had on English music of the eighteenth century; his 'Messiah' alone has ensured him a permanent place in posterity.

'At St Paul's from 1713 onwards, Purcell's Te Deum and Jubilate, hitherto in regular use, alternated with Handel's Utrecht settings, until in 1743 the Dettingen Te Deum superseded both.' It was in the cathedrals that Purcell's music was still to be heard with regularity, and when John Robinson opened the enlarged Westminster Abbey organ in 1730, the choir sang and he played Purcell's 'O give thanks'. The Charterhouse continued to use 'Blessed is the man' as its Founder's Day piece and a number of choirs remained loyal in their selection of his anthems. As late as 1789, ten were still performed in the King's Chapel and nearly 20 were still used at York.[14]

So much for performances of Purcell's music, but what happened to English music after Purcell? We accept that a number of German-born musicians, the most prominent being Handel, settled in England and became an integral and important part of the musical establishment. But what do we know of the other composers, Purcell's contemporaries and the next generation, many of whom contributed richly to the musical life of the country? Before asking why they were not as well known as Handel it is important to remember that at the time it was difficult enough to learn the art of composition, let alone earn a living from it. The kind of patronage which was commonplace in what we now know as Germany hardly existed in England and, when it did, it tended to help only the foreigners. As we know, the wealthy Duke of Chandos appointed Handel and Pepusch to look after his musical requirements at Cannons, and the Prince and Princess of Wales employed the Italian Sammartini. When, later in the century, the young Princess Charlotte arrived in London to be Queen, she invited J.C. Bach to direct her palace concerts; hence his nickname the 'London' Bach. These appointments gave the employee not only financial security, but also opportunities to compose which would otherwise not have been available. The King was the only patron obliged to employ an English composer as the Master of his Musick, but ironically, even he restricted his commands to annual birthday and New Year's odes 'which were heard by few, never repeated and, apart from a handful of overtures, never published'.[15]

Composers like Blow and Purcell and their contemporaries were fortunate in having been choristers in the Chapel Royal, whilst others gleaned what they could at cathedrals or universities. It was therefore in the playhouses that most of the young musicians learned their trade whilst being employed as house composers.

Besides the theatre, there were also regular subscription concerts – both public and private – in London and leading cities in the provinces; and music-making in the home was still an important part of family life for the affluent, fast-growing middle classes. In the eighteenth century, people wanted to hear new compositions – a situation reversed at the present time, so the young composer had a reasonable chance of having his work performed somewhere. But by far the most lucrative opportunities were to be found in writing for the pleasure gardens which had been steadily increasing in popularity since the late-seventeenth century. The best-known were at Marylebone, Vauxhall and Ranelagh. Here in summer, for a small entrance fee, a cross-section of the public were supplied with refreshments, music and other forms of entertainment, and the high spot of the day would be the concert.

Gottfried Keller, who died in 1704, was a German composer, teacher and harpsichordist who had settled in London in the late-seventeenth century. He was a contemporary of Purcell and, had the proposed plans for a Royal Academy in 1695 materialized, he was to have had a teaching post alongside Purcell and Draghi. He was, in all probability, one of the group of 'the best Masters' who performed at the concerts given at the Theatre Royal and York Buildings.

Keller's published works are mainly for wind instruments, which may well be because he wrote many of them for the chamber band of Princess Anne, which included the famous trumpeter, John Shore.

A composer about whom very little is known, but who should not be overlooked, is Robert Woodcock. He must have been born in the late-seventeenth century and died about 1734. He wrote a number of concertos and, when Walsh & Hare published the first three sets of English concertos in which solo parts were allotted to woodwind, the earliest was by Woodcock.

The Moravian Gottfried Finger (*c* 1660–1730) came to England in 1687 as one of the foreign musicians engaged to serve in the Roman Catholic chapel of James II. When James II fled the country the following year, the Protestant rule of William and Mary precluded any further royal employment. Nevertheless, Finger, with some support from the Duke of Manchester, managed to follow an independent career with success.

Finger composed numerous odes, incidental music for plays, and some excellent instrumental music, much of which he had published both in London and Amsterdam. In January 1696 his Farewell for Henry Purcell (using *flatt* trumpets) was performed.

On 21 March 1700, an advertisement appeared in the *London Gazette*: 'Several persons of quality having for the encouragement of musick advanced 200 guineas to be distributed in four prizes, the first of 100, the second of 50, the third of 30, and the fourth of 20 guineas to each master as shall be judged to compose the best.' The contenders would have been challenged to set to music the text of a masque, *The Judgement of Paris* by William Congreve, then one of the leading dramatists of the day. John Weldon won first prize, the others being awarded to John Eccles, Daniel Purcell and Gottfried Finger respectively. Many were of the opinion that Finger should have been given first place, and he was so put out by the decision that he vowed he would no longer stay in England. However, he did stay long enough to attend the first performance of his opera, *The Virgin Prophetess*, which was said to exceed even Henry Purcell's *Dioclesian* in grandiose spectacle.

Jeremiah Clarke (1674–1707) was a child of the Chapel Royal and later took over from Blow as Master of the Choristers at St Paul's Cathedral. In 1700, Clarke and his former fellow pupil William Croft were sworn in as Gentlemen Extraordinary of the Chapel Royal and four years later as joint organists. Although today Clarke is mainly remembered as a composer of church music, he wrote a number of harpsichord pieces and songs, and was also very active in the theatre where his gift for melody and clean, direct instrumental writing served him well. His odes marked not only court celebrations, but also other special occasions, such as 'Come, come along for a dance and a song' composed upon the death of Purcell and performed at Drury Lane Theatre. However, it is through his famous 'Trumpet Voluntary' that his name has been handed down to posterity. This came about when Sir Henry Wood arranged the piece for trumpet, organ and drums and ascribed it to Purcell. It would appear that Wood had consulted a nineteenth-century organ arrangement which mistakenly attributed it to Purcell. Although it may well have begun life as a piece for trumpet and wind ensemble, when published in 1700 in *A Choice Collection of Ayres for the Harpsichord*, it was called 'The Prince of Denmark's March' having been written for Queen Anne's brother-in-law. Clarke's career ended in suicide when he was only 33, the result of an unhappy love affair.

John Weldon (1676–1736), who won first prize in the previously mentioned *Judgement of Paris* competition, received his early training as a chorister at Eton College and must have shown early promise for he was sent to have lessons with Purcell from sometime in 1693. At 18 he was appointed organist at New College, Oxford. During the next few years Weldon composed some vocal theatre music and a number of songs.

When Blow died in 1708, Weldon was appointed an organist of the Chapel Royal, after which his interest in secular music declined. In 1714, he was sworn in as second composer to the Chapel Royal.

Weldon, though a composer of considerable talent,

never quite fulfilled his early promise . . . His melodic range was wide . . . His word-setting was often sensitive and rhythmically subtle, though he over-indulged in lengthy roulades and certain favourite turns of phrase. He could make effective use of chromatic passages and Purcellian plunges into the minor for expressive purposes, but his normal harmonic idiom was rather conventional and his range of modulation restricted.[16]

Another gifted composer, William Croft (1678–1727), was a chorister in the Chapel Royal under Blow, who soon recognized and nurtured what appeared to be an extraordinary talent. Croft was only 22 when he was appointed, together with Clarke, a Gentleman Extraordinary of the Chapel Royal. In 1708, he succeeded Blow as composer and Master of the Children of the Chapel Royal, and in addition was appointed organist of Westminster Abbey.

Croft did write some songs and a few string pieces for the theatre, but they are not especially noteworthy. His harpsichord music 'is smoother and more regularly turned than that of Blow', while his

'Hymn on Divine Musick' from *Harmonia Sacra*, ii (1714), 'is worthily in the line of Purcell's sacred songs but has less intensity of feeling . . .'

It is through his church music that Croft is remembered today. His writing was distinguished by its 'rhythmic vocabulary, contour of phrase, [and] clarity of tonality'. Watkins Shaw claims that 'it was Croft who among composers of his generation most decisively turned a new page in the history of the verse anthem'.[17]

The Italians had always been popular with the English royals and nobility and Giovanni Bononcini was no exception. He was born in Modena in 1670 and came to London in 1720 to take up a post as composer to the Royal Academy of Music on the recommendation of the Earl of Burlington. He met with considerable success in London with his operas, but one of his patrons was a known Jacobite and the cabals against him were so strong that he thereupon left London promising not to return. He did return, however, in 1724, when Henrietta, Duchess of Marlborough gave him a stipend of £500 for life to direct performances at her own private concerts, but in 1731 he went to Vienna and died there in 1747. Bononcini's vast output included a great many dramatic works and solo cantatas, and a few instrumental compositions. 'His graceful arias were very affecting within their dramatic context' and his text setting was 'indescribably expressive of human passions . . . and in the true genius of the Italian language'.[18]

Another very important Italian, Francesco Geminiani, was born in Lucca in 1687 and came to London in 1714 where he scored an immediate success as a violin virtuoso. He went on to become a celebrated teacher whose influence reached a much wider public on account of his writings on the subject. To a large extent, Geminiani was overshadowed by his teacher Corelli and his contemporaries, so that his 'highly original and expressive'[19] compositions tend to be overlooked. Geminiani lived mainly in London until about 1760 after which he went to Dublin where he died in 1762.

A German-born composer who worked in London during the first half of the eighteenth century was John Ernest Galliard (c 1687–1749). In 1706 he came to London as a court musician to Prince George of Denmark, and when Draghi died in 1710, he was appointed organist to Charles II's widow at Somerset House.

Galliard was one of the most outstanding theatrical composers of his day. He worked for some 13 years with Rich at Lincoln's Inn Fields and it was here that he first collaborated with the writer Lewis Theobald in supplying the music for a masque, *Pan and Syrinx*.

It was about 1723 that the first pantomime was seen on the London stage; those written by Theobald and Galliard and produced at Lincoln's Inn Fields and later at Covent Garden were so successful that they provided Rich with his chief source of income. Since the music was continuous throughout, Galliard had ample opportunity to display his considerable gifts. He seems to have been extremely versatile in that, besides his enormous output for the playhouse, he wrote four operas, some church music and several sonatas and concertos, predominantly featuring solo woodwind.

The Londoner, Maurice Greene (1696–1755), was a contemporary of Handel – who nicknamed him 'Dr Blew'. He is remembered mainly for his church music, but he was 'also an important composer of keyboard music, songs and extended vocal works'. Greene came from a well-to-do family and his father was a chaplain of the Chapel Royal. He received his musical training as a chorister at St Paul's under Jeremiah Clarke and Charles King, and was only 18 when he took up his first appointment as organist of St Dunstan-in-the-West, Fleet Street. Four years later he became organist at St Andrew's Holborn, a post previously held by Daniel Purcell. On the death of Croft in 1727, Greene was appointed organist and composer of the Chapel Royal. Before he was 40 he was made Master of the King's Musick.

Greene's music was 'generally buoyant and attractively tuneful . . . more elegant and polished than that of almost all his immediate predecessors and contemporaries'. Like Purcell, Greene had an affinity for setting words to music, and it has been suggested that, had his career taken a different turn, he might easily have become a first-rate composer of opera.

H. Diack Johnstone writes that Greene was 'a born melodist of the front rank, perhaps a shade less individual than Arne, but in no way inferior. Greene undoubtedly was a genius, though the fire of inspiration burnt fitfully.'[20]

A prominent figure in the early eighteenth century was the composer and violinist, Michael Festing. His birthdate is unknown but he died in 1752. Festing was primarily a violin virtuoso, and most of his writing was for that instrument. He was taught at first by Richard Jones, leader of the band at Drury Lane, and later by Geminiani. He then became a well-known teacher of the violin and numbered Arne among his pupils. In 1735 he was appointed a member of the King's Private Band and two years later became director of the Italian opera house. His enthusiastic involvement in concert activities in London meant that his compositions, mostly for sonatas and concertos of moderate difficulty, were in regular demand by the music clubs and amateur societies.

The pleasure gardens, which were then coming into vogue as fashionable places of entertainment, gave Festing yet another platform for his talents. He was appointed musical director of Ranelagh when it opened in 1742, and provided music and led the band there for ten years.

Festing's violin compositions all reflect his sound knowledge of the instrument and contain a great many advanced ideas such as

rapid string crossing between high and low registers with dramatic and abrupt tonal contrasts. Passages of elaborate virtuosity are frequently of an improvisatory nature and reflect the influence of Geminiani . . . His vocal compositions consist mainly of cantatas and songs written for Ranelagh, which were very popular and after his death were included in numerous vocal collections and arrangements for flute, violin and keyboard.[21]

William Hayes (1708–77) was born in Gloucester and showed an early talent for music. He was a chorister at Gloucester Cathedral and in 1731 became organist at Worcester Cathedral. Three years later he was appointed organist and master of the choristers at Magdalen College, Oxford and in 1742 was elected Professor of Music at the university. The Holywell Music Room was opened in 1748 during Hayes's tenure of office, and from this time he directed the weekly concerts which were held there and were to become one of the city's most popular musical events. His activities were not confined to church and university: in 1765 he was elected a 'privileged member' of the Noblemen's and Gentlemen's Catch Club, having already won several prizes offered by that society.

'Hayes's musical style is much indebted to Handel, especially in his large-scale work. French overtures, accompanied recitative, vivid portrayal of emotions such as rage, and the choral writing all reflect Handel's influence . . . His melodic writing tends to lack freshness of inspiration, but he nevertheless ranks highly among English 18th-century composers.'[22]

Charles Avison (1709–70) has been described as 'the most important English concerto composer of the 18th century and an original and influential writer on music'. He was born in Newcastle-upon-Tyne, where he played an important part in all that city's musical activities, most notably the series of subscription concerts under his direction, of which he was appointed musical director at the age of 29. This was a post that he retained, together with that of organist of St Nicholas Church (now the Cathedral) until his death.

Despite this busy schedule, Avison also gave concerts in Durham, Edinburgh, Dublin and London. His reputation was certainly not confined to Newcastle. He had a number of important posts offered him over the years, but he turned them down, preferring to keep his base in the north-east; these included organist at York Minster, two similar posts in Dublin, recommended by his teacher, Geminiani, and the succession to Pepusch as organist at the Charterhouse, London.

As a composer, Avison is best-known for his 60 concerti grossi for strings, in general modelled on Geminiani's. 'Stylistically there is little difference between the early works and the late ones. If somewhat lightweight in texture and in content, Avison's concertos are unusually tuneful; he was a firm believer in the value of "air" or melody.'

Burney tells us that Avison was 'an ingenious and polished man, esteemed and respected by all who knew him; and an elegant writer upon his art.'[23]

The leading figure in English theatrical music in the mid-eighteenth century, was Thomas Arne (1710–78). He was educated at Eton and originally destined for the law, but his musical talent manifested itself very early and his family agreed to allow him to follow a career in music. He was taught the violin by Michael Festing and was said to have an exceptional gift for this instrument, but it was in the theatre that he felt happiest. As a young boy, he would gain admission to the gallery of the Italian opera dressed in livery borrowed from a servant.

In 1734 Arne's masque *Dido and Aeneas* was performed with great success at the Haymarket Theatre and Arne, his brother and sister were engaged to appear at Drury Lane. Arne's *Comus* was an immediate success at Drury Lane and his reputation in the theatre steadily grew. He spent some time in Dublin playing his own and Handel's music and on his return he became the leading composer at Vauxhall, Ranelagh and Marylebone Pleasure Gardens for some 20 years. In 1762, he achieved his greatest success when his opera *Artaxerxes* was produced at Covent Garden, although he achieved immortality by the song, 'Rule, Britannia' in the masque, *Alfred*, given by command of the Prince of Wales.

Arne's prolific output included odes, cantatas, catches, sacred and instrumental music, but his talent was best employed in his dramatic works and songs. Arne's Shakespeare songs have remained an important part of the English musical heritage, and the best of these 'have an elegance and melodiousness that rise above the tide of musical fashion . . . It was indeed Arne's unique gift of melody that made him the most significant English composer of his century.' As a nineteenth-century writer put it:

There was in Arne's compositions a natural ease and elegance, a flow of melody which stole upon the senses, and a fullness and variety in the harmony which satisfied, without surprising the auditor by any new, affected, or extraneous modulation. He had neither the vigour of Purcell, nor the grandeur, simplicity and magnificence of Handel, he apparently aimed at pleasing, and he has fully succeeded.[24]

William Boyce (1711–79) was equally known for his church music as for that he wrote for the theatre. He was 'regarded as the leading English representative of the late Baroque style, and was also significant for his role as a musical antiquarian and editor'. His music has 'a fresh vigour, perhaps of a specially English quality, that distinguishes it from Arne and other contemporaries. It is especially evident in his masterly fugues and in his dance movements, of which the gavottes and gigues are outstanding.'

Boyce was yet another who started as a chorister at St Paul's under Charles King and later became a pupil of both Maurice Greene and Pepusch. He held a number of important posts as organist in city churches and in 1736 was appointed composer to the Chapel Royal, succeeding John Weldon.

For some time Boyce had been writing songs for Vauxhall Gardens and he had also composed an oratorio, *David's Lamentation over Saul and Jonathan*, and in 1740 tackled a short opera *Peleus and Thetis*. It was his serenata *Solomon* that became popular enough not only to receive regular performances but also to be published in full score. At the turn of the century it declined in its popularity owing to the eroticism of some of the text.

Boyce was sworn in as Master of the King's Musick in 1757 and a year later appointed one of the three organists of the Chapel Royal. In the latter part of his life through increasing deafness he concerned himself mainly with editing. His master, Maurice Greene, had started a collection of church music but died before it could be completed. Boyce took over the project and in so doing became the owner of 'a music library without parallel in Britain'. His *Cathedral Music* was published in three volumes from 1760 to 1773. This was, at the time, 'of inestimable value in preserving the tradition of English church music at its best, and it exerted a strong influence on 19th-century taste and knowledge'.[25] However, some composers did better than others; some of Purcell's music, especially his *Te Deum and Jubilate in D*, was almost unrecognizable after Boyce's editing. Only much later did more informed scholars redress the balance.

Another important contemporary of Boyce was John Stanley (1712–86) who, as the result of an accident, was blind from the age of two. His musical gifts were considerable and he became a pupil of Maurice Greene at St Paul's. By the age of 12 he was appointed organist at the church of All Hallows, Bread Street. In 1727 he was made organist to the Honourable Society of the Inner Temple and, according to Burney, his playing of voluntaries at the Temple attracted musicians, including Handel, from all over London. He was also a very fine violinist and for many years directed concerts at the Swan Tavern, Cornhill. In 1729, at 17, he became the youngest person ever to gain the B. Mus. degree at Oxford University.

Stanley is mainly remembered today for his three published sets of organ voluntaries, but his concertos and cantatas are more interesting, as they illustrate the role he played in the transition from the Handelian baroque to the *galant* style associated in England with J.C. Bach, the 'London' Bach. 'The six concertos op. 2 are among the finest English string concertos in the Corelli–Handel tradition, and they were popular enough to be reissued in arrangements for organ and also as solos for violin, flute or harpsichord.'[26]

One of the most respected of the German musicians who settled in London, Carl Friedrich Abel (1723–87), came from a long line of talented musicians who were noted viola da gamba players. Abel came to London in 1758 and from this time spent most of his life there. He followed in the family tradition, playing the viola da gamba on a virtuoso level. At his first public concert in London in 1759, he played the viola da gamba, the harpsichord, Sir Ernest Walpole's newly invented pentachord, and in addition composed most of the music performed. His reputation became established quite soon through his own concerts and those of other artists under his direction.

In 1764 Abel gave a concert together with J.C. Bach and from this point there existed a close collaboration between the two families, leading to the creation the following year of the highly successful Bach–Abel concert series, which continued until 1781. This led to Bach and Abel building their own concert-hall in Hanover Square where they held oratorio evenings, presenting new works by each composer. About 1764, both men were appointed chamber musicians to Queen Charlotte, and held their posts until their deaths.

Abel's music was mainly instrumental, and he naturally wrote well for the viola da gamba. His style was tuneful and light-hearted – he seldom used minor keys. His slow-movements 'usually have elegant lyrical, highly ornamented melodies of considerable breadth'.[27]

Johann Christian Bach (1735–82), son of Johann Sebastian Bach and his second wife, Anna Magdalena, first came to London in 1762, and from this time spent the greater part of his life there. He made a strong impression on the eight-year-old Mozart when he visited London in 1764, and they were said to improvise together on several occasions. As we know, Bach and Abel were the most important influence in the establishment of regular public concerts in London. Unhappily, after some time, the popularity of these declined and Bach suffered considerable financial hardship. Although he had contributed so much to the musical life of London in particular, when he died there in 1782, the event went almost unnoticed.

As a composer, he was one the most versatile of his age. His output was enormous and covered practically every genre, from sacred, dramatic and instrumental to symphonies, concertos, cantatas and keyboard.

He was not ranked among the top echelons but

In a broader historical perspective he can be seen as a highly significant figure of his time, the chief master of the *galant* style, who produced music of elegance, formality and aptness for its social purpose, and was able to infuse it with both vigour and refined sensibility.[28]

One of the most successful composers of his day was James Hook (1746–1827), that rare phenomenon, the child prodigy who fulfilled his early promise. He could play the harpsichord at four and appeared in concerts from the age of six. He was eleven when his father died, and from this time set out to make a career for himself in music. He was soon able to support himself by teaching at a local boarding-school in Norwich and performing at concerts in that city. He also advertised that he could teach guitar, harpsichord, spinet, violin and German flute, compose music for any instrument, and transpose or copy any music put before him; he was even prepared to tune any keyboard instrument. Hook was reputed to be an excellent piano-teacher from which he is said to have earned some £600 a year – a great deal of money in those days.

Hook soon became known as a composer of light, tuneful music for entertainment, and about 1768 he was employed as organist and

composer at Marylebone Gardens. In 1774 he was engaged by
Vauxhall as musical director and held the post for almost 50 years. He
wrote more than 200 songs for Vauxhall and many of these were
published in the annual collection of 'Vauxhall Songs'. Hook was
known for being generous to his fellow countrymen, making many
opportunities for their works to be performed. The Italians living in
London jealously criticized him and accused him of plagiarism. Since
there were no copyright rules at the time, everyone was free to use any
tune that took their fancy; therefore it would seem that it was his talent
they envied, more than what he did with their music.

Hook was a prolific composer in many fields apart from his songs,
theatre music and catches. He wrote odes, cantatas, concertos, works
for keyboard and other chamber music ensembles. He even produced
a complete book of instruction for beginners on the harpsichord or
pianoforte, published in three volumes.

These then were the main composers in the wake of Purcell; many, as
we have seen, were highly gifted, and thanks to the efforts of the music
revivalists, much of their writing has survived and is performed today.
But with the exception of Handel, however enchanting their melodies, or
impressive their dramatic content, not one of them could stand beside
Henry Purcell, truly the 'Glory of his Age'.

References

1. Cummings, *Purcell*, notes opposite p 76.
2. W.D.M. in *Notes & Queries*, 5th ser, 4 (30 October 1875), p 359, in
   Zimmerman, p 261.
3. Bedford, Arthur, *The Great Abuse of Musick*, John Wyatt, 1711, p 196.
4. Cummings, op cit, p 87.
5. Ibid, pp 88–9.
6. North, *On Music*, p 307n.
7. Luckett, Richard, 'Or rather our Musical Shakespeare', *Music in
   Eighteenth Century England*, ed C. Hogwood and R. Luckett,
   Cambridge University Press, 1983, p 64.
8. Fiske, Roger *English Theatre Music in the Eighteenth Century*, Oxford
   University Press, 1986, p 144.
9. Ibid, pp 359–60.
10. Ibid, p 259.
11. Dupré, Henri, *Purcell*, English trans, Knopf, New York, 1928, p 193.
12. Carey, Henry, 'The Poet's Resentment', *The Poems*, ed Frederick T.
    Wood, 1930, p 102.

13. Harman, Alec, and Mellers, Wilfrid, *Man and His Music*, Barrie & Jenkins, 1971, p 514.
14. Luckett, op cit, p 68.
15. *The Eighteenth Century*, ed H. Diack Johnstone and Roger Fiske, Blackwell, 1990, p 11.
16. NG, Vol 20, p 331.
17. NG, Vol 5, p 56.
18. NG, Vol 3, pp 31–2.
19. NG, Vol 7, p 223.
20. NG, Vol 7, pp 684–6.
21. NG, Vol 6, pp 504–5.
22. NG, Vol 8, p 413.
23. NG, Vol 1, pp 749–50.
24. NG, Vol 1, pp 605–8.
25. NG, Vol 3, pp 138–41.
26. NG, Vol 18, p 76.
27. NG, Vol 1, p 13.
28. NG, Vol 1, p 872.

EPILOGUE

In the nineteenth century, interest in Purcell's music declined. A few old favourite anthems such as 'I was glad' and 'Rejoice in the Lord alway' were probably still sung in the cathedrals where both services and anthems would have been less subject to change. But in general, it is unlikely that his church music was much favoured, because it was too flamboyant for the religious revivalists. Conversely, his keyboard music was too primitive for virtuoso exponents of the day. Another problem was that by this time, the scholars and musicians had already lost touch with the performing styles of the classical period, let alone the seventeenth century. Their approach was strictly through nineteenth-century ears, when 'bigness' was worshipped and the pianoforte dominated all musical performance whether amateur or professional. Furthermore, music was veering towards romanticism and once that had taken hold of the scene – in Britain in particular – there was little hope that there would be an interest in the music of an earlier period. After all, Bach was long since forgotten, and he died 55 years *after* Purcell.

None the less, throughout the century there was a growing recognition of the greatness of Purcell by a small minority, and sporadic efforts were made to revive interest in his music and to make it more accessible. At the turn of the century there appeared *The Beauties of Purcell* in two volumes of favourite songs, duets and trios, revised and arranged with a separate accompaniment for the pianoforte and thorough bass. This was compiled by Joseph Corfe, a 'Gentleman of the Chapels Royal' and published in 1805. In his preface he quotes Dr Burney: 'Henry Purcell is as much the pride of an Englishman in Music, as Shakespear in productions of the Stage – Milton in Epic Poetry – Lock [*sic*] in Metaphysics – or Sir Isaac Newton in Philosophy and Mathematics.'[1]

Three years later, John Clarke, a Doctor of Music from Cambridge, also brought out a selection of favourite songs etc under the same title, similarly adapted and arranged with an accompaniment for the pianoforte. Clarke's preface goes into considerable detail which gives an interesting insight into the way in which Purcell was regarded at the time. His main aim is to bring into more general use, the works of 'the unrivalled HENRY PURCELL'. He has selected his pieces from 'the most correct editions' and has added the piano part in order to obviate the difficulties of accompanying from a figured bass; but he assures us that great care has been taken to adhere to the original text. He continues:

In some few instances where the Harmonies have been doubtful, and the passages in the different scores have differed widely from each other, he has endeavoured to adopt those which appeared to be most authentic and to correspond best to the Movement and General Style of the Composition.
In two or three instances a few bars by way of Symphony have been cautiously introduced to relieve the voice . . . it struck the Editor that in the repetition of the sections in the latter movement, a moving Bass would produce *variety*. He has therefore inserted it merely under *that* idea, and not as presumptuously aiming at an improvement in the style of him whose works have seldom been equalled and never surpassed . . .[2]

From 1828 to 1832, Vincent Novello published his five volumes of *Purcell's Sacred Music*, but these, too, were edited versions. During this time a curiously equivocal view of Purcell comes from a series of lectures given by the celebrated composer and organist, William Crotch, at Oxford. He says that Purcell was

sublime, beautiful and ornamental . . . but had he no defects? Yes, – such as Milton had. The mind that at all comprehends him is kept continually on the stretch. It is a strong sight that can take in his designs; he is often incomprehensible; the summit of the mountain is hid in clouds. His sublimity is seldom of the pure and simple kind but vast and complicated. His melodies are often fascinating and bewitching yet not eminently vocal and beautiful. His passages for the trumpet are difficult and not productive of good effect . . . The long divisions for the voice in his songs are ungraceful and tedious; and the frequent repetition of monosyllables, and of small portions of a sentence, are absurd and offensive. These are spots in the sun. But they are spots, not subjects for imitation and praise. His vocal music should never be attempted by foreigners; and it succeeds so little in general even with natives that those who have heard it sung by . . . [eminent singers of the day], can scarcely bear to witness the attempt.

. . . All his anthems are fine, particularly, 'I was glad'; his services also. But the canons to the Gloria Patri, do not sufficiently exemplify the art of concealing art. His sonatas are more scientific and varied, but less pleasing and artless than those of Corelli . . .

. . . His three mad songs in the *Orpheus Britannicus* . . . are the finest of their kind and worthy of the highest praise and admiration. But we cannot speak of many of his songs and rounds on account of the words. Have we no Hercules of the present day to cleanse away this Augean filth, and to render the study and performance of all his vocal music a safe and delightful employment? We ought not to be unacquainted with any work of this man, who was not only the greatest master of his time, but the most extraordinary genius that this nation has ever produced.[3]

In 1836, the 'Purcell Club' was formed by a small group of enthusiasts including the conductor, James Turle. Membership was limited to 20 professionals and 20 amateurs, who met twice a year; in February they dined together and in July they assembled at Westminster Abbey where at the morning service, by permission of the Dean, they assisted in any Purcell music that had been selected for the occasion. On the evening of the same day, members again met to perform secular music composed by Purcell; the soprano parts were sung by choristers from the Abbey, the Chapel Royal and St Paul's, but ladies were permitted to sit in the audience.

In February 1842, Edward Taylor (1784–1863) was elected President. He was a professional singer, teacher, musical journalist and Professor of Music at Gresham College in London, who had long sustained an interest in the works of Purcell, and edited *King Arthur* for the Antiquarian Society which he instituted with Chappell and Rimbault. He was music critic of the *Spectator* for many years, and once wrote:

It would seem as if the view which Purcell had obtained of the powers and resources of his art, and his conviction of what it might hereafter accomplish, had led him to regard all that he had produced but as the efforts of a learner (and we are justified in this conclusion from his own words), fitted to give a brief and transient impulse to his art, and having accomplished this purpose, to be forgotten. It may be that he was right: it may be that we stand, as he stood, but at the threshold of music: it may be that in his 'clear dream and solemn vision' he saw further than his successors: nor will it be denied, that some of its recesses have been further explored by geniuses and talent like his own; but all the great attributes which belong to the true artist, all the requirements which make the true musician, we may yet learn of Purcell.[4]

In 1858, to commemorate what was then regarded to be the bicentenary of Purcell's birth, members of the Club were joined by a number of musicians and amateurs at a banquet followed by a concert of the composer's music at the Albion Tavern, Aldersgate Street, in London. The Club survived until 1863, and when it was disbanded, the valuable library, acquired by gift and purchase, was deposited at Westminster Abbey.

On the initiative of W.H. Cummings, eleven years later, the 'Purcell Society' was founded for the purpose of 'doing justice to the memory of Henry Purcell, firstly by the publication of his works, most of which exist only in MS, and secondly by meeting for the study and performance of his various compositions'. Besides Cummings, the original committee consisted of a number of eminent musical personages including Sir Frederick A. Gore-Ouseley, Sir John Goss, Joseph Barnby, J.F. Bridge and John Stainer. The idea of performance was abandoned quite early on and the Society assumed the form of a body of subscribers to its publications, only two of which – published by Novello – were produced in the first eleven years.

In 1887, the Society was reorganized with Cummings as Editor and W. Barclay Squire as Honorary Secretary, but it was still somewhat pedestrian in achieving its aims. Members were given a variety of works to edit, and, according to the minutes, by July 1894, *The Fairy Queen, Dioclesian*, some organ music, the first and second set of Sonatas, the Harpsichord Lessons and the Instrumental Fantasias had been allocated. But over the next few years, very few editions reached the printing-press and it took until 1923 for the next 20 volumes to be published.

Around this time we see the emergence of another musician who was to bring about a complete revolution in the attitudes to the performance of early music. He was the French-Swiss Arnold Dolmetsch (1858–1940) who had arrived in Britain in 1883. He had attended the Conservatoire in Brussels and studied the violin privately with Vieuxtemps, and was to spend a further two years at the newly opened Royal College of Music in London. His interest in early music had been inspired by his former Director in Brussels, François-Auguste Gevaert, and he was further encouraged by Sir George Grove, Principal at the College, who recommended him for the job of assistant music master at Dulwich College.

Dolmetsch had already acquired a few early instruments and reference books and had begun researches in the Royal College of Music library and the British Museum looking for music

contemporary with these acquisitions. His discoveries were so fruitful
that he decided to concentrate on performing early music on original
instruments, something that had not been attempted hitherto – at least
not outside a private drawing-room. Dolmetsch's discoveries did not
necessarily devalue the work of others in the field: we know that
Mendelssohn had been conducting performances of Bach's major
choral works from 1829, and Carl Engel, A.J. Hipkins, a specialist
employee of Broadwood's, Canon Francis Galpin and Edward
Dannreuter were all, in various ways, promoting interest in early
music. But it is important to remember that in actual *performances*,
including those of Mendelssohn, modern instruments were used,
including a pianoforte for the continuo. Since Dolmetsch had been
trained as a maker as well as a musician, and was also a fine violinist,
he was in a strong position to put his ideas into practice; he could
restore old instruments, and, should the need arise, make reproduc-
tions. It was in the RCM library that Dolmetsch discovered a copy of
Purcell's *Golden Sonata* and some pieces from *The Fairy Queen*, and
proceeded to give – with his boys at Dulwich – what was almost
certainly the first modern performance of these works. A reviewer
commented that 'the music sounded fresh in spite of its age'.

From this point onwards, Dolmetsch devoted himself to giving
concerts on original instruments, of music copied from the original
editions and manuscripts. At first he gave candle-lit concerts in
costume of the period in his own home, but the success of these led him
to giving equally well attended public concerts. By the turn of the
century Dolmetsch had performed some 45 pieces by Purcell on
original instruments, either from manuscript or contemporary
editions.

In 1895, to celebrate the bicentenary of Henry Purcell's death, the
Purcell Society made plans for several performances of his music. *Dido
and Aeneas* was performed by students of the RCM at the Lyceum
Theatre in London, and a special service was held in Westminster
Abbey in which a number of his anthems were sung. The Philharmonic
Society also made their contribution by way of a performance of the
1692 'Ode on St Cecilia's Day'. It is not difficult to imagine that, apart
from the service in the Abbey, the forces were far removed from those
employed in Purcell's day. The music critic from *The World*, was
aware of this situation and did not mince his words:

We reverence his name, and refuse tacitly to have anything to do with him. He
is our greatest musician, we say, and therefore, well, we will occasionally

consent to endure the hearing of one of his little songs . . . Very kind of us, is it not? We, the British, then discover that Purcell has been dead for 200 years and the merit of this proceeding strikes us forcibly . . . Forthwith, for two or three days we prostrate ourselves before his shrine.

The writer goes on to say how the British make feeble attempts to pay homage to otherwise neglected musicians who are brought out occasionally and deified to celebrate an anniversary:

The shade of the dead master must have been smiling ironically at the 'Purcell Week' which caused so many people to 'read up' all about the composer or tell their friends that they had for years been paying him homage, and then inspired them to drown themselves in his 'long-neglected and well nigh forgotten music'. The shade might have ceased to smile though if it had heard 'the solid echoes of *The Golden Sonata* as performed on two modern grand pianofortes, with full orchestra! . . . But we must advance, mustn't we? It does not do to stand still and become obsolete.'

He suggests that we must dress up poor Purcell, as no doubt future generations will dress up Wagner, to 'disguise the leanness of his genius'. The *Golden Sonata*, performed on two violins, a 'cello and a spinet, may have been adequate in an age when there were no railways, but would not be fit for the present generation of music-lovers. We want more 'body' and the Philharmonic Society kindly gives it to us at the expense of the spirit.[5]

Dolmetsch also gave a concert of Purcell's music at the Portman Rooms in Baker Street, and the critic from *The Times* (almost certainly J.A. Fuller Maitland) recognizes a very different approach:

The concert of Purcell's music given last night . . . was a worthy sequel to the recent Festival in the composer's honour, and not the least artistic part of it. The most important feature of the programme was the series of specimens from the concerted works for strings, enabling an instructive comparison to be made between the master's work before and after he came under Italian influence.[6]

The writer then singles out the Fantasia upon one note for five viols, dating from a period shortly before 1682, as being a composition of wonderful ingenuity and *The Golden Sonata*, 'played, of course, on the instruments for which Purcell wrote it, and therefore most effective'.

Perhaps the most interesting revival of all was the performance of *King Arthur* at the Birmingham Triennial Musical Festival in October 1897. The score had been specially edited by J.A. Fuller Maitland for the festival and Hans Richter conducted a large choir and orchestra with principal singers drawn from the top-ranking artists of the day: Madame Albani, Ada Crossley, Ben Davies, Plunket Greene, David Bispham and others. However, when it came to the continuo, Richter clearly made a move towards authenticity by the employment of two harpsichords.

It must therefore have been particularly galling for Maitland when John Runciman devoted two-and-a-half columns to his incompetence in the *Saturday Review*:

'With your permission Mr Maitland,' says Hans Richter at the semi-public band rehearsal . . . on Wednesday afternoon 'we will play *forte* where you have marked *piano* and *piano* where you have marked *forte*.'

Richter would not tolerate such a hash being made out of Purcell's score so he told the orchestra that the whole of Mr Maitland's score would be revised (by Dolmetsch) before the next rehearsal and proper marks of expression would be inserted. Runciman, obviously in agreement with Richter's deposition, writes: 'A more incompetent piece of work it has never been my fate to set eyes upon . . . a mere travesty of Purcell, concocted by a gentleman wholly ignorant of the elementary rules of harmony and of the art of filling in accompaniments from a figured-bass'. Runciman then quotes almost a page of errors with accompanying justification, and furthermore advises Boosey's, the publisher, to 'withdraw at once this deplorable exhibition of bad taste and entire lack of musicianship' on the assumption that their name will suffer as a consequence, and if copies go abroad foreigners will get the wrong impression of English musicianship.

The sting is in the tail of the article. He points out that Maitland, who is the critic of *The Times*, does not wish it to be known that he cannot work out a simple bit of harmony without coming to grief. He suggests that the critics have long known about Mr Maitland's ignorance but he fears to let the general public into the secret. Therefore he would prefer the edition to be withdrawn and the matter hushed up.

Of the performance itself, he criticizes Richter's final cuts and challenges him to do the work in a complete form. The two harpsichord parts 'were excellently played by Mr Dolmetsch and Mrs Elodie Dolmetsch' and it appears that 'a good many unintelligent musical people have complimented Mr Maitland on these parts; but I may take this opportunity of saying that Mr Maitland's parts were discarded for some reason and entirely new ones written by Mr Dolmetsch.' There follows an exchange of correspondence in which Maitland tries to defend himself by quoting an article he has written on the subject in *The Musician*, but Runciman will not have it and gives some valid argument to prove his point. He summarizes in cutting terms:

The mental process which enables him [Maitland] after owning to these alterations, not only to say that he has made no alterations, but also to castigate previous editors for the alterations they have made, is to me an inscrutable mystery. And as that I am content to leave it. I only wish it to be known that Mr Maitland's score is wholly untrustworthy.[7]

In 1901, in an essay on Purcell as an anthem-writer, Myles B. Foster wrote: 'To whatever branch of the Divine Art we choose to direct ourselves, we find that Purcell stands, head and shoulders, above all other English musicians.' In particular, he praises Purcell's works written under the Italian influence and claims that at this period, Purcell was not only the greatest composer in his own country, but of all Europe: 'for you could not find, over the whole Continent at that day, a brighter genius, nor were there any works by contemporaries to compare with his vigour of ideas, his breadth of style and power of expression'. He deplores the fact that 'alas, his glorious works are seldom heard, his name scarcely recognized in these modern days' and he considers it a disgrace to Englishmen that the memory of their greatest composer should be so slighted.

He goes on to quote a Frenchman, M. Amedée Mereaux, who also complains that Purcell has not been paid the tribute justly due to his genius, and comments that he 'is one of the artistic glories of England ... without doubt, the most able and most fertile of all the English composers'.[8]

That same year the Purcell Society noted in their minutes that the King had agreed to continue his subscription to the Society, and would also allow MSS from Buckingham Palace to be deposited at the British Museum for the use of its editors. There is also a little note which tells us that for 'a small fee to be paid from the editing fund, Mr Paul England has been requested to alter the words' of the song 'Good neighbour, why do you look awry?' from *The Canterbury Guests*. The song, like so many others, was published in the bowdlerized version in the Purcell Society Edition.

Very few meetings are recorded from this date until 1922 when

Novello announced they had incurred a loss of £400 on Volume XXII alone. The following year, Squire was succeeded by Gerald M. Cooper who was responsible for four more publications. On his own account, Cooper began the publication of the Purcell Society Popular Edition in a format for practical performance, but in other respects the Society remained inactive until 1957 when Anthony Lewis brought about its revival and saw to it that the remaining volumes were published to make a complete set of 31.

In 1899, the composer, Martin Shaw (1875–1958), whose interest in English music, when that of almost any foreigner was preferable, founded the Purcell Operatic Society. His main aim was to mount a performance of *Dido and Aeneas* in the form of an oratorio with orchestra, soloists and choir. He chose as his stage- director Gordon Craig, the man, who, 'by example and precept, was to revolutionize the modern theatre'. But Craig envisaged it as a theatrical production and managed to convince Shaw that it was a more viable proposition. However, there were problems. They knew of no suitable theatre and lacked the money with which to engage an orchestra, a choir and singers who could also act.

However, it seems that these difficulties were finally overcome, although the entire preparation and rehearsals took six months, which, at the time, was unheard of in the theatre. They engaged an orchestra, and a choir and minor soloists, all of whom were amateurs, the majority of whom had untrained voices and no stage experience, and two professional singers, who could also act, in the parts of Dido and Aeneas.

Their choice of venue was the hall of the Hampstead Conservatoire (now the Embassy Theatre) where the stage was designed in a series of rising terraces as is customary for seating an orchestra. On the back step, Craig assembled a wide trellis resting on several vertical scaffoldings which he used for the main setting, and, as and when required he had the performers arranged on the various terraces. Martin Shaw wrote: 'They had to sing their choruses crawling, leaping, swaying, running – any way that Craig fancied. How they did it I do not know, but they did.'[9]

However, if Craig's demands on the actors were unusual, the lighting was completely revolutionary. He used no lighting from the wings and dispensed with footlights. For the main lighting he built a bridge behind the proscenium arch and placed the lights so that they shone on to the stage from above. (It is generally believed that this type of lighting originated in Germany, but it was first used at this performance in Hampstead and was adopted by the Germans some years later.) Craig also placed two spotlights at the back of the hall so that the beams passed over the heads of the audience to shine directly on to the actors' faces.

It is difficult today to imagine how daring it was to put on an English opera when the Covent Garden audiences were steeped in operas by Italian, German and French composers. But it turned out to be an enormous artistic success. Whether it was also a financial success, is doubtful, as Shaw remembered having to sell most of his books immediately after the performance. The critics were most enthusiastic and praised Craig for his ingenuity, and the way in which by subtle suggestion and evocation he allowed the public to use their own imagination. He achieved his effects by transforming the scenic image in colours, lines, movement and lighting; the costumes, based on the harmonizing of simple colours matched to the draperies, blended with the overall spectacle. Mabel Cox wrote: 'Colours and lighting for Craig do not represent a means of expressing natural history but rather a way of supporting the dramatic element. It is not by chance that the scarlet cushions of the throne in the first act are changed to black in the last scene when Dido mourns the loss of Aeneas.'[10]

There were a few revivals of Purcell's semi-operas in the early part of the twentieth century. *The Fairy Queen* was performed in a concert version at Morley College under Gustav Holst in 1911, and *King Arthur* was produced in Cambridge in 1928 by Dennis Arundell, conducted by Cyril Rootham with the soprano Margaret Field-Hyde making her solo debut. She was later to become one of the leading exponents of Purcell's music.

When Covent Garden opened a season of opera in English in 1948, they chose Purcell's *Fairy Queen* for the opening night. Under the direction of Constant Lambert, Frederick Ashton and Michael Ayrton, 'it was in the safest possible hands, for the presentation of it on the modern stage, to a Covent Garden audience soaked in Puccini and Strauss, needed all the resources of scholarship, imagination and humanity.' Despite its sumptuous scenery, and modern machinery, Covent Garden was unable, perhaps owing to the water shortage, to reproduce cascades and fountains rising twelve feet high, which had been such a feature of the Dorset Garden's production. There were cuts, too, which caused unfavourable comment; Dent deplored the omission of certain sung episodes such as the scene of the Drunken Poet and Corydon and Mopsa's duet, but even so, 'they were two hours of Purcell and continuous delight'.[11]

Finally we must return to the Purcell Society, which by 1950 had become not only much more active, but also authentic in its approach to how the music should be performed. This was due to the efforts of a strong and well-informed committee with Edward J. Dent as Chairman and Anthony Lewis as Honorary Secretary. The other members were Dennis Arundell, Clive Carey, Thurston Dart, Arnold Goldsborough, Philip Radcliffe, Michael Tippett, J.A. Westrup and Ralph Vaughan Williams. At a meeting in March 1950 they decided to ask for support from the Arts Council to enable the publication of five further volumes which were still unpublished. A further appeal to the Arts Council was in a proposal by Anthony Lewis that they should jointly sponsor eight programmes of Purcell's music to be incorporated in the Festival of Britain which was planned for the following year. Needless to say, the motion was carried *nem con*.

Six of the concerts were given in the newly equipped concert-room at the Victoria and Albert Museum, one in the Chapel of the Royal Hospital in Chelsea and one at Westminster Abbey, all under distinguished conductors with Anthony Lewis as artistic director. The programmes covered a wide range of the composer's music, from catches, songs, masques, odes and string fantasias to the great *Te Deum and Jubilate* in D in Westminster Abbey sung by the Abbey Choir and the Choir of King's College, Cambridge. The artists performing included the singers Margaret Ritchie, Margaret Field-Hyde, Alfred Deller, Owen Brannigan, Norman Walker; and instrumentalists Frederick Grinke, David Martin, James Whitehead, Arnold Goldsborough, Geraint Jones and many others, all prominent in their respective fields.

At this juncture it might be interesting to consider a view expressed in a novel of this same year when one of the characters is giving advice to another on the delights of singing:

Purcell! What a genius! And lucky, too. Nobody has ever thought to blow him up into a God-like Genius, like poor old Bach, or a Misunderstood Genius, like poor old Mozart, or a Wicked and Immoral Genius, like poor old Wagner. Purcell is just a nice, simple Genius, rollicking happily through Eternity. The boobs and the gramophone salesmen and the music hucksters haven't discovered him yet and please God they never will. Kids don't peck and mess at little scraps of Purcell for examinations. Arthritic organists don't torture Purcell in chapels and tin Bethels all over the country on Sundays, while the middle classes are pretending to be holy. Purcell is still left for people who really like music.[12]

In the Arts Council's publication of the eight programmes, several musicians contribute their views on Purcell. Michael Tippett considers him one of the greatest masters in setting the English language and gives examples of how Purcell places the strong syllable on the strong beat so ensuring that 'the musical phrase, however long, shall end in such a way that the word can be spoken at the very end of its natural rhythm'. He further describes this 'word-painting':

In the opening chorus of the Ode to St Cecilia, 1692, 'Hail Bright Cecilia', after the opening words the poem continues, 'fill every heart with love of thee and thy celestial art'. The word which took Purcell's imagination in this way is 'celestial'. At first it is only lightly treated, but later he carried the voice high up into the celestial air. Perhaps the visual image Purcell had in his mind was of the altar incense thinning out as it rises, while the aural image would be of the thin sound of the high organ pipes and of the high boys' voices. Therefore, he probably meant us to sing these phrases not louder as they rise, but softer, even though the instinct to make a *crescendo* may be a strong one. I think we must often deny ourselves that if we want the real Purcell.

It would be interesting to know whether in choosing words for long vocalisations, Purcell was conscious of the vowels he used. For example, in the 1692 Ode to St Cecilia, by far the greatest proportion of vocalisations are of the vowel *oo*, in words like 'flew', 'true', 'move' and 'music'; and there is only one vocalisation to the open *ah*, – that to the word 'charms'. [His final sentence sums it up perfectly:] Yet as Purcell's music reaches our ears, it embodies a great tradition of sensitiveness to the sound of our language, which is not the least of its claims to greatness, nor of its lessons to us today.[13]

A further contribution came from the singer, Norman Platt who confirmed what so many others have claimed over the centuries:

Purcell had a profound understanding of the rhythmic nature of the language and grasped its essential flexibility . . . [he] realised, too, that the singer is a hybrid, a cross-breed between musician and actor – a proposition which remains true even in the case of a singer who never approaches the operatic stage; for a singer's material is always a combination of the basic stuff of the actor – words, and that of the musician – notes.[14]

Many twentieth-century scholars have diligently researched and written about Henry Purcell's music, notably Arundell, Buttrey, Holland, Luckett, Laurie, Price, Westrup and Zimmerman. Of this aspect, there is little more to contribute. Biographers will presumably continue to suffer the deprivation of source material, unless some miraculous discoveries are made. However, when it comes to the question of the *performance* of Purcell's music in our present time, we are fortunate in having a number of musicians who have made a special study of Purcell's period and performing style. As a result, we can expect to hear performances that will get even closer to the sounds and style heard by Purcell himself.

References

1. Corfe, Joseph, *The Beauties of Purcell*, 2 vols, Preston, 1805.
2. Clarke, John, *The Beauties of Purcell*, Rt. Birchall, 1808.
3. Crotch, *Substance of Several Courses of Lectures on Music*, Longman, Rees, Orme, Brown and Green, 1831, pp 105–9.
4. Cummings, *Purcell*, p 95.
5. *The World*, 27 November 1895, pp 24–5.
6. *The Times*, 21 December 1895.
7. *Saturday Review*, 9 October 1897, pp 386–7.
8. Foster, Myles B., *Anthems and Anthem Composers*, Novello, 1901, pp 56–7.
9. Shaw, Martin, *Up to Now*, Oxford University Press, 1929, p 26.
10. Bablet, Denis, *Edward Gordon Craig*, L'Arche, Paris, 1962, pp 52–9.
11. Dent, Edward J., Preface, *The Fairy Queen*, as presented at the Royal Opera House, Covent Garden, ed Edward Mandinian, Lehmann, 1948, pp 17–18.
12. Davies, Robertson, *Tempest-Tost*, The Salterton Trilogy, 1951, Penguin 1986, p 149.
13. Tippett, Michael, 'Purcell and the English Language', *Eight Concerts of Henry Purcell's Music*, Arts Council of Great Britain, 1951, pp 46–9.
14. Platt, Norman, ibid, 'Purcell and the Singer's Art', pp 25–6.

BIBLIOGRAPHY

Arundell, Dennis, *Henry Purcell*, Oxford University Press, 1927.
—— *The Critic at the Opera*, Benn, 1957.
Ashbee, Andrew, *Lists of Payments to the King's Musick in the Reign of Charles II (1660–1685)*, Ashbee, 1981.
—— *Records of English Court Music (1660–85)* Vol 1, Ashbee, 1986, Vol 2, 1987, Vol 3, 1988.
Aston, Anthony, *A Brief Supplement to Colley Cibber, Esq; his Lives of the Late Famous Actors and Actresses*, for the author, Dodesley, 1889.
Bablet, Denis, *Edward Gordon Craig*, L'Arche, Paris, 1962.
Baker, David Erskine, *The Companion to the Playhouse*, Vol 1, T. Beckett, 1764.
Baldwin, David, *The Chapel Royal, Ancient & Modern*, Duckworth, 1990.
Beaver, Alfred, *Memorials of Old Chelsea*, Elliott Stock, 1892.
Bell, W.G., *The Great Fire of London in 1666*, 2nd edition, Bodley Head, 1951.
—— *The Great Plague in London in 1665*, 3rd edition, Bodley Head, 1951.
Betterton, Thomas, *An Account of the Life of that Celebrated Tragedian, Mr Thomas Betterton*, J. Robinson, 1749.
Blom, Eric, *Music in England*, 2nd edition, Penguin, 1947.
Borgman, Albert S. *The Life and Death of William Mountfort*, Harvard Studies in English, Vol 15, Harvard University Press, Cambridge, Mass., 1935.
Boswell, Eleanor, *The Restoration Court Stage*, Harvard University Press, Cambridge, Mass., 1932.
Bridge, Frederick, *Twelve Good Musicians*, Kegan Paul, Trench, Trubner 1920.
Brown, Thomas, *Works*, 9th edition, Vol 2, 1760.
Bryant, Arthur, *King Charles II*, Longmans, 1949.
Burney, Charles, *A General History of Music*, Beckett, 1789.
Campbell, Margaret, *Dolmetsch: the Man and his Work*, Hamish Hamilton, 1975.
Chamberlayne, E., *Angliae Notitia, or the Present State of England*, 15th edition, Sawbridge, 1684.
Chan, Mary, *Music in the Theatre of Ben Jonson*, Clarendon, 1988.

Cibber, C., *An Apology for the Life of Mr Colley Cibber, Comedian. With an historical view of the stage during his own time. Written by himself*, Printed for the author, 1740.

Cleaver, James, *The Theatre Through the Ages*, Harrap, 1946.

Crotch, William, *Substance of Several Courses of Lectures on Music*, Longman, Rees, Orme, Brown and Greene, 1831.

Cummings, William H., *Purcell*, Sampson Lowe, 1881.

—— *The Words of Henry Purcell's Vocal Music*, private publication.

Davies, Robertson, *Tempest-Tost*, The Salterton Trilogy, Penguin, 1986.

Davis, W.J. and Waters, A.W., *Tickets and Passes of Great Britain and Ireland*, Spink, 1974.

Dent, E.J., *Foundations of English Opera*, Cambridge University Press, 1928.

Dobrée, Bonamy, *John Dryden*, Writers and their Work, no 70 (for the British Council), Longmans, 1961.

Downes, John, *Roscius Anglicanus*, ed Judith Milhous and Robert D. Hume, Society for Theatre Research, 1987.

Dryden, John, *The Indian Emperour*, Herringman, 1665.

—— *King Arthur*, Tonson, 1691.

—— *Examen Poeticum*, Tonson, 1693.

Dupré, Henri, *Purcell*, English trans, Knopf, New York, 1928.

Eight Concerts of Henry Purcell's Music, Commemorative Book of Programmes, Notes and Texts, Arts Council of Great Britain, 1951.

Elkin, Robert, *The Old Concert Rooms of London*, Arnold, 1955.

Evelyn, John,*The Diary of John Evelyn*, ed Ernest Rhys, Dent, 1945.

—— *The Diary of John Evelyn*, ed E.S. de Beer, Vol 4, Clarendon, 1955.

Fiske, Roger, *English Theatre Music in the Eighteenth Century*, Oxford University Press, 1973.

Fraser, Antonia, *Cromwell, Our Chief of Men*, Methuen, 1985.

Gildon, Charles, *The Lives and Characters of the English Drammatick Poets*, Tho. Leigh, 1698.

Grove's Dictionary of Music and Musicians, 5th edition, ed Eric Blom, Macmillan, 1954.

Harley, John, *Music in Purcell's London*, Dobson, 1968.

Harman, Alec, and Mellers, Wilfrid, *Man And His Music*, Barrie & Jenkins, 1971.

Harris, Ellen T., *Henry Purcell's Dido and Aeneas*, Clarendon 1987.

Hawkins, J.A., *A General History of the Science and Practice of Music*, Novello, 1875.

Hogwood, C. and Luckett, R. eds *Music in Eighteenth Century England*, Cambridge University Press, 1983.

Holland, A.K., *Henry Purcell, The English Musical Tradition*, Penguin, 1932.

Holst, Imogen, *Purcell, 1659–1695, Essays on his Music*, Oxford University Press, 1959.

Hume, Robert D. ed *The Development of English Drama in the Late*

Seventeenth Century, Clarendon, 1976.

—— *London Theatre World*, Southern Illinois University Press, 1980.

Hutton, Ronald, *Charles II, King of England, Scotland and Ireland*, Oxford University Press, 1989.

Johnstone, H. Diack, and Fiske, Roger eds *The Eighteenth Century*, Blackwell, 1990.

Lafontaine, Henry Cart de, *The King's Musick, A Transcript of Records Relating to Music & Musicians*, (1460–1700), Novello, 1909.

Lawson Dick, O. *Aubrey's Brief Lives*, Secker & Warburg, 1958.

Leacroft, Richard, *The Development of the English Playhouse*, Methuen, 1988.

Loewenberg, Alfred, *The Annals of Opera*, 2nd edition, Societas Bibliographica Geneva, 1955.

The London Stage, ed William van Lennep, Emmett L. Avery, Arthur H. Scouten, Southern Illinois University Press, Carbondale, 1965.

Luttrell, Narcissus, *A Brief Historical Relation of State Affairs from September 1678 to April 1714*, Oxford University Press, 1857.

Mandinian, Edward, ed *The Fairy Queen, as presented at the Royal Opera House, Covent Garden*, Lehmann, 1948.

Milhous, Judith, *Thomas Betterton and the Management of Lincoln's Inn Fields (1698–1708)*, Southern Illinois University Press, Carbondale, 1979.

Moore, Robert Etheridge, *Henry Purcell and the Restoration Theatre*, Heinemann, 1961.

Morley, Thomas, *Plaine and Easie Introduction to Practicall Musicke*, Short, 1597.

Motteux, P.A. ed *The Gentleman's Journal: or The Monthly Miscellany, By Way of a Letter to a Gentleman in the Country*, Baldwin, 1692–4.

Muller, Julia, *Words and Music in Henry Purcell's First Semi-opera, Dioclesian, An Approach to Early Music through Early Theatre*, Edwin Mellen, New York, 1990.

The New Grove Dictionary of Music and Musicians, ed Stanley Sadie, Macmillan, 1980.

Nicoll, Allardyce, *British Drama – An Historical Survey from the Beginnings to the Present Times*, Harrap, 1951.

—— *Memoires of Musick*, ed Edward Rimbault, Bell, 1846.

—— *Autobiography of Roger North*, ed Augustus Jessop, Nutt, 1887.

North, Roger, *The Musicall Grammarian*, ed Hilda Andrews, Humphrey Milford, 1925.

—— *Roger North on Music*, ed John Wilson, Novello, 1959.

Pepys, Samuel, *The Diary of Samuel Pepys*, 10 vols, ed R.C. Latham and W. Matthews, Bell, 1970–83.

Pope, W.J. Macqueen, *Theatre Royal Drury Lane*, Allen, 1945.

Powell, Jocelyn, *Restoration Theatre Production*, Routledge & Kegan Paul, 1984.

Price, Curtis A. *Henry Purcell and the London Stage*, Cambridge University Press, 1984.

—— ed *Henry Purcell: Dido and Aeneas, An Opera*, Norton, New York, 1986.

Pulver, Jeffrey, *A Biographical Dictionary of Old English Music*, Novello, 1927.

Rimbault, Edward F., ed *The Old Cheque-Book, or Book of Remembrance of the Chapel Royal*, Da Capo, New York, 1966.

Rowse, A.L., *The English Past*, Macmillan, 1951.

Royal Encyclopaedia, Macmillan, 1991.

Scholes, Percy A., *The Puritans and Music in England and New England*, Oxford University Press, 1943.

Shaw, Martin, *Up to Now*, Oxford University Press, 1929.

Southern, Richard, *Changeable Scenery: Its Origin and Development in the British Theatre*, Faber & Faber, 1952.

Trevelyan, G.M., *England under the Stuarts*, 19th edition, Methuen, 1947.

Turner, F.C., *James II*, Eyre & Spottiswoode, 1948.

Van Der Straeten, Edmund S.J., *History of the Violoncello, the Viol da Gamba, Their Precursors and Collateral Instruments*, Reeves, 1971.

van der Zee, Henri and Barbara, *William and Mary*, Macmillan, 1973.

Ward, Charles E. *Life of John Dryden*, University of North Carolina Press, Chapel Hill, 1961.

—— ed *The Letters of John Dryden*: with letters addressed to him, Duke University Press, Durham, North Carolina, 1942.

Westrup, J.A., *Purcell*, 'The Master Musicians', Dent, 1960.

Wheatley, Henry B., *Round About Piccadilly and Pall Mall*, Smith, Elder, 1870.

White, E.W., *The Rise of English Opera*, Lehmann, 1951.

—— *A History of English Opera*, Faber & Faber, 1983.

Wood, Anthony, *The History and Antiquities of the University of Oxford*, ed John Gutch, Oxford, 1786.

Zimmerman, Franklin B., *Henry Purcell, 1659–1695, An Analytical Catalogue of his Music*, Macmillan, 1963.

—— *Henry Purcell, 1659–1695, His Life and Times*, 2nd edition, University of Pennsylvania, Philadelphia, 1983.

All quotations from journals and reports, etc are detailed in *References*.

INDEX

COMPOSITIONS BY HENRY PURCELL MENTIONED IN TEXT